THEOLOGY

and

THE NEW HISTORIES

THEOLOGY
and
THE NEW HISTORIES

Gary Macy

Editor

THE ANNUAL PUBLICATION
OF THE COLLEGE THEOLOGY SOCIETY
1998
VOLUME 44

Maryknoll, New York 10545

Co-published by the College Theology Society and Orbis Books, Maryknoll, NY 10545-0308

Manufactured in the United States of America

Orbis/ISBN 1-57075-239-7

Contents

PART I
NEW METHODOLOGIES

PART II
NEW READINGS OF OLD TEXTS

Editor's Preface

Gary Macy

There is a Calvin and Hobbes cartoon in which Calvin marvels at the wonder of an evolutionary process which through aeons of time has struggled to produce that apex of natural development which is, of course, Calvin himself.

Calvin's arrogance, humorous as it may be, represents, in a nutshell, the difficulty exposed by what are sometimes termed the "new histories." Women's history, ethnic history and different forms of deconstructionism have all challenged the idea that history is the simple process of recording "what happened in the past." Since history is written, inevitably, by "us" and is driven by "our" interest in "our" past, these historians suggest that history may tend to be less about "what happened in the past" and much more about how historians explain and justify the present cultural location of their own society or group. History, assumed to be so firm, through these eyes becomes both slippery and suspect, suffused through and through with self-interest, power and politics.

Several insights follow. First of all, history is irredeemably present. We have only what now remains from the past in the present to judge what the past may have been like. And those remains are not (usually) random leavings. Politics, wars, and other forms of cultural struggle determine what survives and what does not. Those elites who could write and whose writings have been preserved are much more likely to catch an historian's interest, for instance, than the mute scraps of material remains that attest to the illiterate majority. Power determines whose history gets written.

Power also determines which of those bits of the past left in the present historians feel it is worth writing about. Historians must pick and choose both which evidence they will look at and which topics they will research. Different historians from different cultures will prefer some evidence over others and even use the same evidence to tell quite different versions of the past. "Our" history differs, you might say, depending on who "we" are. A classic example of this would be those histories of the United States which begin with the Pilgrim "Fathers," despite the presence of both Native Americans and Spanish Catholics hundreds of years (or millennium) before the Pilgrims' mothers were born. These histories tell "our" story and neither Native Americans nor Hispanics nor Roman Catholics, nor, for that matter, mothers are the "us" these historians have in mind.

History, from this standpoint, can no longer be assumed to be "just the facts." Political agendas pervade historical remains as well as the histories constructed from those remains. The illusion that there is a value-free history which can be gradually and finally gleaned from past remains has been shown to be an illusion. It is probably more correct to say that there are many "histories" and, actually, always have been. Each of these histories, moreover, is not only a narrative, but a narrative which must make moral choices in its very valuing of some evidence and some topics over others.

The matter is not quite so simple as that, however. Is history then pure fiction? Are there then any number of possible histories? Are all histories credible? What criteria are there for deciding which histories are accurate and which merely convenient or lazy fictions? In what way can or should historians fulfill the moral obligations which the "new histories" ascribe to their task?

These questions are magnified for historians of theology. The history of Christianity, or as it more commonly is known, the "tradition of the Church," is considered by many Christians, and certainly by Roman Catholics, to be a form of revelation. Must we say, then, that there are many traditions in the Church that themselves make up "the Tradition"? Can there be a "tradition" of pluralism? Can historians challenge the "teaching of the Church" or "Tradition" based on new readings of "the traditions"? Can God really speak to modern Christians through such a polyphany of voices? Or to put the question another way, what is the relation of this new way of writing history to theology, to faith and to magisterial teaching?

This volume is an attempt to wrestle with these issues both by discussing the challenges made by the "new histories" and by providing examples of what such histories might be. The essays need no introduction from the editor; they speak eloquently for themselves. Yet it would be hypocritical in such a volume not to reveal the structure the editor has created for arranging the essays. All historians, as I have suggested, have an agenda and this editor is no exception.

The first essay, "Practicing History, Practicing Theology," was the presidential address given by Terrence Tilley at the 44th Annual Meeting of the College Theology Society. The theme of that meeting was "Theology and the New Histories" and this volume is a collection of papers given at the conference. In a scholarly and concise argument for the proper relationship between theological and historical claims, Tilley's wit and clarity offer an engaging entree into this new and challenging world. The reader may not agree with all that Tilley proposes, especially his evaluation of the editor's own work, but then all introductions ought to be an invitation to further discussion and correction.

Each of the next three sections of the book begin with one of the three plenary addresses given at the conference. The first of these sections presents three discussions of the theory behind the practice of the "new histories." Justo González's plenary address, "The Changing Geography of Church History," invites the reader to examine this new "shifting ground" of church history as both frightening and exhilarating. Michael Barnes makes a compelling case for limits to the relativism suggested by some proponents of deconstructionism in his essay, "Universalist Pluralism and the New Histories." Based on anthropological and historical data, Barnes offers some suggestions for determining the common ground shared by all humans. In "History or Geography? Gadamer, Foucault, and Theologies of Tradition," Vincent Miller proposes that an analysis of the philosophies of Hans Georg Gadamer, Edward Schillebeeckx, Michel Foucault and Mary McClintock Fulkerson offers insights into how "new histories" might be used in appropriating Christian tradition.

The second section of the book moves from theory to practice. Four writers offer examples of how the "new history" might look when used to "reread" classic Christian, and specifically Roman Catholic, texts. Elizabeth Clark in her plenary address, "Rewriting Early Christian History," first presents an astute summary of the debate over "new histories" from an historian's point of view. She then offers an intriguing and convincing analysis of how the insights provided from the new approaches might be applied to recovering the "Monica" which St. Augustine skillfully created in his writing about his sainted mother.

Even more challenging is Barbara Green's reconstruction of the riddles presented by the prophet Amos. "How the Lion Roars: Contextualizing the Nine Riddles in Amos 3:3-8" deliberately confronts the reader with the same awkward moral bind that may have faced the original readers of Amos. Anne Riggs's careful "retrieval" of Karl Rahner's theology rejects the accusation of dualism sometimes made of his theology. Her essay, "Rahner and the 'New Histories': Everything Old is New Again," reveals, in fact, that Rahner might have been quite at home in the post-modern world of the "new histories." "Meaning and Praxis in History: Lonerganian Perspectives" locates the tradition of another influential Roman Catholic theologian, Bernard Lonergan, within the larger discussion of history and tradition. Donna Teevan suggests in this essay that, like many of the "new histories," Lonergan's concept of praxis in history posits a role for morality in history.

The third section of the book suggests new and unexpected historical sources for Christian tradition. James Fisher's claim in his plenary address that "the 'Christ is in the shapeup' scene from *On the Waterfront* offers the most powerful representation of modern Catholic social teaching ever presented to a national audience" is well supported in his careful analysis of the role of Fr. John Corridan in the making of this famous movie. Movies as sources for Christian tradition may seem an odd thought until you read "The Priest in the Movie: *On the Waterfront* as Historical Theology" (and then, I strongly suggest, race out to rent the movie). Literature as well can carry theological insights, as is movingly shown in Pamela Kirk's essay, "Uncovering Resistance in the Third Reich: Luise Rinser's *Prison Diaries*." As is only now being recognized, Luise Rinser, both in her life and in her work, embodied Christian resistance to evil. Just as inspiring is the transformation of Clarence Jordan, "an ordinary, Southern Baptist good-old-boy" into a leader for racial reconciliation and the inspiration for the now famous "Habitat for Humanity" program. Ann Coble introduces this impressive witness in her essay, "Cotton Patch Justice, Cotton Patch Peace: The Sermon on the Mount in the Teachings and Practices of Clarence Jordan."

The fourth and final section of the book suggests how the writing and teaching of history might recognize and fulfill the moral obligation which such practices, it is argued, necessarily entail. Franklin H. Littell's plenary address, "Liberty in an Age of Coercion and Violence," tags the twentieth century with the harsh epithet, "the Age of

Genocide." Christians must ever be on their guard against even the beginnings of this great evil and such watchfulness begins with an honest evaluation of our own past. In "Celibacy and Sexual Malpractice," Brian Linnane argues convincingly that clerical sexual malpractice is more than a reprehensible breach of professional ethics, it is also "simply a blatant example of the destructive logic of patriarchy." Linnane ends his essay with a suggestion of how this structural evil might be confronted by the Church's own tradition. The College Theology Society has always claimed a dual role as a community of both scholars and teachers. Therefore it is fitting that this volume includes an essay introducing the "new histories" into the classroom. In "Experiential Learning in Service of a Living Tradition," Margaret Pfeil describes her experience of teaching social justice as a graduate student instructor. In particular, she details the surprising corroboration between the students' gradual acquisition of critical textual skills and their personal confrontation with the effects of social ills through experiential learning.

In many respects this volume raises more questions than it even purports to solve. But that perhaps, is the point. We don't know how future histories will look (in other words, what our past will become); we don't know how these histories will affect future theology. What we do know is that that future will not look like the present, not even the past(s) which that future will recall. This very uncertainty, frightening as it is, surely is also equally liberating. We may be tied to the past, but we are not bound to it. The very multiplicity of the Christian past can be an ally in freeing us to choose from any number of possible Christian futures.

Acknowledgments

I wish to thank all my colleagues who so graciously and promptly reviewed the manuscripts submitted for this volume. I would as well like to thank each of those who submitted manuscripts and all of the contributors. Deadlines were met, formats were followed and queries were answered in full, on time and with a delightful professional courtesy. Few editors have had, I suspect, such a gratifying experience. Special thanks goes to Susan Perry of Orbis Books for her gentle yet firm shepherding of the volume through the publication process.

Introduction:
Practicing History, Practicing Theology

Terrence W. Tilley

As a prelude to the central argument of this essay, I would like to ask the readers to engage in the exercise of remembering some of the communities which have shaped them as academics. Each of us can recollect people without whom it would have been impossible for us to be who we are, to get where we are, to do what we can now do. We each have lived, do live, and will live in communities that shape our characters. We have learned the virtues of the mind[1] because we have been trained in those virtues by others who have made commitments to us and to our development. We learn intellectual as well as moral virtue by participating in communities of character.[2]

The first community to remember is the family. Each of us owes a huge debt to "family." This may be our natural family, our adopted family, our religious family, or our congregational family. If no one else would teach us, the Godfather would: "Family comes first." Family members need to support each other in every way imaginable. When families fail, their members' characters can become warped, distorted, and broken. Yet at their best, families teach us how to form a life together, how to raise children, and even how to die well. Christian families are schools of virtue that properly teach us the skills we need to live and work together *ad majorem Dei gloriam*. The honesty, integrity, and practical wisdom we learn (or, tragically, fail to learn) as members of those intimate familial communities are components not only of our moral lives, but also of our intellectual lives.

The second community to remember is the community of our friends. The wild variety of the ways we have friends, the uncountable sorts of debts we owe them, and the ways we often unwittingly shape our friends' lives, make this the most difficult group to characterize quickly. While our family can and should teach us how to be virtuous in regions of intimacy, our friends help us to learn how to exercise virtue in civic realms beyond the intimacy of the family. Compared to our families, in which we tend to "find" ourselves, the communities of our friendships are more "made." The virtue(s) of sociability we learn (or, tragically, fail to learn) as friends expands the realm of the virtues we begin to learn in the family.

The third community to remember is the community of scholars. Each of us owes a monumental debt to teachers who have exemplified virtue in the professional craft we learn. School teachers showed me ways that a vocation to teaching could be lived responsibly. As an undergraduate, I learned as much about faithful and tough love of the church as about the history of Catholicism from the late Monsignor John Tracy Ellis. From my Anabaptist "doktorvater," Jim McClendon, I learned how to discover, understand and (when necessary) work to creatively transform the convictions of the Christian community.[3] His practice taught me not only what incisive, yet healing and clarifying, criticism could be,[4] but also showed me how to live out those crucial virtues of open-mindedness, intellectual courage, and intellectual sobriety.[5] Whatever clarity in thinking and writing we have, whatever abilities we have as teachers and scholars, we owe to those who have brought us into the community of scholars and taught us how to exercise the virtues of the mind in our craft. As we mature as scholars, we begin to teach others, both those beginning students we meet in the classroom and the advanced students we meet in convention. For we are all students and all teachers of each other. That is what a community of scholarship like the College Theology Society is about.

The CTS is, in this sense, a true community of scholars and the cornerstone of my professional life. To be frank, the CTS may not have the *cachet* of some other societies, but its members produce good scholarship in the context of real friendship. The meetings of the CTS are not about ecclesial politics, not about intellectual one-ups-manship, not about pretentious posturing by academic peacocks and peahens. The CTS is about the shared tasks of doing and teaching theology and religious studies openly, creatively, courageously, and carefully. As a scholarly community, it is a splendid example of an advanced "school of intellectual virtue."

Presuming this understanding of the academic life as one of exercising intellectual and moral virtue learned and practiced in communities of scholars in the background, I want to consider the specific responsibilities found in the historian's craft and the theologian's work.

One of the most important themes of twentieth-century theology has been the relationship of "faith and history," explored in light of recent scholarship in history during the forty-fourth Annual Meeting of the College Theology Society under the rubric, "Theology and the New Histories." Adapting the analysis of Avery Dulles, S.J., I find that the relationship between faith and history has been construed as following four patterns or models in this century: history against faith, history and faith irrelevant to each other, history as ground of faith, and faith as interpreted history.[6] While I recognize the utility of such a construction, especially for understanding the ways historians of the scriptures and traditions of Christianity have approached their tasks, I also find its basic essentialist approach unhelpful for understanding the relationships of "faith" or "theology" and "history." The disciplines of history and the practices of discipleship (including doing theology) are related in ways far more complex than such a schema allows. History is *not* a discipline, but a field of disciplines with the major tasks of excavating and analyzing the material remains of the past (including texts) and constructing a story about the way things might well have been in order to make that past useful (in various ways) in the present for the future.[7] Construals which essentialize "history" and "faith" or "theology" unfortunately obscure the variety of the practices, findings, and goals of the historians and the variety of types of assent to religious and theological claims ingredient in the practice of faithful discipleship.

In our era, reflective academics, inspired especially by continental philosophies, tend to take hermeneutics as the master key for opening every disciplinary door. Hermeneutics is everything and everything is hermeneutics. Hence, we seek to ferret out the hermeneutical presuppositions which inform the works which academics produce in order to understand and assess those works. This practice is certainly revealing and, at its best, an exercise of great intellectual interest. But we have become so obsessed with scholars' hermeneutical theories and methods that students get doctorates today without doing any history, theology, or sociology—they "do method" or "specialize in hermeneutical theory." Well, far be it from me to kill the messenger— Hermes, the god of thieves, liars, and tricksters is important after all— but I am not so sure that asking the question of the hermeneutical presuppositions and methodological foundations of a piece of scholarship always gets us the insights we seek. I am suggesting that the question of a scholar's interpretation theory or method may not be the most fruitful question to ask about the works a scholar produces. In particular, *now that we know no history is presuppositionless*, perhaps our quest for the historical presuppositions behind every historical text may be the wrong approach for understanding the relationship of "history" and "faith" or "theology," especially when "history" seems to be in conflict with or in support of "faith," i.e., the relationships suggested by the theme of the convention.

Criticism of historians often focuses on their hermeneutical presuppositions. For instance, John Boswell has been criticized for finding just what he was looking for in *Same-Sex Unions in Premodern Europe*.[8] Boswell is accused, justly or not, of allowing his own gayness to lead him to read his own agenda into ambiguous material. More importantly, the "Jesus" that emerges from the newest phase of the Quest for the Historical Jesus looks strikingly contemporary. For instance, Marcus Borg has written what I find to be a rather deceptive popular book, *Meeting Jesus Again for the First Time: The Historical Jesus and the Heart of Contemporary Faith*.[9] He proposes to sketch "what we may surmise" about Jesus "as a historical person." He then claims that "I will introduce you to the pre-Easter Jesus."[10] Here Hermes the trickster seems to stand between the reader and the past. Borg's uneschatological "spirit person" who "mediates the sacred" as a healer and sage is a figment of Borg's imagination just as the Jesus who merely taught "the fatherhood of God and the brotherhood of man" was a figment of Adolph Harnack's imagination. George Tyrrell's pithy diagnosis of Harnack's ahistorical historicism could be applied *mutatis mutandis* to this Newest of the New Questers. In 1909 Tyrrell wrote, "The Christ that Harnack sees, looking back through nineteen centuries of Catholic darkness, is only the reflection of a Liberal Protestant face, seen at the bottom of a deep well.[11] So do Borg and some of his colleagues in the Jesus seminar see and present as the "real Jesus" a figure who remarkably reflects much of their own social locations and academic imaginations.[12]

However, neither the brilliant Harnack, the provocative Boswell, nor the evangelizing Borg fail as historians because they *have* historical methods and hermeneutical presuppositions peculiar to their social locations. Rather, they are especially vulnerable to being accused of *allowing* their presuppositions to *control* their results. Yet similar accusations can easily be leveled against almost any "revisionist" historian whose reconstructed history challenges the tradition a community recollects in ritual and story. The accusation of such bias is an undiscriminating weapon which can be used against almost any academic target. Because our discourse valorizes hermeneutics as the master key for all the humanities, attacks on hermeneutical presuppositions are the master strokes for dismissing the works of historians when those works challenge received wisdom. My point is that however useful analyses of hermeneutical presuppositions might be, attacks on historians' presuppositions too easily uproot the wheat as well as the tares—and do not really get at the important issues when historical claims and faith claims seem to conflict.[13]

My claim is that we should take a different approach. I believe that historians' failures and successes are *not* so much attributable to their methods or hermeneutical presuppositions, but to their carrying out or not carrying out the role-specific responsibilities of historians. My argument is that an evaluative approach that centers on academics' responsibilities and their conclusions, rather than on their presuppositions and their methods, holds more promise for discriminating helpfully among historical works.

In theology, the language of "role-specific responsibilities" is attributable especially to Van A. Harvey. In 1966, Harvey produced a book I still find extremely important, *The Historian and the Believer*.[14] Harvey found two radically different "moralities of knowledge," the historian's and the believer's. He found not merely two hermeneutics or two methodologies. The key difference was two incompatible "ethics of judgment."[15] The historian warranted her claims on the basis of arguments utilizing field-specific evidence and warrants. The orthodox believer who holds a religious belief about history, but who refuses to allow warranted historical claims to count against his belief, by contrast, "is intellectually irresponsible, not so much because he wants certainty, as because he continually enters objections to our normal warrants for no principled reasons."[16] Given the claims that God acts in history, given what Harvey called the Protestant understanding of faith, and given the different practices of the historian and the believer, he found that the liberal theologians of the end of the nineteenth century, the "New Questers" of the fifties, and the neo-orthodox theologians popular when he wrote were all trapped by what we can call Harvey's paradox. They wanted both to affirm historical truths about the historical Jesus and simultaneously to affirm that historical investigations proper to forming judgments about historical figures could not warrant theologically significant truths about Jesus.[17] Unfortunately, Harvey's attempted solution, an adaptation of H. Richard Niebuhr's distinction between "inner" and "outer" history, didn't resolve the paradox.[18]

Adopting Harvey's approach teaches us that it is not the methods or the presuppositions of the Boswells, Borgs, and Harnacks that are at fault. Rather, their concrete judgments fail to meet the role-specific responsibilities of historians. They employ unhistorical, even ideological, warrants for their historical claims as much as "believers" do. In short, I find that the problem with these historians is not that they are liberal or gay or revisionist, or that their methodologies are flawed, but that they engage in argument and analysis as historically "irresponsible" as those Protestant believers Harvey criticized. Like Harvey's "irresponsible" believers, they allow their own faith or presuppositions to warrant their historical claims and thus make claims that go far beyond those which can be supported by the proper practice of historians.[19] They fail not *because* they have value-laden presuppositions, but because they *allow* such beliefs to warrant claims that are not warrantable by the practice of historical investigation and reconstruction. They are "intellectually irresponsible" in their roles as historians.

In contrast, what the responsible historian does is to allow the possibility that historical investigation can change her presuppositions as a practitioner of history. As an example of such historical responsibility, I cite a methodological point in Elizabeth A. Clark's *The Origenist Controversy:*

> [W]hen I began my research on the Origenist controversy in 1985, before I had encountered Evagrius Ponticus, I imagined that I might explain the controversy with little reference to theological "ideas" of any sort. But my introduction to Evagrius's *Kephalaia gnostica* in its unexpurgated form challenged my early, purely social understanding of the Origenist dispute. By situating Evagrius as a central force in the Western (i.e., Latin-speaking) Origenist debate, I signal my chastened reconsideration of the importance of both theology and an ascetic spirituality for the controversy.[20]

Clark did not allow her materialist and social-historical presuppositions to warrant the claims she made. Nor did she allow those presuppositions to control the questions she asked of the monuments and texts from the past. Rather, her investigation itself revealed that those presuppositions needed to be factored out in order to do justice to the evidence and to construct a narrative of the controversy that did justice to that evidence. The difference between Clark and the others cited above is that she fulfilled the role-specific responsibilities of the historian by the standards of the historian's craft because she did not allow her personal presuppositions or her theological views to function as illegitimate warrants or controls in asking her questions, making her arguments, or constructing her narrative. She does not look down the well of sixteen centuries of Catholic darkness to see her own face, her own social location, or her own methodological predilections reflected back at her. It is not that she had or has or did not have or does not have hermeneutical presuppositions, but that she did not allow them improperly to control her historical questions or warrant her historical claims.[21] The way to evaluate historians' claims, then, is not so much to evaluate their presuppositions, but to evaluate whether they have been responsible historians by warranting their claims in ways appropriate to the disciplines of history.

But engaging in the historian's craft responsibly does not resolve Harvey's dilemma. The historian and the believer still have seemingly incompatible ethics of judgment, even in an era in which historical reconstruction is widely recognized as a construct. Exercising the historian's craft—whether utilizing the methods of microhistory, biography, sociology, psychology, economics, or other disciplines—can still result in the production of narratives which have severe tensions with living the faith of the believer. As Justo González points out, both the multiplicity of the historical maps and the variety of topographies they present can undermine our understanding of our religious traditions.[22] And this brings us to pass from examining aspects of historians' work to analyzing one part of the theologian's craft. Particularly, I want to consider how theologians reflect on Christian believing in an era in which historical investigations have cast long shadows on particular religious beliefs and practices by examining a recent controversy.

Some theologians have made unwarranted attacks on our sister society, the Catholic Theological Society of America in *Commonweal* earlier this spring.[23] Avery Dulles, S.J., for instance, asserted that an "orchestrated chorus . . . rejected fundamental articles of Catholic belief regarding priesthood and Eucharist. . . .[24] Dulles attacked historian Gary Macy, among others. Macy has done meticulous and challenging work on popular devotion to and medieval theologies of the Eucharist. In so doing he has revealed a true diversity of doctrine and practice in the Middle Ages. With regard to St. Thomas Aquinas, Macy claimed, "Thomas's work, interesting as it remains, was an idiosyncratic voice in thirteenth century eucharistic theology and by the end of that century, a voice which ceased to convince."[25] In his remarks, Dulles presumed that the historians like Macy are attacking the faith. "These views were set forth with a certain display of historical erudition as though doctrines could be invalidated by tagging them chronologically."[26] But as Dulles knows, and as Mary Ann Donovan pointed out so well in response to his essay, "to adduce historical evidence for earlier stages of doctrinal development is not to attack doctrine."[27] *Pace* Dulles, for a historian to show that there is diversity in the tradition is not to attack the tradition. No one has shown, to my knowledge, that Macy has failed to substantiate his historical claims using the tools of the historian's craft. He is a responsible historian, the preeminent American historian of medieval eucharistic theology; he does not use his own theological beliefs as presuppositions for warranting historical claims; nor does he ever claim, so far as I know, that his historical excavations, analyses, and reconstructions show it unreasonable for us to accept contemporary doctrinal claims.[28]

What such critics do is to fail to distinguish the descriptive accounts of the historian from the normative recommendations of the theologian. But why? Is the answer implicit in Roger Cardinal Mahony's letter to *Commonweal* on this subject? Mahony writes:

> Theologians are to be commended for continuing the church's efforts to articulate ever more deeply and fully its eucharistic faith—a task that needs to be done in each age. In carrying forward this effort, some disagreement is unavoidable. But how we treat disagreements among us speaks loudly to the entire world about the depth of our faith and our trust in the Holy Spirit working within the church.[29]

Have the critics allowed their faith and trust in the Spirit to be undermined by historical argument? Do they think that some will lose their faith because historians warrant claims about diversity in our tradition? Do they believe that our contemporary debates about the Eucharist are more pluralistic, confusing, and divisive than the medieval debates?[30] One hopes the answer to each of these is "no."

Such critics unfortunately buy into the confusion about argument and warrant that brings historians and Catholic believers into apparent conflict. They seem to think that historians' theological presuppositions control their historical claims. Of course, in some cases the accusation that historians' non-historical beliefs control their work may be true. I have noted some above. But I do not see any evidence that it is true in the present case.

My diagnosis is that theologians like Dulles continue to construe the problem of "faith" and "history" in much the same terms Harvey described in 1966. This very construal is the problem. "Faith" and "history" seem to be construed as univocal concepts that name some essential ideas or practices that can be modeled as related to each other in constant and specific patterns. Dulles's response to the problem, given his models, seems to reproduce the strategies of the neo-orthodox theologians of the past, who wanted to "save" belief by insulating it from historical inquiry (except historical inquiry that supported, enhanced or nuanced that belief), an approach that falls afoul of Harvey's paradox noted earlier.[31]

I believe Van Harvey has also indicated a way out of this situation, a way that is especially fitting for Catholics. In his 1979 essay on the Victorian debate on the ethics of belief among John Henry Newman, Leslie Stephen, William George Ward, James Clifford, William James and others, Harvey points out that the responsible believing and responsible practice are "role-specific."[32] What went wrong in that earlier debate, Harvey claimed, was that from John Locke through William James the question of what constitutes responsible belief was asked as though it were a univocal question, applicable to all instances of believing, no matter what the strength of the believing, the content or type of the belief, the way in which the belief was formed, or the social significance of holding the belief. What Harvey proposed as a remedy, then, was to look at the social (including intellectual) roles we play, and the duties incumbent on those who would fulfill the responsibilities of that role well.

In the present case, the historian warrants hypotheses as well as she or he can on historical grounds. The historian does not and cannot responsibly claim to introduce us to the "pre-Easter Jesus," but only to offer a hypothesis about the way the actual Jesus might have been, a hypothesis which has some warrant, but can never be certain. Gary Macy does not and cannot responsibly claim to refute church doctrines or invalidate church practice on the grounds of his hypotheses. He does show us, with a high level of probability and strong textual warrant, extensive diversity about the Eucharist in our tradition, especially in the high medieval period. Historical work may indeed indirectly undermine confidence about the unchanging character of some specific beliefs or practices. But for those of us who live in a sacramental universe, a universe in which tracing the way things have been may indeed be encountering traces of the divine, a view central to Catholic faith and theology, the historian's hypotheses may help us, if we have the eyes of faith, to see how God may have been working in our past.

The role-specific responsibility of the theologian is *not* to accept the hypotheses of historians—or sociologists, social psychologists or ethnographers—as vetoes on faith and practice or as sufficient warrants for expressions of faith and patterns of practice. Rather the theologian must accept these hypotheses as indicators of varying reliability of how the faith has been lived, been practiced, been incarnated both "there and then" and "here and now." The theologian can then make her own recommendations for reformation or restoration—*but empirical claims, even if fully warranted, are not sufficient, and may not even be necessary, to warrant theological recommendations.*

As an example of this, consider the traditional Christian belief that Jesus knew that he was God's son.[33] Historical investigation of the New Testament has reached something of a consensus that any christologically significant use of the title "son of God" cannot be reliably attributed to the actual man Jesus himself, but is almost certainly a product of early Christians' reflection on him and his significance.[34] What this means is that this belief cannot be historically warranted on the basis of what the New Testament reliably tells us about Jesus. Insofar as the tradition has warranted that belief on the basis of the New Testament text as portraying Jesus' "consciousness," the tradition has used warrants we cannot reasonably accept today. Yet it can be claimed with a very high degree of historical reliability that the writers of the New Testament used this title and others to express Jesus' significance. The strong historical warrant for the claim about Jesus' self-understanding, then, is not what the New Testament text says about Jesus, but what it shows us about the beliefs of the inspired writers of the New Testament. If indeed they "consigned to writing everything and only those things which He [God] wanted"[35] (a theological claim about the status of the Scriptures), there is excellent historical warrant that *they* believed that Jesus had presented himself to them or to their informants as God's "son" (and thus making not unreasonable the inference that he may well have known or believed he was God's son). The combination, then, of theological warrant (inspiration) and historical warrant (what we can infer about the writers of Scripture and their informants) may well go far to warrant the traditional claim about Jesus' knowledge even though there is no reliable "direct" warrant from scripture about his self-consciousness.[36]

This principle that empirical historical claims, even if fully warranted, are not sufficient, and may not even be necessary, to warrant theological recommendations also applies to a more tender issue about the tradition. Whatever "ordination" has meant—and it has meant many things—if it can be demonstrated historically that the church "ordained" women in the past, that is neither necessary nor sufficient warrant for "ordaining" women today. If it could be demonstrated that the church never "ordained" women in the past, that would not be necessary or sufficient warrant to prohibit the ordination of women today. While theological arguments often can and should be influenced by historians' excavations, analyses, and reconstructions, normative theological claims cannot stand or fall solely on the basis of historical warrant. Dulles and his colleagues seem to think either that the theologians in the CTSA are confused on this issue or that the faithful are simple enough to be duped into thinking so. If they think the former, they fail to understand that the distinct responsibilities of historians and theologians as they are carried out by that group of scholars—very well in my judgment—are not confused by them. If they think the latter, jeremiads against the Catholicity of our sister society are hardly effective remedies.[37]

Moreover, *pace* the critics, theologians cannot and do not responsibly set up an "alternative magisterium" in the contemporary sense of "magisterium." Those who think theologians do so confuse academic responsibility and authority with ecclesial responsibility and authority (however that is exercised in a given polity). These are different responsibilities, ingredient in different roles, undertaken for different purposes. Theological recommendations often can and should influence ecclesial belief and practice, just as historical investigations influence theological recommendations, but theologians' proposals are neither necessary nor sufficient to warrant church belief or practice. While such responsibilities and authority can be exercised by the same person who happens to exercise more than one role, collapsing them into each other is confused.

From the foregoing, it is clear that I see significant overlaps in our practices. Indeed, one person may be both historian and theologian and priest or pastor. Such a person participates in different practices and has responsibilities in each of them and must practice each of them as faithfully as possible—just as many of us engage responsibly in the roles of parent, teacher, researcher, minister. This is not to deny that our roles may not occasionally generate conflicting responsibilities, not only with other practitioners, but within our own hearts. The results of our historical work may indeed challenge our religious beliefs. But there is no algorithm for settling such conflicts, whether internal to an individual or shared in a community. And broadside attacks on faithful theologians and historians struggling to see and show God's truth are not only unedifying, as Cardinal Mahony notes, but tend to be self-destructive. For which of us pastors are not theologians and historians to some extent? Which of us theologians do not engage in history and shape students' beliefs pastorally? Which of us historians are innocent of ideology and want to avoid shaping our students practices? Neither conflating the roles and responsibilities of historians, theologians and pastors nor attacking their practices is sufficient to resolve the conflicts. Even if we avoid the dead end of thinking presuppositional analysis is all we need and turn to examining intellectuals' role-specific responsibilities and how well we carry them out in specific cases, another approach is needed to help us resolve the conflicts our practices generate. Given that rarely are properly formed historical and theological claims—properly understood—directly in conflict with each other because they just do emerge from different "ethics of judgment," how can we resolve those conflicts when they do occur?

I have argued elsewhere that the proper approach to answering that question is to rely on that shared practical wisdom, that virtue Aristotle identified as *phronesis* and Aquinas as *prudentia*. I have written at length about this in *The Wisdom of Religious Commitment*. Here I will merely restate my main thesis as applicable for the present discussion: *Phronesis* is the ability to come to and act on hard judgments in the face of conflicting claims.[38] We learn this virtue in the communities of our families, friends, and fellow-scholars. We teach each other how to do history and how to do theology responsibly. Our ability to work through hard conflicts depends on learning *phronesis* in and through the communities in which we celebrate, remember, and believe. When hard conflicts arise as a result of our work as historians or theologians that make religious commitment difficult, no simple method of adjudication will do, no examination of presuppositions or hermeneutical theory will turn the trick, no wholesale acceptance or rejection of the religious, historical, or theological practices we engage in will suffice, no appeal to the rights of this or that group will trump the opposition.

And that takes us back to the beginning. I focused on the communities of family, friends, and scholars as schools for virtue. That led us into the exercise of considering the ways we responsibly practice history. And that exercise led us to the exercise of theology, of working at refining, restoring, renewing, rethinking our beliefs and practices. And that led us to consider briefly the virtue of *phronesis*, a virtue we learn from family, teachers, students, colleagues, and friends when we find there are no easy solutions to our apparent conflicts, especially conflicts of principles. Learning to be *phronimoi*, people of prudence, is the only hope for us who live in a world of conflict but who are committed to work *ad majorem Dei gloriam.*

So what does this mean? Why should we take such an approach in which everything seems to be at risk, in which we must rely on the prudence of our colleagues who all too often seem imprudent? One reason for taking the risk is that it is just the postmodern condition: everything *just is* at risk. One reason for trusting to prudence is that it is just the only way available: *scientia*, however understood, no longer applies in these cases, if it ever did. But there is another, deeper reason as well, one that involves my deepest theological conviction as a Catholic theologian.

If we live in a sacramental universe—and I do—it means that my life must live out the conviction that God has given us to each other as family, friends, and teachers. It means that we can be signs of God for each other, if we would recollect and revere each other. It means that we can and must practice our crafts humbly and responsibly according to our roles with and for each other. It means that we can do this because we as theologians responsibly live out our conviction that all the world—the natural world, the human world, the interior world—is charged with the grandeur of God. This God has created the world, been incarnated in it, and remains with us, among us, and in us as the Spirit of Wisdom. This Spirit whom we celebrate this Pentecost comforts us even as we seek to understand God's ways in the past and present and to live in God's ways now and forever.

Some would worry that an approach that puts everything at risk is so constructivist that it gives up on realism in epistemology and merely invokes God as a mantra to hide the fact that it gives up on "real truth" altogether. A full defense of my view would go far beyond the space available here, but to put it simply, I accept "constructivism" and "contextualism," but with a very important twist—the conviction that we live in a sacramental universe. Because of this "twist" I can and do accept an important insight of pragmatist Wilfrid Sellars. Sellars made the comment that he found Richard Rorty's anti-realist approach in epistemology congenial, but that Rorty had not considered that accuracy of reference might not be a criterion of the truth of a claim, but an effect of our getting things right.[39] I understand this to mean that constructivists in epistemology are right to say that all of our knowledge is constructed; are right to note that we cannot control the way things are; are right to claim that it is not in our control whether our claims match (reflect, accurately represent, accurately refer to) the way things are. What we *can* do is to warrant our claims as well as we can in the discursive communities in which we participate.[40] If we do live in a thoroughly sacramental universe, however, we can be confident that our fully warranted claims are as true to the way things are as they can be. In short, my view is that strong constructivism is compatible with strong realism in epistemology if the universe is sacramental.

In a sacramental universe, however sinful, raucous, charged with disagreement, confused, and torn we are, we can be confident that God's polyphonic and multicolored truth will always be present, both hidden and revealed. We can do our work with confidence together for we are members of the body of Christ, of a communion of saints and scholars, of a household of God, and of academic societies. In these communities together we nurture each other in the virtues of the mind appropriate to the roles God has given us to live out. In "practicing history and practicing theology," we cannot do more and we dare not do less.

Notes

[1] This phrase acknowledges the very important work of Catholic philosopher Linda Trinkaus Zagzebski, *Virtues of the Mind: An Inquiry into the Nature of Virtue and the Ethical Foundations of Knowledge* (Cambridge: Cambridge University Press, 1996). Her work shows how the strengths of the various strands of classical and contemporary epistemology can complement each other in a theory that focuses on the responsible epistemic subject and her intellectual virtues. Zagzebski's work makes *phronesis*, practical wisdom, central to epistemology (see especially pp. 211-31 in her book) as I make it central for wisely making and holding religious commitments (see Terrence W. Tilley, *The Wisdom of Religious Commitment* [Washington, D.C.: Georgetown University Press, 1995]).

[2] This phrase acknowledges the work of Stanley Hauerwas, but emphasizes that we do not and cannot live or thrive in one community, but are constituted as subjects in many communities of discourse, a point important for understanding how the historian's craft is related to the work of theologians as discussed below. Among his many works, for this point see especially S. Hauerwas, *A Community of Character: Toward a Constructive Christian Social Ethic* (Notre Dame: University of Notre Dame Press, 1981).

[3] This clause pays tribute to McClendon's definition of theology. Among his early works, see James W. McClendon, Jr., and James M. Smith, *Understanding Religious Convictions* (Notre Dame: University of Notre Dame Press, 1975); revised edition: *Convictions: Defusing Religious Relativism* (Valley Forge, Pennsylvania: Trinity Press International, 1994), 184.

[4] As one example, on the first page of the first draft of the first chapter he saw of my doctoral dissertation some quarter century ago—a page jumbled with nervous prose—he wrote down the margin in his distinctive left-handed scrawl words that made me laugh and showed me how to think and write better: "Backward run sentences 'til reels the mind."

[5] See Zagzebski, *Virtues of the Mind*, 185. Because she is exploring the shape of a virtue-based epistemology, Zagzebski does not attempt to offer a comprehensive list of intellectual virtues, but offers various candidates for inclusion in such a list. This is one small set, adapted from John Dewey.

[6] Avery Dulles, S.J., "Historical Method and the Reality of Christ," *The Craft of Theology: From Symbol to System*, New Expanded Edition (New York: Crossroad, 1996), 212-22.

[7] I do *not* offer this as a "definition" of history, but as a rough and ready description of what historians actually do when they work as historians. Some practices, e.g., doing oral histories, would need to be explored more fully to make this description more nuanced. Some historians would also not accept the purpose as stated, preferring not to say that they "construct" history, but instead "tell it like it was." But on the account I offer below Rankean objectivity can find a place even if history is more literature than science, a point made by Elizabeth A. Clark in a

plenary address to the 1998 CTS Convention, "Rewriting Early Christian History" (see pages 89-111 of this volume).

[8] John Boswell, *Same-Sex Unions in Premodern Europe* (New York: Villard Books, 1994). I am unable to locate the source for this criticism, but recollect it from casual reading of book reviews.

[9] Marcus J. Borg, *Meeting Jesus Again for the First Time: The Historical Jesus and the Heart of Contemporary Faith* (San Francisco: HarperSanFrancisco, 1994). I see no reason to believe this deception was intentional, but, having read the text with a number of students, I find them consistently to be deceived in the ways I describe below as a result of reading the opening chapters of the book.

[10] Borg, *Meeting Jesus Again*, 20.

[11] George Tyrrell, *Christianity at the Crossroads*, (London: George Allen and Unwin, Ltd., 1963), 49.

[12] Lest it be thought that I reject historical approaches to Jesus altogether, let me affirm that I find the work of E. P. Sanders to be much nuanced, reliable, and far more convincing than any of the works of the Jesus Seminar members. See his (relatively) popular summary, *The Historical Figure of Jesus* (London: Penguin, 1993) and the historically nuanced scholarship that lies behind it, especially *Jesus and Judaism* (London: SCM Press, 1985). Luke Timothy Johnson, *The Real Jesus: The Misguided Quest for the Historical Jesus and the Truth of the Traditional Gospels* (San Francisco: HarperSanFrancisco, 1996) interestingly says nothing about Sanders's work.

[13] This must not be construed as rejecting the value of learning or exercising proper methods in history or in any other discipline. Good methodology is necessary, but not sufficient, to produce good work in any field.

[14] Van A. Harvey, *The Historian and the Believer: The Morality of Historical Knowledge and Christian Belief* (New York: Macmillan, 1966).

[15] Harvey, *The Historian and the Believer*, 104. Harvey presumes a deontological ethical approach. Along with Zagzebski, I would subsume this "rule governed" approach into a "virtue ethic" applying both to moral and intellectual virtues. As "virtue ethics" was not resurrected in philosophy or theology until about a decade after Harvey wrote, this should not be taken as implying any criticism of Harvey.

[16] Harvey, *The Historian and the Believer*, 118. This claim is severely limited. It applies to some believers in some cases. Harvey is quite correct in noting that the believer has a rather different "ethic of judgment" from that of the historian, but that does not make the believer "intellectually irresponsible" unless the believer fails to exercise the virtue of wisdom in her or his faith. I have argued that believers can fail to be prudent in their judgments, as in the case Harvey notes, but that this is not characteristic of all religious believers or religious judgments (see Tilley, *The Wisdom of Religious Commitment*, chapter 4).

[17] See Harvey, *The Historian and the Believer*, 196-97. Avery Dulles takes a similar position in "Historical Method and the Reality of Christ": "The postcritical approach . . . does not rule out the legitimacy of efforts to reconstruct the person and teaching of Jesus by 'presuppositionless' methods acceptable to nonbelievers.

The resulting pictures of the 'historical' Jesus are always intriguing and sometimes useful in illuminating aspects of the life and personality of the Redeemer. But in no case does the method provide a religiously adequate portrait, one that can take the place of Jesus Christ as proclaimed by the Church and received in faith" (224). The problem with Dulles's account is that it seems to insulate faith from historical work that might cast shadows on theological claims.

[18] See H. Richard Niebuhr, *The Meaning of Revelation* (New York: Macmillan, 1960; first edition 1941), especially 32-66.

[19] This is a large claim which requires significant argument and analysis to warrant it fully. Space does not allow redeeming this claim fully here. To do so I would use the work of Luke Timothy Johnson and the many discussions and reviews of the Newest Quest and argue that their criticisms are most warranted if they are seen not as "wholesale" criticisms of method and presuppositions, but as "retail" criticisms about specific claims the Newest Questers make not on the basis of historical investigations, but on the basis of their own ideologically informed social locations.

[20] Elizabeth A. Clark, *The Origenist Controversy: The Cultural Construction of an Early Christian Debate* (Princeton: Princeton University Press, 1992), 6-7. I find similar revisions of theoretical presuppositions by the data in the evolution of Robert Orsi's work; compare "'Mildred, is it fun to be a cripple?' The Culture of Suffering in Mid-Twentieth Century American Catholicism," *South Atlantic Quarterly* 93/3 (Summer 1994): 547-590 with *Thank You, St. Jude: Women's Devotion to the Patron Saint of Hopeless Causes* (New Haven, Conn.: Yale University Press, 1996).

[21] In discussion of her paper, "New Footsteps in Well-Trodden Ways: Religion and Gender in Irish America," presented to the American Catholic Life and Thought Section of the Annual Meeting of the College Theology Society, May 31, 1998, Kathleen A. Sprows of the University of Notre Dame noted that she could not make progress in her own work on gender roles until she stopped trying to answer the ideological questions often put to her. People would ask her (and she evidently began her work with such questions) questions like, "Weren't the roles constructed for Catholic women in that context repressive (or 'suffocating' or 'liberating' or 'supportive')?" But these are questions that can only come *after* one reconstructs the actual shape of those roles, the effects they had on women's and men's lives, and *after* one develops a notion of what essentially contested terms like "liberating" or "repressive" mean. If one tries to get historical investigations to provide answers to such ideological questions, one cannot proceed properly in the craft of the historian. These questions can only come logically later, after the excavation, analysis and reconstruction is well under way, if not complete. Sprows's answer to these questions is, if I understood it correctly, that those roles were "liberating" and "repressive" in different ways, at different times, for different people—and sometimes *both* simultaneously.

[22] Justo L. González, "The Changing Geography of Church History" (see pages 23-32 of this volume).

²³ Avery Dulles, Mary Ann Donovan, Peter Steinfels, "Disputed Questions: How Catholic is the CTSA? Three Views," *Commonweal*, 125/6 (March 27, 1998). Letters on these essays, both attacking and defending the CTSA and its members, have appeared in the April 24, 1998 and May 22, 1998 issues of that magazine. Further letters have been submitted; whether they will be published remains to be seen at the time of this writing.

²⁴ Dulles, "Disputed Questions," 13.

²⁵ Gary Macy, "The Eucharist and Popular Religiosity," *CTSA Proceedings* 52 (1997): 52.

²⁶ Dulles, "Disputed Questions," 14.

²⁷ Mary Ann Donovan, "Disputed Questions," 16. Msgr. M. Francis Mannion finds her defense uncompelling, "because, though it appears to refute Dulles, she ends up for the purposes of defense placing herself in a position considerably to the "right" of the operative convictions of American sacramental theology—a position I do not believe she generally inhabits" (Correspondence, *Commonweal* 125/8 [April 24, 1998], 30). Mannion, like Dulles, conflates Donovan's theological views with her historical and textual analysis. Where she stands on the issue of sacramental theology is irrelevant to the debate at this point; her theological views factor out of this argument. She is not, indeed, "taking a stance" at all.

²⁸ I recommend consulting his work and the modern and medieval sources he cites in "The Eucharist and Popular Religiosity." Macy does note that there was a renegotiation of ritual power in the late twelfth and early thirteenth centuries and that there is reason to think that there may be a ritual renegotiation occurring today (56-58), a state of affairs about which he confesses optimism and enthusiasm in his peroration. That admission, however, neither substantiates nor undermines his historical arguments; rather, it expresses in a plenary address to a theological society his valuing the present ferment in debate and practice as being as interesting and exciting as that of the thirteenth century, and his optimism for the church in this era. Neither of these are historical judgments.

²⁹ Cardinal Roger Mahony, Correspondence, *Commonweal* 125/10 (May 22, 1998): 4.

³⁰ Peter Steinfels, "Disputed Questions," makes the point that there is real reason for concern by moderate and conservative theologians. In language Macy uses, there *is* a renegotiation of ritual power in the church today. In language Steinfels uses, this renegotiation is resulting in a "diffusion" of the power of the minister into the congregation. But this "diffusion" is not new, as Macy shows, nor are the theologies that reflect these practices completely new. Rather, the monochromatic and concentrated practice and theology of the Eucharist which we have considered as *the* tradition is being revealed as merely one color in the Catholic theological rainbow in past and present. This seems to be a clearly warranted historical claim. The worry about the diffusion of the tradition and the possible loss of Catholic identity through loss of distinctiveness in our culture is as legitimate as the worry about excessive centralization and the loss of Catholics' ability to identify with the tradition because of petrification of traditional practices and

beliefs. Yet this worry is a religious one, important whether or not the historical claim is accurate. And neither Dulles's hint that the schism of a remnant group from the CTSA might be preferable nor Steinfels's suggestion that more "balanced" theological presentations are needed will resolve those real worries about Catholic identity. For what the plenaries at the CTSA Meeting of 1997 did was to present an authentic, but neglected, strand of the tradition which "emphasizes the entire eucharistic liturgy as celebrated by the whole gathered people of God. To present and explain this growing consensus, in scholarly papers at a theological convention, is the proper work of the Catholic theologian" (Mary Ann Donovan, "Disputed Questions," 16).

[31] Dulles, "Historical Method and the Reality of Christ," 222-24, clearly subordinates "history" to "faith," allowing "faith" a trump over "history" in the way neo-orthodoxy privileges "belief" over "history" according to Harvey's analysis in *The Historian and the Believer*. While I think Dulles's theory needs significant modification to do justice both to the practice of faith and to the practice of history, I nonetheless wholeheartedly agree with Dulles when he points out that the Quests for the Historical Jesus cannot provide a "religiously adequate portrait" or an acquaintance with the real Jesus, and that "faith and intelligence, dogma and history, can and must be integrated" (224).

[32] Van A. Harvey, "The Ethics of Belief Reconsidered," *The Ethics of Belief Debate*, ed. Gerald D. McCarthy, AAR Studies in Religion 41 (Atlanta: Scholars Press, 1986), especially 194-203. McCarthy's book collects many of the Victorian essays and some contemporary reflections; Harvey's article was first published in *The Journal of Religion* in 1979.

[33] For a brief, but helpful, discussion of Jesus' self-knowledge, see Elizabeth A. Johnson, *Consider Jesus: Waves of Renewal in Christology* (New York: Crossroad, 1990), 35-47.

[34] For a brief discussion of this title and the consensus about its historical significance (which has not, so far as I know, changed in any significant way since I wrote), see Terrence W. Tilley, *Story Theology* (Wilmington, Del.: Michael Glazier, Inc., 1985; reprint edition, Collegeville, Minnesota: Liturgical Press, 1990), chapter seven, "The Stories of Jesus: III," especially 121-27.

[35] *Dei Verbum* § 11; as in Walter M. Abbott, S.J., ed., *The Documents of Vatican II* (New York: Guild Press, America Press, Association Press, 1966), 119. The position developed here is intended to be fully consistent with the teaching of *Dei Verbum*.

[36] The skeptical historian will, of course, reply that this is no "historical" proof about what Jesus knew. But the skeptical historian has no warrant for the claim that Jesus *did not* know or *could not* have known he was in a christologically significant sense the "son of God." Proving the absence of a singular belief is practically historically impossible. The skeptic will claim that the belief is attributable to the early Christian community. The traditional believer will agree— but, at least in this case, will see no reason not to think that however the belief emerged in their discourse, the process was inspired by God. The difference

between them has nothing to do with historical warrants and arguments, but with ideological issues about the ultimate inspiration for some historical events.

[37] I am certainly *not* claiming that only well-warranted claims have been made at gatherings of the CTSA or any other society. I have heard claims made at meetings of theological societies that are far more outrageous than any Marcus Borg makes. But such claims are usually recognized for what they are and die from malnourishment as competent theologians refuse to feed them with their attention.

[38] For a description of *phronesis* as "intellect in action," see Tilley, *The Wisdom of Religious Commitment*, 93-160; also see Zagzebski, *Virtues of the Mind*, 211-231, for historic discussions of *phronesis*.

[39] Sellars made this comment at a symposium devoted to a discussion of Richard Rorty, *Philosophy and the Mirror of Nature* (Princeton: Princeton University Press, 1979), at the Annual Meeting of the Eastern Division of the American Philosophical Association in Boston in 1980. I am not aware of its being published.

[40] For my view of the standards we can use, see *Story Theology*, 182-213.

Part I

NEW METHODOLOGIES

The Changing Geography of Church History

Justo L. González

As a central image for describing and discussing the changes that are taking place in church history, I have decided to use the metaphor of geography. However, in a way this is more than a metaphor, for there is indeed a connection between history and geography. If history is a drama, then geography is the stage on which the action takes place. No matter how much one focuses on the plot, it is impossible to understand or to follow the action without its setting on the stage. Indeed, much of the plot has to do with the placing of the various actors on the stage, with their entering and exiting, with the various props that establish the setting, with the movement of the actors up- or downstage. Likewise, I learned many years ago that it is impossible to follow history without an understanding of the stage on which it takes place.

In my own academic career, I must confess that in my early years of study, the subject that I most disliked was history. And then I realized that one of the reasons why I disliked it was because I was trying to understand events only in their chronological sequence, as if the geography or the stage in which they took place were unimportant. Thus, what ought to have been the fascinating study of people's lives became a series of names and dates hanging in mid-air, of disembodied ghosts parading through my textbooks in rapid and confusing succession. It was only when I began seeing them as actual people with their feet on the ground, and when I began understanding the movements of peoples and nations, not only across time and chronology, but also across space and geography, that history became fascinating to me.

As a professor, I have become convinced that one of the main obstacles in the teaching and the learning of church history is that the geography in which that history takes place is alien and unknown to

most students. I may be fascinated with the theological and hermeneutical contrasts between Alexandria and Antioch, and spend an hour
explaining those contrasts and their consequences for Christology or
for soteriology, only to find at the end of the hour that many of my
students do not have the faintest idea where to place Alexandria or
Antioch on a map of the Roman Empire.

My wife also teaches church history. Some years ago she began to
suspect that one of the reasons why some students had enormous difficulties understanding the history of the ancient and medieval church
was that they lacked even a basic understanding of geography. One
year, at the very first class, before saying even the first word about
history, she handed out maps of Europe and the Roman Empire, and
then asked the students to locate on those maps a list of cities and
places. Almost all knew enough geography to place Rome somewhere
in the boot of Italy. Most knew that Jerusalem was somewhere towards the eastern edge of the Mediterranean. But there their knowledge ended. One student put Ireland in the Ukraine. Another moved
Spain to Germany, and Egypt to Spain. Alexandria drifted all the way
from Egypt to Great Britain, and the unfortunate Lybians were freez-
ing north of Moscow.

Having had our laugh at beginning students of theology, it is time
that we historians and professors of theology look at the beam in our
own eye. True, we know more or less where to place Alexandria on
the map, and we would never place Spain east of the Rhine; but, are
we sufficiently aware of the manner in which the map of the church
has changed during our own lifetimes, and the manner in which that is
beginning to affect the reading and the writing of church history?

The changes in the map of Christianity should be evident to anyone
who is aware of the manner in which Christianity has evolved during
the last few decades. At the beginning of this century, half of all Christians in the world lived in Europe. Now that figure is less than a quarter. At the beginning of the century, approximately four out of five
Christians were white. At the end of the century, less than two out of
five. At the beginning of the century, the great missionary centers of
Christianity were New York and London. Today more missionaries
are sent from Korea than from London, and Puerto Rico is sending
missionaries to New York by the dozen. At the beginning of the century, Christianity was confident of its future in the North Atlantic, and
was hoping to carve a future in the rest of the world. Today, there is

malaise and often even despondency in the North Atlantic, and hope and enthusiasm in the rest of the world.

What this means is that the map of Christianity on which we operated a few decades ago is no longer operational. That was a map in which the center was the North Atlantic—Europe and North America. Apart from a few churches whose interest was mostly as relics of an ancient past, there was little outside the North Atlantic to attract the attention of historians. And these historians themselves were either persons from the North Atlantic, or persons who, as myself, had been trained into the North Atlantic reading of history.

It is true that it was only in my courses in church history that I learned that there are in places such as Ethiopia and Armenia churches that are at least as ancient as most churches in the West.

Still, when I review the manner in which I first studied church history, and the cartography that lay behind that history as an unspoken presupposition, I am surprised and dismayed at the degree to which I allowed that telling of the narrative to become part of my story, even though in fact in many ways it marginalized me and my community.

One example should suffice. Just about every textbook on church history that was used when I first studied the subject tended to reduce the significance of the sixteenth century to the Protestant Reformation and its Roman Catholic counterpart. That was understandable. These were mostly Protestant books, written at a time when there was still great alienation between Protestants and Catholics, and they were also books from the North Atlantic, written from a perspective in which the North Atlantic was the new *mare nostrum* of the new imperial civilization. However, even Roman Catholic histories followed the same pattern. Significantly, even though I had studied the history of the conquest and colonization of the Western Hemisphere ever since I was in the second grade, as I read those books in seminary it did not occur to me that there was here a great omission. Today, I cannot speak of the history of the church in the sixteenth century without taking into account that on May 26, 1521, the same day that the imperial Diet of Worms issued its edict against Luther, Hernán Cortés was laying siege to the imperial city of Tenochtitlán. And today, after the Second Vatican Council and a number of developments in Latin America, many would agree that the jury is still out as to which of those two events will eventually prove to be more important for the history of the church at large.

Today, I must work with a different set of maps. Indeed, today I must work with a map that no longer places the North Atlantic at the center, but is rather a polycentric map. This is perhaps the most radical change that has taken place in the cartography of church history. In the past, we could speak of a center, or at most of two centers, and tell the story from those centers outward. Today that is no longer possible. Today there are many centers, both in the actual life of the church and in the way the past history of the church is being written.

It may be helpful to stop and think about the polycentric nature of today's Christianity. To a degree without parallel in the history of the church, today the centers of vitality are not the same as the centers of economic resources. And those centers are more than one. In times past, there have been many changes in the geography of Christianity. Already in the New Testament, we see the center shifting from Jerusalem to Antioch, and even towards Asia Minor. Yet at that time it is also clear that as the importance of the church in Jerusalem wanes in comparison with the rest of Christianity, so also do its economic resources wane, so that a significant part of Paul's mission is to collect funds for the saints in Jerusalem. Later, when the Islamic invasions and the Carolingian renaissance shift the center to Western Europe, it is clear that there is a new center, not only in vitality, but also in economic resources.

Today the situation is quite different. There is no doubt that the vast majority of the financial resources of the church are still in the North Atlantic. Indeed, the endowment of some of our major colleges and seminaries in the United States is larger than the entire budget of many a national church overseas. And some parishes in the United States own buildings that are worth more than all the holdings of entire dioceses elsewhere. The same is true of the number of magazines and books published, resources invested in the media, etc. And yet, proportionately speaking, the number of Christians in the North Atlantic continues to dwindle, while there is an explosion in church membership in traditionally poorer countries.

That is the first dimension of what I mean by affirming that the emerging geography of Christianity is polycentric. From the point of view of resources, the centers are still in the United States, Canada, and Western Europe. From the point of view of vitality, missionary and evangelistic zeal, and even theological creativity, the centers have been shifting south for some time.

The second dimension of the new polycentric reality is that even in the South there is no new center. There are exciting new theological insights coming from Peru as well as from South Africa and the Philippines. There is phenomenal growth in Chile as well as in Brazil, Uganda, and Korea. No single place can now be called *the* center of Christianity, nor even one of the few centers.

This new map of Christianity in turn implies a different reading of church history at least on two points.

The first of these is that it is no longer possible to separate the history of the church from the history of missions or the history of the expansion of Christianity. The manner in which church history has been traditionally read, written, and taught, not only in the North Atlantic, but even throughout the world, made it appear that North Atlantic Christianity was the goal of church history, and that therefore everything that did not lead to it was part of a different field of study, usually called the "history of missions," or by some other similar name. Thus, the conversion of the Roman Empire and the conversion of the Germanic tribes were part of church history; but the conversion of Ethiopia and the planting of Christianity in Japan were part of the history of missions. The controversy over the presence of Christ in the Eucharist during the Carolingian period was part of church history, but the controversy over the Chinese rites in the Roman Catholic Church was not; the debates over the veneration of images in eighth-century Europe were part of church history, but the debate over the veneration of ancestors in nineteenth-century Asia was not.

Such distinctions are no longer possible. Precisely because Christianity has become polycentric, church history has become global and ecumenical in a way that would have been inconceivable a few generations ago.

This takes us to the second point at which the new map of the church leads to a different reading of church history. This has to do with the ideological framework that stands behind the map itself, and therefore behind the discipline of church history.

This is not the first time the cartography of church history has changed. Indeed, the map of the church has changed repeatedly through the centuries. From a sect limited to Palestine and its surroundings, it soon spread throughout the Roman Empire and beyond. By the fourth century, the map had come to include Ethiopia, Armenia, Georgia, Persia, and perhaps even India. By the eighth century, China was part of the map. Then came the age of the great expansion of the European powers, and the map changed even more radically, rapidly including Africa, Asia, the entire Western Hemisphere; then Australia, New Zealand, and the islands of the Pacific.

But although these changes have taken place in the map of Christianity in purely geographic terms, in ideological terms the map remained the same since the times of Eusebius. The map of Eusebius was clear. It went just one step beyond Justin, Clement, and Origen. They had said that God, through the logos, had provided two streams leading to Christ: the Jewish tradition, especially the Hebrew Bible, and Greco-Roman culture, especially philosophy. These two lead to Jesus, and are now the property of the church. What Eusebius did was to add the political dimension to this view of God working in more than one way towards a single goal. The way Eusebius tells the history of the church, God's plan was not only that Jewish revelation and Greco-Roman culture would come together in Christianity, but also that Christianity and the empire should come together in Constantine. The church and the empire were meant for each other. Therefore, Eusebius reads the preceding centuries as leading towards this joyous unity and peace which he himself experienced, and towards Constantine as the new David. The map of Eusebius was monocentric and providential, for he saw all events in the past leading towards the situation which he experienced, and which he believed to be the work of God.

Ever since that time, while the map has been expanding, its ideological structure has not changed. It is a bigger map; but it has usually remained a monocentric and providential map, one in which the historian stands at the apex and looks back at history as somehow culminating in the present—and specifically in the historian's present. What cannot be seen as part of that movement has little or no place in the narrative of history, and must at best be seen as a matter of condescension, a white man's burden, a responsibility which it is the duty of the historian's community to discharge in a sort of noblesse oblige.

The new map is very different. As Christianity has become a truly universal religion, with deep roots in every culture, it is also becoming more and more contextualized, and therefore out of its many centers come different readings of the entire history of the church. The result is frightening and exhilarating.

I find it frightening, because in many ways it means that I have constantly to relearn much of my own discipline. I can no longer read the past out of a single perspective or out of a single context. I must somehow listen to those voices from other centers, and from the margins, that speak from a different perspective and see a past that is not exactly the same that I see. In fact, I can no longer speak of a single past, for out of these many centers and many perspectives come many pasts. Sometimes the chaos is such that one even fears that the entire discipline of church history might explode into a thousand fragments, and no one will be able to put it together again.

On the other hand, this is an exhilarating time in which to be doing church history, for it clearly shows that church history is not already done. The very fluidity of our maps, and the ensuing fluidity of the past, means that we have the freedom and the necessity to write church history all over again. Each time I read what I have written on church history, I wish I could write it all over again, for the story is not quite right, for there is another insight from another perspective that must be taken into account.

Geography, then, is not flat. We have a constant reminder of that fact in the need to project the globe on a flat surface, and how every such projection somehow distorts reality. And it is not only the globe that is not flat. Geography includes, not only flat maps, but also topography, mountains and valleys. And in that respect too the geography of church history is changing.

The topography of the church history that I studied was almost exclusively orography—it was concerned mostly with the mountains and mountain chains; with towering peaks such as Innocent III and Thomas Aquinas, and with lofty chains such as the great abbots of Cluny. As we looked at the fourth century, we saw Athanasius struggling against all odds in defense of the Nicene faith. But we paid little attention to the host of people, mostly Copts or native Egyptians, who supported him and who made his cause defensible. We knew that when things got too difficult he hid among the monks of the desert. But we paid little attention to the background from which those monks came, or why they would wish to support a fellow Copt in defiance of imperial decrees.

As we looked at the thirteenth century, we saw St. Francis and the emergence of his order, St. Thomas and his imposing synthesis, the great Gothic cathedrals. But we paid very little attention to those who actually built the cathedrals, or to the peasants of Rocasecca who made it possible for the family of St. Thomas to live as they did. We paid attention to the Fourth Lateran Council and to the manner in which it sought to guide the life of the faithful; we took note of what it said regarding the doctrine of transubstantiation; but we did not look very deeply into the actual faith and devotion of the masses of the faithful.

Likewise, we studied the Reformation under the headings of Luther, Melanchthon, Loyola, Calvin, and a few others, and we thought we had studied the Reformation!

What we had in fact done in studying such orographic church history was to skip from mountain top to mountain top without ever descending into the valleys, much as a flat rock skips and bounces over the water without ever really getting wet.

We now see the shortcomings of such history in ways that were generally invisible to church historians a few generations ago. The main reason for this new vision is not that new sources have been discovered or that new methods have been developed—which they have—but rather that those who are now writing church history, and those for whom church history is being written, very often find themselves more at home in the valleys than on the mountaintops.

The changing topography can readily be seen in some of the emphases and directions that have developed in the field of church history in the last few decades.

Among these, the impact of the increasing number of women engaged in the study of church history must be noted. When I studied church history at Yale, there were "Three Great Cappadocians"; now we know there were four, for no one would dare ignore Macrina, whose brother Gregory called "the Teacher."

Likewise, the poor and their concerns are making their presence felt in the new topography of church history. Again, when I was a student at Yale, under some of the best church historians of the time, I was taught to read Ignatius of Antioch, Ambrose, John Chrysostom, and the rest of those whom we then called the "Fathers" of the church, asking them "theological" questions. By "theological" questions were meant items such as the presence of Christ in communion, or the doctrine of the Trinity. The question of why some are inordinately rich, while others starve to death, was not a theological question, and therefore one that most of us never thought to ask of the so-called "Fathers." And, because we never asked, they never told us! Today, however, church historians are asking such questions. And they are asking them, not simply as "ethical" questions, apart from "theology," but as central theological questions.

The shifts here have been enormous. Whereas in years past our most valued sources for the study of church history were the writings of ecclesiastical leaders and the archeological remains of churches and cathedrals, we are now making more use of documents and other sources that speak to us of everyday life. The discovery of an ever increasing number of papyri in Egypt dating from ancient times, the study of tax documents and population records from the Middle Ages, and an archeology much more interested in everyday life, have all contributed to a changing topography in church history, in which we are increasingly able to speak, not only of bishops and cathedrals, but also of small village churches, and of the daily life of common, everyday lay Christians.

This changing topography of church history then forces us to look anew, not only at issues such as the role of women in the life of the church, Christian understandings of wealth and poverty, and everyday Christian devotion and practice, but also at some of the items that have always been central to the history of Christianity. For instance, have we properly understood the issues at stake in the Trinitarian controversy as long as we cannot make sense of Gregory of Nazianzen's comment, that one could not get one's shoes fixed without getting into a discussion as to whether the Son was *homoousios* or *homoiousios* to the Father? If in Gregory's time the common people in a cobbler's shop were eager to get into the argument over the iota in homoiousios, this is a sign that we probably have not understood what was actually at stake from their point of view. And that in turn is a sign that we have not really understood the development of the doctrine of the Trinity, about which so many books have been written!

What all of this means is that the changes in the geography of church history are nothing short of cataclysmic. Entire centuries which were earlier submerged in obscurity are now arising, like continents emerging from the ocean. Others that we considered important for one reason are now seen as important for other reasons, much as a continent tilting in a different direction. When the next generation of historians looks at the sixteenth century, will they see first of all the Reformation, or will they see the Conquista? When they look at the nineteenth century, will they look primarily at the great liberal theologians of Europe, or at the process whereby Christianity for the first time became a truly global religion?

I do not know the answer to those questions. But one thing I do know: I know we are standing on shifting ground. I know not only that history has a geography but also that geography has a history. Just as history must be understood in the context of the geography in which it occurs, so must geography be understood as a changing reality. I well remember the map of Africa I studied years ago. It was a map with the allure of far-away places—so far away that many of them no longer exist: Rhodesia, French Equatorial Africa, the Belgian Congo. These have all disappeared. In their stead other places have appeared: Zimbabwe, Namibia, Burkina Fasso. In my own lifetime, I have seen geography change prodigiously. And if geography has a history, this means that a new reading of history may also be subversive of the present reading of geography; that a reading of the history of national borders, for instance, reminds us that all existing borders are the result of historical circumstances; that, just as all mountains are eventually eroded, the present topography of any society is at best provisional; that, just as continental plates shift, so do centers of power and influence.

That is what I find exciting about church history and its changing geography. It is what I find exciting, but also what I find terrifying, as each day the history I learned yesterday has to be relearned. That is probably what makes it so difficult for so many historians to acknowledge the new configurations of the emerging geography. Yet, if any should be able to survive such cataclysmic changes, it should be those of us who claim to be heirs to the faith of the Psalmist who long ago sang: "God is our refuge and our strength, a very present help in trouble. Therefore we will not fear, though the earth should change, though the mountains shake in the heart of the sea."

Universalist Pluralism and the New Histories

Michael Horace Barnes

The theme of this annual meeting is "the new histories." The old histories usually emphasized the acts of powerful people and philosophies, and treated these as pieces of a single human story with some all-embracing meaning, direction, or purpose.[1] The old histories tended to treat these acts as the main human story, as the embracing truth of human activities. The new histories are called new because they uncover many forgotten or repressed human activities. The new histories represent an interest in telling the story of ordinary people, of the society as a whole and not just the powerful, or the story of the marginalized whose life patterns have been ignored, or the stories of local or ethnic groups whose lives have been omitted from the standard histories. The new histories are clearly quite valuable. They are better history because they include more of human reality. They are better social instruments because they give presence and power to many who have previously been left socially mute and weak.

The new histories can be written from different perspectives. For those of a universalist bent, the new histories could be thought of as way stations towards an eventual new single all-embracing history of human activities. This single but more inclusive history would investigate the activities of both the powerful and the weak, men and women, different ethnic and racial groups, both the heterosexual and homosexual, and out of this wider-ranging set of histories produce a new and broader outline of the patterns of human life. Call this the universalist impulse in the writing of history.

For those of a relativist bent, a universalist impulse would be both incorrect and harmful. Older cultural relativism simply proclaimed that different cultures are irreducibly different. The postmodern form of relativism adds that universalist histories are inevitably incorrect because they are also inevitably interpretations. Every interpretation arises from the social context of the interpreter. To claim that any history is the universal truth is an ideological position, i.e., a false belief in the universal validity of that which in fact is socially situated and constructed. Postmodernism says attempts at a universal history are also harmful. The rich complexity of human traditions and various locally shared identities are too significant an aspect of human life to be submerged again in some single universal story of humankind. It is humanly much better that the varied complexity of human life patterns be accepted as distinct forms of life. Male and female differences, Anglo and Hispanic, African American and Italian American, gay and straight, Christian and Jew, Hindu and Muslim, must each be respected for their distinctiveness. Each of these loses something if its story is contorted to fit within some universal framework.

There is a third possibility between the universalist and the relativist in writing histories. I will call it a universalist pluralism. It is a pluralism inasmuch as it respects differences, cherishes the variety of culture, community, and context, just as relativism does. It is universalist, however, in that it also tries to uncover and celebrate what we humans have in common. The name "universalist pluralism" is not so oxymoronic as it first sounds. This approach appears in such works as Robert Schreiter's *The New Catholicity: Theology between the Global and the Local* or David Krieger's *The New Universalism: Foundations for a Global Theology*.[2] As is evident from the titles, both are interested in discovering values or ideas that humankind might share on a global or universalist scale. But both also argue that the correct way to do this is not to obscure or diminish the rich array of differences among people because of religious, ethnic, racial, or sexual identity. They seek a pluralistic universalism.

Postmodern relativism also values pluralism highly, but it legitimizes differences or otherness by arguing that there are no universal standards or reference points at all, from which one might interpret, much less evaluate, any given culture or community. By default, in the absence of any such universals, the only standards by which a culture or community can legitimately be understood and judged are its own. Religious forms of relativist pluralism appear in the often-cited *The Nature of Doctrine*, in which George Lindbeck argued for a postliberal theology, and more recently in Kathryn Tanner's *Theories of Culture: A New Agenda for Theology*.[3] To argue in favor of a universalistic pluralism, I need first to describe relativistic pluralism at some length, to explore its nature and origins, the justifications given for it, and what I see as its dangers. Both kinds of pluralism have their limits, even their dangers. But of the two I think that relativist pluralism is the less coherent and the more dangerous.

Anthropological and Postmodern Relativisms

Current relativism has roots in anthropology, in the functionalism promoted by Franz Boas, Ruth Benedict, and others after the First World War in this country.[4] Functionalism argued that each culture was an independently functioning unity. Though many aspects of this or that culture might look very strange to European-trained eyes, those aspects could be truly understood only as part of a larger network of cultural norms and processes. Within their own context even the strangest aspects of a culture might be highly constructive. In one social context, the issue of marriage is settled by rules of exogamy that are tied to patterns of clan identity. In another social context marriages are arranged by the parents for the sake of political and financial connections. In a third social context the issue of marriage is left to individual choice with few explicit rules at all. Given such diversity of well-functioning models of marriage and other aspects of life, it is foolish to interpret other cultures by applying the standards of the anthropologist's own culture.

The most extreme position, perhaps, is the claim that differences between some cultures are so great as to be "irreducibly different."[5] Levy-Bruhl set the stage with his famous claims that primitive thought represents a prelogical mentality of "mystical participation"[6] radically different from the rational mentality of the modern European. The British anthropologist Peter Winch pressed this sort of claim quite strongly. In his discussion of the Azande oracle procedure, for example, he refers to it as "completely unintelligible to us." He argues that when translating from a European to an African language "much of what may be expressed in the one has no possible counterpoint in the other."[7]

As the twentieth century wore on, other elements contributed to what would become postmodern relativism. Nietzsche's ghost drifted about after the First World War, spreading suspicion about the self-interest hiding within supposedly objective moralities. The Frankfurt school in philosophy explored ways in which knowledge is constructed as part of social processes. In the United States Sellars and Quine elaborated an anti-foundationalist interpretation of knowledge as part of a network of ideas.[8] Meanwhile, back on the continent, Foucault uncovered hidden histories in order to show how the interests of the powerful had imposed their self-serving interpretations on the marginal.[9] Derrida deconstructed both texts and the subject who reads the texts, arguing in his fight against structuralism that the most basic structures of human life are given by language, and that language is both a product of history and creates history, and is thereby creating human consciousness from era to era and place to place.[10] One of the firmest walls against relativism was breached when Thomas Kuhn convinced many people that science itself had feet of social convention rather than hard objectivity, feet that trod a steady path most of the time, but often tripped, got up, and then moved off in a new direction as the somewhat subjective and social consensus of scientists directed it. Rorty used all this as part of his own anti-foundationalist neo-pragmatism.[11]

The result is the postmodern conviction that all the facts we think we see are interpretations guided by the supposed truths given to us by our culture, and the truths are interpretations produced by the history of the culture, but the history *as we know it* is also an interpretation. After that it is interpretation "all the way down." There is no way to interpret any aspects of life and culture except by using methods of interpretation which are produced by some other historically conditioned interpretation. What can we do then? "We just interpret, with a full recognition of the contingency and arbitrariness of our interpretive position."[12]

There is an additional dimension to human diversity or difference. The human world is not composed of neatly coherent societies, each with its dominant life-form distinct from that of other societies. Variety occurs as much within any given society as it does cross-culturally; each of them has some degree of change and internal disagreement. Neither Sri Lankan Buddhism nor Cornell University Humanism nor the Moose Clubs of Itasca County in Minnesota are single coherent life-forms. Moreover, each community has porous boundaries; each may adopt ideas and practices from its neighbors over time; each may lose members to other communities and take in strangers who carry with them new and odd ideas. Such variety occurs even with each individual person, who belongs to more than one social group, whose life continuously changes and crosses boundaries.[13]

Postmodernism finds relativism not only correct but constructive. Belief in universally valid truths and values, say the postmodernists, is all too easily a tool of oppression. North Atlantic imperialist male-dominated culture proclaimed itself to possess the objective truth of things, to have the way of life best for all people everywhere. With this conviction, the North Atlantic forces have gone out into the world to oppress peoples everywhere in the name of their truth-claims and values. Postmodernists often argue that if we expose the socially constructed nature of these truth-claims and values, this will prevent men from insisting that women should be judged by the standards that give power and authority to men but not to women, or that power and authority are good social standards in the first place. This will prevent the capitalist from claiming that this form of economics can legitimately be imposed on societies everywhere. This will prevent missionaries from disrupting societies to open them to Christian belief and practices. This will prevent white people of European origin from claiming superiority to other races. This will prevent heterosexual people from declaring that those with a homosexual orientation are ontologically or morally inferior. All this is more likely to be achieved, say many of the postmodern voices, if we demythologize the whole idea of universally valid truth-claims and values, and unmask it as a false state of consciousness.

Problems with Relativist Pluralism

Relativism has serious problems, however, both because of internal incoherence and because the anthropological information to which it sometimes appeals will not sustain relativism, as I will discuss a bit later here. Relativistic pluralism is internally incoherent in two distinct ways. The first point of internal incoherence is its universalist claim that all cultures everywhere are socially constructed, interpretations produced by historical processes. This is indeed accurate, even though it may not be the whole truth of things. But as a universalist claim, it identifies at least this one way in which all cultures are alike.[14] The relativist might respond that this is the only universal; that all else is relative to the culture. Even so, at least here is one point of human identity that we all share as a basis for further communication and positive interaction. The second point of internal incoherence is similar to the first. When relativists are also pluralists, they appeal to a single universal value; they promote the right of peoples everywhere to basic human dignity and respect. But relativism has no way to justify giving respect to other people, except as the interpretation of life that happens to have been constructed by the history of the society that thinks all people are deserving of basic human respect. Postmodern relativism in particular can only say that the other cultures have different interpretations of what is morally legitimate, and no interpretation has a privileged place.[15] A culture that objects to slavery, of course, can try to persuade other cultures to agree. But they would then seem to be promoting anti-slavery as a universal value. Moreover, they would face the question of justifying this moral theory that all people deserve freedom from slavery.

The point is not merely a theoretical one of logical internal inconsistency. It is a practical one. A true relativism undercuts the sense of human solidarity needed to sustain the universal respect for human dignity that pluralism requires.[16] We human beings show a strong tendency to favor what we think of as our own kind, and to demean or even destroy those who are not like us.[17] The tragedies of recent years in Rwanda, Bosnia, Cambodia, Northern Ireland, India, and Somalia all remind us of this aspect of our human nature. It is a seemingly universal tendency of us humans to identify some people as "other." Postmodernist thinkers recognize this clearly; and ask us all to respect what is other. A highly moral concern for the other is a major motivation behind postmodern thought. But relativism by its nature claims there is some degree of irreducible otherness among peoples and cultures. If the others are irreducibly alien, a positive pluralistic attitude will not come easily. The other must be able to be recognized as also the same in some way, like us enough to provide a basis for a sense of solidarity or mutual sympathy, strong enough to outweigh the differences, even as those differences continue.[18]

One path forward is offered by Habermas and his belief that if we all keep talking to each other in spite of what divides us, we will be able to create more peace and justice. But this has a double dose of universalism within it already. It supposes that peace and justice, for example, rather than glorious war or exploitive rule by the powerful, are values we can share broadly enough to make them predominate. It supposes, moreover, that the conversation must follow certain universal rules of openness and equality and honesty.

Because relativism has bad consequences, however, does not mean it is incorrect. Our cultures might in fact make us so different in our thoughts and behaviors that there is no real basis for human solidarity. Here, fortunately, the second problem with relativism comes forward: the anthropological data do not support the claim that different histories and different cultures make us radically different in our thoughts and values.

Anthropology and Human Commonalities

Let me modestly back away a bit from talking of human "universals." Even within individual societies people differ enough from each other that the word "universal" is a bit too ambitious. Let me refer instead to "commonalities." By these I mean aspects of human life, thought, and behavior that are common enough that most people in every society have some experience of them as a significant part of their own lives or at least of the lives of people around them. In the face of the many differences among cultures, such common elements could provide a basis for common human understanding, for mutual acceptance, for mutual sympathy.

Recall the claim by Levy-Bruhl that primitive people have a pre-logical mode of thought that is quite different from the scientific rationality of Europeans. Most of the examples of such thought given by Levy-Bruhl, however, are beliefs that magical powers and spirit beings influence events. This is not really hard for a European to understand, even though the European may often not share the belief. A small percent of Levy-Bruhl's examples concern statements about participation in nature, as in the famous Bororo claim "I am a red parakeet." But it is also not hard to understand how a group can identify themselves with various beings. My own father was proud of being a Moose and my uncle was a devoted Elk. Evans-Pritchard once said that Levy-Bruhl told him he thought that European Jews and Christians also indulged in this primitive pre-logical thought. So apparently it is not very strange to the "European" mind after all.[19]

Recall also the claim by Winch that some cultures are so foreign to each other they cannot communicate. There may certainly be a significant degree of incommunicability in cases where non-literate people come face-to-face with literate and technologically advanced cultures. After all, it takes years of formal schooling for those of us raised in such a culture to come to understand most of the basics of it. But this is a result of the sheer volume and complexity of knowledge. The kinds of cases to which Winch appeals seem readily communicable to me. I think that I can understand the Azande belief that feeding a certain poison to a chicken can help determine the guilt of an accused person. I am highly skeptical that this oracle works the way the Azande say it does, but I think I understand quite well what they are doing and why.

Let me appeal here not to my own conviction of what I can understand, however, but to others in a position to make more authoritative judgments. Kwasi Wiredu, an African philosopher, is a native of Ghana whose first language is Akan. He declares that there are many concepts he learned from French culture that have no equivalent in Akan. But he has usually found it possible to communicate ideas from French to Akan and vice versa nonetheless, albeit sometimes by way of extensive circumlocutions. Wiredu addresses many problems in translation and communication. "But overriding all such problems is the fact, which is surely one of the more remarkable facts about language, that we can understand even what we cannot translate." And in the same context he adds: "The fundamental fact here is that, because of the biological unity of mankind, any human being can participate or imaginatively enter into any human life form, however initially strange."[20]

An anthropologist concurs. Donald Brown appeals to his own experience in the field, as well as to a report by a young anthropologist named Steadman, who lived with the Hewa, a New Guinea tribal group living in a "restricted" area, one closed by the government to all outsiders except anthropologists. Steadman had been taught a theory of "cultural determinism" that told him to expect it would be enormously difficult to grasp the Hewa way of life. After a few weeks of learning the language the anthropologist discovered it was not at all difficult to communicate with the Hewa. After a few months he reported his surprise that the Hewa turned out to share the same concerns, interests, and needs as he did, that their common humanness was quite evident.[21]

To cite one more case, Bradd Shore at first experienced great psychic differences between his own culture and that of the Samoans among whom he lived and worked. But as he learned their ways, he concluded, "I was discovering the importance of basic human processes of meaning construction and information processing." The particular contents of their cultural hoard was strange to Shore, but the workings of the minds of the people was not.[22]

Two anthropologists and one Akan philosopher, however, do not add up to a truly thorough case for belief in human commonalities.[23] But we can explore similarities further, in two directions. The first is to search for ways in which we humans all share issues and experiences in life, regardless of the variety of our responses. The second is to identify any common human ways of thinking about issues and experiences.

Common Human Issues and Experiences

The annotated bibliography of Donald Brown's book *Human Universals* can help us greatly on the exploration for common human issues or topics or experiences. Here is a list of "human commonalities" gleaned from the notes of just four of the entries in that bibliography:

Commonalities Based Directly on Biology
General physiology
- bipedal walking, no flying like birds or breathing underwater like fish
- need for food; digestion processes; processes of elimination
- need for water source(s)
- susceptible to weather extremes
- opposable thumbs
- sleep; dreams
- limits to endurance; tiredness
- binocular vision
- adequate sense of smell
    —recognize locales and people
- directional hearing
- taste: fondness for sweets and fats
- touch: tactile information and pleasure
- pleasure and pain feelings; comfort and discomfort
- sexual interest and arousal

Emotions
- midbrain basic responses: fear, anger, calmness
- emotional states mediated by same range of neurotransmitters
- facial expressions correlate with emotions
- personality range: from shy to outgoing, from angry to cheerful

Evolutionary epistemological specifics
- language use
  - —innate neonatal attentiveness to language sounds
  - —innate tendency to practice sounds
  - —some degree of universal grammatical forms
- story telling / narrative as basic means to interpret reality
- kin favoritism
  - —inclination to favor those with whom we are raised
  - —tendency to think of self as a part of a clan-like group
- anthropomorphizing natural forces and things
- belief in entities not directly observed or observable

Dimensions of Sociality
- distinction between self and others
- status and roles in general
- division of labor and other roles by age and/or sex
- group regulations of sex, marriage, and other behaviors
- rules and leadership for allocation of scarce or important resources
- activities by dyads, of equal or unequal status, cooperative or in conflict
- family; extended family; kinship terms and rules
- supervision or leadership practices
- early socialization, especially by parents and close kin
- interaction with children; care giving, affection
- distinction between public and private
- adjusting joint activities to the personalities involved
- etiquette
- using facial and bodily expression to communicate
- using hands interpersonally: fight, stroke, groom

Human Commonalities in Fact
- games
- ritual
- artistic expression
- joking
- procuring and processing raw materials
- tool use
- use of fire
- containers
- body decoration
- the association of art with ritual
- metaphor

- the concept of "specialness" or of "making special"
- daily routines
- need for novelty
- distinction between people and the rest of the world
- problem solving by trial-and-error, insight and reasoning
- feelings of being in a quandary
- recognition of signs, in nature and by others
- trade and transport of goods
- subject/object
- in control/under control (causing involuntary action)
- conscious awareness of memory
- making decisions
- self-responsibility
- psychological language
- classification of things
- consciousness of birth and death
- care of ill or injured
- knowledge of relationship between sickness and death
- positive death customs
- curiosity about one's nature

Some Specific *Overlapping Social Commonalities*
- the need to impose order among people, things, and the world
- social structure influenced by accumulated information
- leadership: moderators; vs. force; vs. charism; vs. familiarity
- consultation and collective decision making; informal vs. formal consultation
- band (or derivative organization) distinct from family
- nonlocalized social rules
- intimate property vs. non-property and "loose" property
- inheritance rules
- equation of social and physiological maternity
- prohibition of mother-son incest
- other incest prohibitions that yield exogamous groups
- each household has at least one adult in charge
- modeling transactions with remote (larger) groupings or those in intimate (small) social groups
- mutual influence of personality and social role
- ascribed vs. achieved status
- a pool of inner "state parameters"

                —degrees of uncertainty, freedom of choice,
            urgency, pleasantness, anxiety, and seriousness

Commonalities in Modes of Thought

To the list of common human issues and experiences we can add
the limited range of basic human modes of thought. We have seen that
Levy-Bruhl and Winch argue for the existence of quite different modes
of thought. In this vein, postmodernists often claim that the rational
approach of modern European thought is a product of Western culture, and is not necessarily valid in other cultures. Even if we humans
share a large number of common issues in life, our ways of thinking
about them may be irreducibly different. On the other hand we have
the work of philosophers like Piaget and Lonergan, each arguing that
human beings in general have only a few basic modes of thought. A
relativist response to Piaget and Lonergan, of course, is to point out
that both of these people are socially situated. These men of North
Atlantic culture manage to discover that European patterns of intellectual development are patterns that human beings in general either
do or should follow. But once again there is relevant anthropological
and historical evidence to support this. Let me use Piaget's categories
here, because his ideas have been the object of extensive study in a
variety of cultural contexts. There are many arguments about the validity of Piaget's theories, and perhaps about the empirical validity of
Lonergan's also, but the arguments are not about the general adequacy
of Piaget's descriptions of different modes of thought.[24] They can serve
as good heuristic devices in looking at history.[25]

A quick reminder of some distinct categories of thought-styles in
Piaget's analysis will allow us then to see how well they may illumi-
nate history.[26] The pre-operational thought-style which we possess at
the age of three is good for learning information but relatively poor
about logical consistency among those ideas, or even how plausible
the ideas are, especially ideas with some appeal. The tooth fairy and
talking mice inhabit this mental world. Vivid imagination and the authority of big people are the major criteria of truth. Most people do not
entirely grow out of this imaginative stage entirely, fortunately; imagination is a precious resource. But most people also develop critical
ways of evaluating what they imagine.

The concrete operational mode of thought, which begins around the age of seven, is much better at organizing ideas into coherent categories and recognizing things that are highly implausible. First-hand experience is a major source of knowing what is true, but the authority of parents and elders as well as the tradition they represent, is usually the final arbiter of truth. Most adults everywhere rely mainly on this mode of thought. It is a practical and usually trustworthy mode of thought for most of life's problems. This seems to match with what Lonergan calls "common sense."

Formal operational thought skills begin to develop somewhere around twelve. They extend the everyday logic which even concrete thought possesses into more complex methods of analysis. It requires a fairly long and difficult training of some sort, and a cultural context which provides that training. (Piaget treated this as a natural developmental stage; but it is quite possible that the natural human capacity for formal operational thought requires certain cultural contexts for its development.[27] We will see a bit about this in a moment.) Those who find themselves fairly adept in this mode of thought also find it a tool for critically testing traditional or authoritative truth-claims. This seems to be what Lonergan means by "theory."

Late formal operational thought is formal operational thought capable of systematic analyses of ideas. But it also includes a recognition of the conditional nature of evidence and reasoning. It is therefore less dogmatic and more likely to exercise caution in making truth-claims. It can more readily acknowledge the legitimacy of plural approaches to conclusions, especially where the evidence or logic is not highly compelling. This seems to fit with what Lonergan labels "method."

We can find these four modes of thought in cultures around the world and through time. This is especially true of the first two. We humans all seem to start life with the same pre-operational and then concrete operational modes of thought. Extensive testing of the Piagetian categories in pre-literate and literate cultures allows us to say that humans everywhere, as children and as adults, share in these two modes of thought as at least part of our repertoire of cognitive tools.[28] What is more in question is the extent to which we human beings share in formal operational modes of thought. This style of thought has been called peculiarly Western, part of the Enlightenment heritage.

But the rational style of formal operational thought can be found even in ancient times and in several cultures. The shift from reliance on common sense and concrete operational thought alone, to the additional use of formally systematic and logical thought took place in several major world cultures about 2500 years ago. This was the time of the composition of the principal Upanishads in India, of Thales and Pythagoras in Greece, of the writer of the first chapter of Genesis in Babylon or Jerusalem, of the first assembling of the Tao Te Ching text in China. This was the general period in human history when the idea of a single ultimate unity or pattern to all things caught the imagination of an intellectual elite in all these major cultures.[29] There had been sparks earlier—Ikhnaton's single sun god, perhaps Zoroaster's Ahura Mazda. But now an intellectual fire broke out. In India the principal Upanishads built upon a few, probably late lines in Book X of the Rig Veda and reflected on the origin of everything in an ultimate incomprehensible Source. In China Taoist texts spoke of the single incomprehensible and formless Tao from which arise all the things with form. In Jerusalem or Babylon a priestly writer proclaimed that the God of Israel is the single Creator God of the whole world. The Greek philosophers constructed cosmologies to explain the nature and structure of the entire universe. Old beliefs in the spirits and gods were challenged. That new supposition was that there is an ultimate single source or power or structure in terms of which all else can be understood. The gods are multiple powers, each contending with others. No one of them has all the power there is. No one of them constitutes the fundamental explanation for everything else. Belief in a single Ultimate, whether called God or Brahman or the Tao or the Logos, to use the Stoic term, relativizes the gods. If they survive at all, their finiteness is apparent.

This was also the time when the intellectual elite of several major cultures struggled self-consciously with the criteria of rationality. This elite began to think about their thinking. Formal criteria for arriving at truth were proposed in India, China, and Greece. In India the Samkhya school, which can be dated at least prior to 300 B.C.E., explored basic universal principles of cause and effect, and constructed rules for determining truth. The name Samkhya in fact means "enumeration" or "calculation."[30] In China, Mohist thought from the fourth century B.C.E. proposes three standards for truth: by testing an idea against tradition, by comparison with empirical evidence as seen by people in general, and by whether it works in practice.[31] Now the authority of tradition was not enough; it had to compete with explicit additional rational criteria. In the third century B.C.E., the Yin Yang school, more philosophical than its companion Taoist movement, produced commentaries on the ancient Book of Changes, commentaries that describe the universe as a rational whole, intelligible through rational thought.[32]

From this time onward in all three areas of the world, there were periods of analytical reflection, of philosophical speculation guided by canons of logic and evidence. Chinese Buddhist philosophizing in the fourth century, or ninth-century theological philosophy in India, or the late medieval intellectual rebirth in Europe are all major instances of universalist rational reflection, using common human criteria of logical coherence and, usually, compatibility with empirical evidence. The rationality of the European Enlightenment was just one more expression of a common human capacity to learn methods of rational analysis that has had periods of flourishing in various cultures at various points in history, and that flourishes today to our benefit.

Interestingly, we can also see in ancient China, India, and Greece moments of what today might pass as early forms of postmodernist protests against universalist claims (though not so motivated by social justice concerns as current day postmodernism). In India the Carvaka school, from as early as 600 B.C.E. perhaps, denied the validity of logical inferences about the world. They emphasized sense experience as the only basis for knowing what is true, but like David Hume so many centuries later in quite a different social context, they noted that there is no way of proving that what has consistently happened so far must necessarily continue in the future or be the case everywhere. One cannot logically establish the reality of universals, they argued.[33] Similarly, in China the fourth-century B.C.E. group known as the Logicians busily deconstructed language use.[34] The Logician Hui Shih, for example, is noted for showing that a white horse is not a horse. (If a yellow horse is different from a white horse, then a yellow horse is different from *a* horse—i.e., from the white horse. But if a yellow horse can be different from a horse, so also a white horse can be different from a horse.)[35]

In ancient Greece the school of thought known as the Skeptics were also precursors of current postmodernism.[36] They were what today would be called both anti-foundationalists and relativists. They took their stand against the "dogmatists," i.e., the Stoics and Epicureans who provided long rational arguments to show that they were correct.

The skeptics took a critical stance towards their own knowledge. They pointed out that all truth-claims were inevitably caught in an infinite regress, with every idea dependent on some other idea, and every piece of evidence dependent on some presupposition, and that presuppositions varied from culture to culture. Not all of them collapsed into relativism, however. Their division into two main schools, in fact, provides instruction for our own times.

The extreme skeptics followed Pyrrho's example, and refused to take a position on anything. They recommended following the customs of wherever a person happened to be. Because no one could know the truth of things, time-tested tradition would have to provide the framework for life. They would be at home, I suspect, with Lindbeck's cultural-linguistic proposal.

The moderate skeptics followed Carneades and his "New Academy." Carneades was not fully skeptical, in our modern sense of the word. Carneades was a probabilist. Though we cannot know anything with dogmatic certitude, he said, we can nonetheless form reliable judgments by applying a careful method. First, distinguish among degrees of plausibility. A coiled rope in a dark room might be a rope or a snake. Either is a plausible judgment at first. But one can then inspect or "scrutinize" the object with degrees of care. A second look may show that it looks more like a rope. A further inspection of color, texture, flexibility, and its lack of motion all add up. One can then consider whether there are contrary indications of any kind to "distract" one from the judgment that it is a rope, whether in the form of conflicting evidence, or in the form of alternative theories that might also fit the evidence. The New Academy thus gives probable assent to appearances which are 1) plausible, 2) scrutinized, and 3) "undistractable."[37] The skeptical probabilism of Carneades is not far from the method of science today, which seeks plausible accounts of things, scrutinizes them by public long-term testing, and seeks to rule out all alternative accounts (all "distractions").[38]

Skepticism did not prevail in any of the great cultures of the world. In each of the many periods in history when a classical rationalism flourished, the usual goal was to transcend mere opinion and probability, to achieve certitude based on philosophically secure foundations. But just as axial age rationalism demythologized earlier traditions, and undercut tradition itself as a reliable method for knowledge, now postmodern thought has demythologized classical rationalism. It has done so by an approach that is anti-dogmatic, like ancient skepticisms. But postmodernism today is passing over the opportunity to recognize the power of probabilism to produce reliable truth-claims of even universal validity.

This helps us see that there can be two forms of postmodernism, two different responses to the reflexive self-awareness that lies at the basis of postmodernism. One is the deconstructive form, which undermines and even attacks any hopes for universally valid criteria of truth and values. This is what is usually meant by the word "postmodern" today. There is also the possibility, however, of a constructive postmodernism, as David Griffin labels it,[39] or even a "reconstructive" form, to use Robert Kegan's more ambitious word. What Griffin and Kegan share is a confidence that the end of rationalism is not the end of rationality.[40] Let rational*ism* be the name for a conviction that by rational methods it is possible to arrive at comprehensive certitude and completeness of understanding. Rationality can take a more modest form than this, as Carneades has shown by his probabilism. When we attend to the nature of the method of modern science, we can see that it also should best be understood as a probabilist rationality. To many postmodern thinkers, modern science is the epitome of an arrogant ideology, not a modest rationality, so it is good to remind ourselves of the limits of science. It cannot express what the arts and literature can. It is restricted to what can be tested empirically, which means it has no competence about metaphysical, aesthetic, and moral dimensions. Bias and interests will influence what is studied and how the results are applied, for better or worse. The conclusions of science are probable, not philosophically certain; the scientific system of knowledge will always be incomplete at the edges; and the human mind is endlessly open to challenge whatever conclusions science arrives at.

But in the end, Western rationality is not really Western; it is human. The common sense that precedes and accompanies rational methods is not primitive; it is human. The reflexive self-awareness that allows for deconstructive relativism or for a reconstructive probabilism is not peculiarly contemporary; it is human. All of us within even this social context will differ among ourselves on how we mix these modes of thought in our own lives. People everywhere mix these modes in their own ways. But we humans all share in some capacity for all of them, though our culture's modes of education will indeed have a great effect on which of the modes of thought we are able to use.

This has been a search for human commonalities. The long list derived from Brown's annotated bibliography contains mostly topics, aspects of life which we humans share. The review of modes of thought, guided by Lonergan and Piaget, through history and across cultures, suggests that we humans also share ways to think about the aspects of our lives. Let me repeat: the new histories have enormous value because they tell a fuller story and because they give voice to the silent and weak. But this can be done through a pluralism that respects differences among people precisely because it recognizes some universal—or at least general and common—human concerns and modes of thought.[41] As the new histories are written, they should indeed articulate the local concerns of various communities, especially of those who have been marginalized. But I hope that in the long run these histories will also contribute to a larger sense of human solidarity, with trust in the common human capacity for both mutual sympathy and rational reflection.

Notes

[1] William Dean , *History Making History: The New Historicism in American Religious Thought* (Albany: SUNY University Press, 1988), emphasizes the transcendent framework of older religious histories, and celebrates what he calls the relativism without nihilism of the new religious histories. He thinks that an American theology built according to the perspective of Foucault and Derrida would recognize that American thought about God is the product of a national community, formed from within the American context (144).

[2] Robert Schreiter, *The New Catholicity: Theology between the Global and the Local* (Maryknoll, N.Y.: Orbis Books, 1997). David Krieger, *The New Universalism: Foundations for a Global Theology* (Maryknoll, N.Y.: Orbis Books, 1991).

[3] George A. Lindbeck, *The Nature of Doctrine: Religion and Theology in a Postliberal Age* (Philadelphia: Westminster, 1984). Kathryn Tanner, *Theories of Culture: A New Agenda for Theology* (Minneapolis: Fortress, 1997).

[4] Robert B. Edgerton, *Sick Societies: Challenging the Myth of Primitive Harmony* (New York: The Free Press, 1992) attributes the first modern declaration of anthropological relativism to William Graham Sumner in 1906. I will use Boas as a symbol of U.S. functionalism, however. Franz Boas, *The Mind of Primitive Man* (New York: Macmillan, Boas's 1938 revision of the 1911 original). Chaps. 1 and 2 summarize the anti-racist basis for his functionalism.

[5] The text here will discuss Winch's ideas, but the phrase "irreducibly different" comes from Thomas S. Kuhn, who claims that "the heavens of the Greeks were irreducibly different from ours." For a recent statement by Kuhn, see his "The

Natural and the Human Sciences," in David R. Hiley, James F. Bohman, and Richard Shusterman, eds., *The Interpretive Turn: Philosophy, Science, Culture* (Ithaca: Cornell University Press, 1991).

[6] These are the major relevant works: Lucien Levy-Bruhl, *Primitive Mythology: The Mythic World of Australian and Papuan Natives,* Brian Elliott, trans. (New York: Queensland University Press, 1983; originally *La Mythologique Primitive,* 1935). *How Natives Think* (New York: Allen and Unwin, 1926; Princeton University Press reprint, 1985), introduction by C. Scott Littleton; trans. Lilian A. Clare of *Les Functions Mentales dans les Sociétés Inferieures* (Paris, 1910). *Primitive Mentality* (New York: Macmillan, 1923), trans. Clare of *La Mentalité Primitive*; *The Notebooks on Primitive Mentality,* trans. Peter Rivière (New York: Harper and Row, 1975). In notes dated 1938 he is still struggling for clarity on what he means by "prelogical." See espec. 37-43, 56-57.

[7] Peter Winch, "Understanding a Primitive Society," 78-111, in Brian Wilson, *Rationality* (New York: Harper and Row, 1970), 91.

[8] The often-cited locus for Sellars is his article "Empiricism and the Philosophy of Mind," in Herbert Feigl and Michael Scriven, eds., *The Foundations of Science and the Concepts of Psychology and Psychoanalysis,* Vol. I of the Minnesota Studies in the Philosophy of Science (Minneapolis: University of Minnesota Press, 1956), 253-329. The standard reference to Willard V. O. Quine's thought is his *From a Logical Point of View: Logico-Philosophical Essays* (New York: Harper and Row, 1961, 2nd edition), espec. 20-46.

[9] I rely on Gary Gutting, ed., *The Cambridge Companion to Foucault* (Cambridge: Cambridge University Press, 1994), especially Gutting's introduction, for my sense of Foucault's various positions over time.

[10] Jacques Derrida, *Writing and Difference* (Chicago: University of Chicago Press, 1978, from the 1967 French original), 5. Translation with notes by Alan Bass.

[11] Richard Rorty, *Philosophy and the Mirror of Nature* (Princeton: Princeton University Press, 1979). He objects to the notion that the objects confronted by the mind or the rules that constrain inquiry, as he puts it, are common to all discourse, 315-16. By this he distances himself even from Habermas's form of hermeneutics.

[12] Claire Colebrook, *New Literary Histories: New Historicism and Contemporary Criticism* (Manchester; New York: Manchester University Press, 1997), vi.

[13] This is a major point of Kathryn Tanner's *Theories of Culture.*

[14] Anthony C. Thiselton, *Interpreting God and the Post-Modern Self: On Meaning, Manipulation, and Promise* (Grand Rapids: Eerdmans, 1995) is one of many to make this argument against relativism. See 111-17. The book is directed mainly against Rorty and Lyotard.

[15] Roberto S. Goizueta, *Caminemos con Jesus: Toward a Hispanic/Latino Theology of Accompaniment* (Maryknoll, N.Y.: Orbis Books, 1995) has an excellent critique of postmodernism along these lines, 163-71.

[16] Richard Rorty, *Contingency, Irony, and Solidarity* (Cambridge: Cambridge University Press, 1989) says there is no rational argument available why all people should grant basic respect to one another, but he hopes to be able to develop

effective rhetorical appeals to create feelings of pity and benevolence for all people, 193.

[17] The "co-evolutionary model" of C. J. Lumsden and E. O. Wilson, *Genes, Mind, and Culture* (Cambridge, Mass.: Harvard University Press, 1981) and *Promethean Fires: Reflections on the Origin of Mind* (Cambridge, Mass.: Harvard University Press, 1983), offers a sociobiological analysis of "enthnocentrism," why we tend to divide everyone into us and them, and hate them.

[18] Michelle M. Moody-Adams, *Field Work in Familiar Places: Morality, Culture, and Philosophy* (Cambridge, Mass.: Harvard University Press, 1997) notes the oddity of Rorty's position, a relativist who places such confidence in the universal relevance and value of what he calls his ethnocentric starting place, 25-26.

[19] See E. E. Evans-Pritchard, *Theories of Primitive Religion* (New York: Oxford University Press, 1965), 91. For more on Levy-Bruhl, see my brief analysis in "Rationality in Religion," 375-90, *Religion* 27 (1997): 377-78 and notes.

[20] Kwasi Wiredu, *Cultural Universals and Particulars: An African Perspective* (Bloomington, Ind.: Indiana University Press, 1996), 85-86, 103-4 in a chapter entitled "Formulating Modern Thought in African Language," 81-104.

[21] So reports Donald Brown, in his *Human Universals* (Philadelphia: Temple University Press, 1991), 4, on what Lyle B. Steadman said in his *Neighbours and Killers: Residence and Dominance among the Hewa of New Guinea*. Ph.D. diss., Australian National University, 26. Brown gives no date for Steadman's work.

[22] Bradd Shore, *Culture in Mind: Cognition, Culture, and the Problem of Meaning* (New York: Oxford University Press, 1996), 7.

[23] James B. Wertsch, *Voices of the Mind: A Sociocultural Approach to Mediated Action* (Cambridge, Mass.: Harvard University Press, 1991) emphasizes cultural diversities but also describes shared human traits of learning and thinking.

[24] On the current criticism of Piaget's theories, see Kurt W. Fischer and Louise Silvern, "Stages and Individual Differences in Cognitive Development," *Annual Review of Psychology*, Mark R. Rosenzweig and Lyman W. Porter, eds., 36 (1985) (Palo Alto: Annual Reviews): 613-648, an inclusive summary of significant studies and the state of the question at the time. Michael and Marjorie Rutter, *Developing Minds: Challenge and Continuity across the Life Span* (New York: Basic Books, 1993), begin by saying that Piaget's theory is wrong, but a careful reading reveals that they think his overall descriptions are correct. Their major complaint is that Piaget's theory was a bit neater than real development in individuals. See also Robbie Case and Wolfgang Edelstein, eds., *The New Structuralism in Cognitive Development: Theory and Research on Individual Pathways* (New York: Karger, 1993).

[25] For another excellent example see the descriptions of stages of faith development given by James Fowler, *Stages of Faith* (San Francisco: Harper and Row, 1981), espec. 149-50, 172-73, 182-83, 197-98. Fritz K. Oser and Paul Gmunder, *Religious Judgment: A Developmental Perspective* (Birmingham: Religious Education Press, 1991), report on a major research project using Fowler's categories and find them valid. See also Fowler's more recent book, *Faithful*

Change: The Personal and Public Challenges of Postmodern Life (Nashville: Abingdon Press, 1996), in which he compares individual stages of faith development to stages in Western culture, from the Enlightenment to postmodernism, 145-75. For another set of labels, see Karen Strohm Kitchener, "Cognition, Metacognition, and Epistemic Cognition: A Three-Level Model of Cognitive Processing." *Human Development* 26/4 (July-Aug., 1983): 222-32, though she does not apply her schema to historical development.

[26] For brief summaries by Piaget see his *The Child and Reality: Problems of Genetic Psychology*, trans. Arnold Rosin (New York: Grossman, 1973), 57-61; or Barbel Inhelder and Jean Piaget, *The Growth of Logical Thinking: From Childhood to Adolescence* (New York: Basic Books, 1958), 245-57.

[27] Kieran Egan, *The Educated Mind: How Cognitive Tools Shape Our Understanding* (Chicago: University of Chicago, 1997), 29, argues for this. I suspect he is correct.

[28] See Pierre R. Dasen and Alastair Heron, "Cross-Cultural Tests of Piaget's Theory," *The Handbook of Cross-Cultural Psychology*, Vol. 4 "Developmental Psychology" (Boston: Allyn and Bacon, 1981), Chap.7, 295-341; as well as Harry C. Triandis and Alastair Heron, *Handbook of Cross-Cultural Psychology*, Vol. 4, 425-71; Raoul Naroll, "Holocultural Theory Tests," in Raoul and Frada Naroll, *Main Currents in Cultural Anthropology* (New York: Appleton-Century-Crofts, 1973), 309-84; and John W. Berry, *Human Ecology and Cognitive Style* (New York: John Wiley and Sons, 1976).

[29] A useful work on this topic is S. N. Eisenstadt, ed., *The Origins and Diversity of Axial Age Civilizations* (Albany: SUNY University Press, 1986). There are also specific comparative studies such as Geoffrey Lloyd's analysis of the axial shift in China and Greece, the topic of his *Demystifying Mentalities* (New York: Oxford University Press, 1990).

[30] A summary and commentary can be found in Gerald J. Larson and Ram Shankar Bhattacharya, eds., *Samkhya: A Dualist Tradition in Indian Philosophy*, Vol. IV of the Encyclopedia of Indian Philosophies (Princeton: Princeton University Press, 1987). Richard Gorbe calls it "one of the oldest philosophies in the Indian tradition" because reference to it appears in the Arthasastra of Kautilya, which he dates to ca. 300 B.C.E. In "Critical Review of Interpretations of Samkhya," 15-22, in Larson and Bhattacharya, 15. The classic formulation of Samkhya principles once existed in the text *Samkhyakarika* attributed to Isvarakrshna. The original text is not known. We have a Chinese copy translated ca. 560 C.E. And Shankara's much later rejection of Samkhya contains many lines from the missing text. For comments on logic in ancient India, see I. M. Bochenski, *A History of Formal Logic*, trans. Ivo Thomas (New York: Chelsea Publishing, 1970; reprint of 1961 Notre Dame "revised" translation of 1956 German work), Part VI, "The Indian Variety of Logic," 416-47. He cites numerous particular arguments from different sources, and finally sums up his conclusion: "That it really was a formal logic is shown by the fact that the formulae constructed by the Indian thinkers concern the fundamental question of logic, the question of 'what follows from what.' These formulae, moreover, were thought of as universally valid" (446).

[31] See Wing-Tsit Chan, *Source Book in Chinese Philosophy* (Princeton: Princeton University Press, 1963) , 211-26, for examples of Mohist thought.

[32] Liu Wu-chi claims that while the Analects of Confucius and the Book of Tao are just conglomerates of ideas, "extensive, carefully organized, and well-developed discourses" based on them are extant shortly thereafter. *Introduction to Chinese Literature* (Bloomington: Indiana University Press, 1996), 38. Cho-yun Hsü, "The Unfolding of Early Confucianism: The Evolution from Confucius to Hsün-Tzu," 23-38, in Irene Ebert, ed., *Confucianism: The Dynamics of Tradition* (New York: Macmillan, 1986), describes a development of Confucian thought up to the time of Hsün-Tzu which is increasingly philosophical in content, form of expression, and its criteria of validity.

[33] Sarvepalli Radhakrishnan and Charles Moore, eds., *A Sourcebook in Indian Philosophy* (Princeton: Princeton University Press, 1957), 227; 228-35 provides texts from this school.

[34] Joseph Needham claims that arguments about the relative value of empirical investigation and theoretical deduction were plentiful. *Science and Civilization in China*, Vol. 2, "The History of Scientific Thought" (Cambridge, Mass.: Cambridge University Press, 1956), 72-73. Needham even says that the work of the school of Logicians in the third century B.C.E. was superior to that of Plato and Aristotle on issues of scientific method (186-88). (In this context Needham tells a wonderful Taoist story on the danger of theoretical thinking. A man was told not to build his house of green wood. But he reasoned it out: green wood is hard and grows softer with age; plaster begins soft but grows harder with age. If he combined the two of them they would make a perfect house. So he built his house of green wood and plastered it well inside and out. Before long it fell down.)

[35] Wing-Tsit Chan, *Source Book*, 233-37, for this and other examples.

[36] See Myles Burnyeat, ed., *The Skeptical Tradition* (Berkeley: University of California Press, 1983), 78-85, for background to skepticism. Burnyeat includes Protagoras the Sophist (c.490-420 B.C.E.), who was active when Socrates was still a child. Fragments from him and Gorgias (c.480?-c.380) reveal strong doubts not only about the gods but also about certainty of knowledge or morals. David Sedly, "The Motivation of Greek Skepticism," in Myles Burnyeat, ed., *The Skeptical Tradition*, 9-29, provides a history of skepticism, with his own arguments as to what this or that ancient skeptic must have thought or should have thought. For the main source on ancient skepticism see *Outlines of Scepticism* by Sextus Empiricus, trans. Julia Annas and Jonathan Barnes, with the British spelling "Scepticism" (Cambridge; New York: Cambridge University Press, 1994). Also see Julia Annas and Jonathan Barnes, *The Modes of Scepticism* (Cambridge; New York: Cambridge University Press, 1985), for informed analyses of the formal "modes" or arguments used by various skeptical groups.

[37] Book I, 227-29. Annas and Barnes, 60. R. G. Bury translates the three criteria in simpler English in the 1939 Loeb edition, 41 (Cambridge, Mass.: Harvard University Press): "probable, tested, and irreversible" [*'aperispaston*]. Sextus then observes that while Carneades would give strong assent to ideas which passed this

triple test, Arcesilaus and he are both closer to true Pyrrhonic skepticism, neither assenting nor not assenting.

[38] Giovanni Reale, *A History of Ancient Philosophy*, Vol. III, The Systems of the Hellenistic Age (Albany: SUNY University Press, 1985), 337-38, sums it up as a matter of first accepting evidence, then looking for other evidence to confirm or disconfirm, and if time allows then connecting the impression thus received with other relevant impressions. His reference is to Sextus Empiricus, *Adversus Mathematicos*, 7.166-189 (LCL 2:91-103). In the realm of values, Cicero proposes a similar goal: "The aim of a skeptic is not to destroy ethical hypotheses, but to undermine the certainty with which they are held, and substitute probability in its place" (*De Officiis*, John Higgenbotham, trans. [Berkeley: University of California Press, 1967], 20).

[39] E.g., as in David Ray Griffin and Richard Falk, eds., *Postmodern Politics for a Planet in Crisis : Policy, Process, and Presidential Vision* (Albany: SUNY University Press, 1993), SUNY series in "constructive postmodern thought."

[40] Robert Kegan, *In Over Our Heads: The Mental Demands of Modern Life* (Cambridge, Mass.: Harvard University Press, 1994), 321-25, makes a distinction between deconstructive post-modernism and reconstructive post-modernism, as he calls it. He cites Nicholas Burbules and Suzanne Rice, "Dialogue across Differences: Continuing Conversation," *Harvard Educational Review*, 61 (1991): 393-416, for a similar distinction between an "anti-modern" post-modernism, which Kegan is calling deconstructive, and a kind of post-modernism that tries to "re-appropriate modernist categories (reason, freedom, equity, rights, self-determination) on less absolutistic grounds."

[41] One more topic would be highly relevant: the degree to which humankind shares also in certain basic options about what makes anything good or bad. There has been extensive cross-cultural work with Kohlberg's categories, with good results. But that is another and very large story. See John R. Snarey, "Cross-Cultural Universality of Social-Moral Development: A Critical Review of Kohlbergian Research," *Psychological Bulletin*, 97/2 (1985): 202-32, for a review of over thirty studies.

History or Geography?
Gadamer, Foucault, and Theologies of Tradition

Vincent J. Miller

The history which bears and determines us has the form of a war rather than that of a language; relations of power, not relations of meaning.

Michel Foucault, "Truth and Power"

Introduction

It is certainly far from controversial to suggest that a theology of tradition has much to learn from Hans-Georg Gadamer; the same cannot be said of Michel Foucault. As one who asserted that meaning is ultimately a comforting illusion that obscures the real dynamisms of history—chance and violence—Foucault seems, at first glance, to have little to offer for reflection on the nature of the handing on of the gracious message of Jesus of Nazareth. While this essay will not follow Foucault completely in arguing that meaning is illusory, it will seek to show that his illumination of the location of all discourse in networks of power has much to contribute to an adequate conception of the complexities of the handing on of the Christian tradition. I will argue that any adequate understanding of the dynamisms of the Christian tradition must encompass both meaning and power. That is, it must take into account the fact that discourses persist both because they bear classic meanings and because they are kept in play by relations of power, relations which, in addition to their productive potential, can distort meanings or cause discourses to function in ways unrelated and even opposed to the meanings they bear.

This paper will seek in the philosophies of Gadamer and Foucault resources for addressing these two aspects of discourse. Gadamer's philosophical hermeneutics will be explored as a sophisticated meaning-centered approach to discourse. Its theological usefulness will be illustrated through an exposition of Edward Schillebeeckx's later theology. We will attend carefully to both the instances where Schillebeeckx fruitfully employs Gadamer, and those times when his theological project requires that he supplement his thought with other perspectives. Foucault's archeological and genealogical discourse analysis will then be explored for resources to address the lacunae of the Gadamerian approach. Mary McClintock Fulkerson's theological analysis of the discursive practices of Appalachian Pentecostal women will provide an illustration of the productive potential of Foucault's method of analysis. The essay will conclude with a discussion of the relationship between the two perspectives.

Problems Facing a Contemporary Theology of Tradition

In order to better evaluate the contributions of the theologies of tradition this paper will review, it is necessary to outline several problems which face contemporary theological reflection on tradition. Two significant problems flow from the rise of historical consciousness in the West. First, historical-critical research into Christian origins has led to questions concerning the development of Christianity and doctrine—as can be found in the seminal writings of Möhler and Newman and countless projects since. An intense area of theological reflection on tradition in the past thirty years in Catholicism has revolved around a second, related theme: the question of contemporary innovation in the tradition. The epochal shifts of the Second Vatican Council gave rise to widespread questions of the relationship between tradition and change. How should the identity of a changing community be conceived? This question of identity also arises in a third problem: the relationship between diversity and inculturation. How can local forms of Christianity be evaluated in a way which both respects their legitimate alterity and takes seriously their relationship to other forms of Christianity? Can difference be valued without reducing it to a repetition of the same?

A tension between identity and difference underlies each of these problems. Yves Congar's distinction between Tradition (with a capital T) and the many, diverse traditions (with a small t) which embody it has proven to be an attractive way of addressing the issue.[1] It affirms the limited human character of the Christian traditions while respecting their claims to mediate transcendence. Thus the identity of the one great Christian Tradition is not thrown into question by developments or even ruptures in the various human traditions which mediate it. Unity is preserved amidst plurality. The problem with Congar's distinction is that it is largely idealist. While it is valuable to affirm in the abstract that the Christian tradition will always be diverse and plural in nature, concrete evaluations of identity and difference are much more difficult (as is witnessed by perennial Vatican avowals of inculturation in the abstract and hesitance to allow it in the concrete). While this abstract idealism is troubling, the inescapable eschatological element in discussions of unity and diversity makes it to some extent unavoidable. This side of the eschaton we will always be uncertain which changes are authentic innovations and which are corruptions.

This idealist tendency in theologies of tradition is fundamental to a fourth problem, the one with which this essay is most concerned: the relationship between meaning and power. Here there is a danger of an eschatological short circuit. Hopeful trust in the ultimate triumph of grace must not obscure our responsibilities in the anguished present. Such a short circuit is manifest in a methodological tendency to speak of the tradition as the handing on of a message or meaning without attending adequately to the technologies, institutions, and power structures in which this handing on takes place. Talk of incarnation or inculturation is not adequate if these terms serve merely to invoke the concrete in an abstract manner. What is needed is a way of conceiving the dynamics of the Christian tradition that takes into account both the saving meaning it claims to bear and the location of its discourses within the power inequalities that mark human existence.

This is more than an abstract academic question. Each conception of the dynamics of the Christian tradition brings with it a particular vision of the tactics of the handing on of the faith: that is, how to effectively preach the gospel in a given situation. Once one has, with Congar, asserted that the Holy Spirit is the transcendent subject of the Christian tradition and the church is the historical subject, one must come to an understanding of the nature of the task of this historical subject.[2] This question is unavoidable unless one concludes that ecclesial quietism is the best response to the Spirit—a position few advocate (at least for themselves). One's answer will vary greatly whether one thinks of the tradition as the Spirit-led *Gemeingeist* at work through history, the active reception of a classic meaning across different cultural horizons, or the persistence of a particular set of utterances over time through a host of varied discursive formations which are inescapably tied to particular institutions and power relationships. Thus, the descriptive task of this essay has a tactical purpose. It is hoped that a more adequate analysis of discourse will provide more sophisticated tactics for the contemporary handing on of the Christian tradition.

Having outlined some of the problems facing contemporary theological reflection on tradition, let us explore various attempts to address them. We will begin with Hans-Georg Gadamer, a thinker whose influence on the topic has been seminal. He provides an example of a very sophisticated meaning-based conception of tradition.

Hans-Georg Gadamer

Gadamer's philosophical hermeneutics grounds a theory of interpretation in a phenomenological account of the location of the subject. In its ability to address both the way contemporary believers relate to the textual witnesses of the past and the formation of the believer in the tradition, it is a particularly appealing resource for a theology of tradition. Although Gadamer understood his project to be a rejection of historicist methods (with their emphasis on reconstruction of the mind of the author or the historical context of the text), he shared with them an emphasis on the meaning borne by historical texts and the ability of a historically located interlocutor to come to an understanding of that meaning.

Drawing upon insights into the location of consciousness from Nietzsche, Husserl, and Heidegger, Gadamer emphasized the pre-understanding at work in any understanding, including hermeneutics. Enlightenment and Modern ideals of disinterested knowledge notwithstanding, the knowing subject is always already involved and situated. In response to those who criticized this portrayal of knowledge as too subjectivist, Gadamer stated that his concern was "not what we do or what we ought to do, but what happens to us over and above our wanting and doing."[3] He desired not to eliminate preunderstanding but to thematize it so it could be thrown into play in the risk of interpretation. In order to let the text speak on its own terms, Gadamer's hermeneutics aims to foreground the preunderstanding and prejudices of the reader so that they can be challenged by the text rather than remain hidden as silent and unquestioned arbiters of meaning.

Gadamer described this awareness of the historical location of consciousness as *wirkungsgeschichtliches Bewusstsein*—"historically effected consciousness." It encompasses two levels: 1) the situatedness of the interpreter in history—the way her or his consciousness is produced in a particular context, and 2) awareness of this fact. This second dimension can never be accomplished once and for all. One never leaves history and enters the realm of absolute knowledge. The further thematization of one's historical situation is a change in the very situation that one is attempting to thematize.

Historically effected consciousness is the opposite of solopsistic reflections on one's own particularity. We come to consciousness of our location only through encounters with something different. Gadamer named this dynamic the "fusion of horizons." Any full encounter with a strange text or interlocutor requires more than an attempt to understand the other by reconstructing its horizon. If that is all one does, one is not taking the text or speaker seriously as a potentially destabilizing source of truth. "By factoring the other person's standpoint into what he [or she] is claiming to say, we are making our own standpoint safely unattainable."[4] True historical consciousness requires an encounter with the other where one's own particularity is brought into play. Such encounters involve a projection of one's own horizon as much as attention to that of the other. "Hence the horizon of the present cannot be formed without the past. There is no more an isolated horizon of the present than there are historical horizons which have to be acquired. *Rather, understanding is always the fusion of these horizons supposedly existing by themselves.*"[5]

This thematization of one's own historical location is not its disavowal. One engages one text or another with a fundamental interest, with a presumption that it has something of value to one's own situation. Thus, Gadamer held up those particular fields of interpretation that involve application, such as legal and biblical hermeneutics, as examples of interpretation that took seriously both the meaning borne by texts and the interested location of the interpreter. He described the process of interpretation as dialogical, where the traditional text can speak as a decentering "thou."[6] Interpretation is dialectical. It begins with a negative experience of misunderstanding, of the strangeness of a text. This strangeness calls the assumptions of the reader into question and serves as instigation to read the text more carefully on its own terms. Thus, the fusion of horizons should not be read as comprehension of the other solely on one's own terms.[7] Preunderstanding and interest are challenged and transformed in the hermeneutical process. "Openness to the other, then, involves recognizing that I myself must accept some things that are against me, even though no one forces me to do so."[8] True experience is characterized by disappointment of expectations. Gadamer goes so far as to describe the painfulness of such openness in terms of suffering and tragedy.

This description of historically effected consciousness is as much an account of the knowing subject as it is a description of the practice of hermeneutics. As in Hussurl's "lifeworld" and Heidegger's "being-in-the-world," the subject is located and involved in history, language, and tradition. "Language is the universal medium in which understanding occurs."[9] It is through this linguisticality of consciousness that the past has effects in the present. It is the "concretion of historically effected consciousness."[10] For Gadamer, tradition is precisely this continued presence of the past in the linguistic formation of consciousness in the present. We exist within language, within traditions that have arisen from ages of experiences. "We are always situated within traditions . . . and we do not conceive of what tradition says as something other, something alien. It is always part of us. . . ."[11]

This relationship between tradition and preunderstanding is the basis upon which Gadamer attempts to rehabilitate the notion of authority. Rather than understand it in Enlightenment terms as prestige and obedience, as purely obscuring prejudice, Gadamer conceives authority and prejudice in the positive sense of pre-judgement or pre-apprehension, as that which enables us to engage the world in a meaningful way. Thus his statement: "authority has to do not with obedience, but rather with knowledge."[12] Understanding is not an individual, subjective act but a "participating in an event of tradition."[13]

This association of understanding, authority, and prejudice must be understood in terms of Gadamer's conception of the fusion of horizons. Within traditions, this process is continually occurring. Hermeneutic knowledge is not simply reproduction of past meanings but, in the fusion of horizons, production of new ones. True experience is marked by its future orientation, by its dialogical openness to the new. Thus, the formation of consciousness in tradition does not result in an endless repetition of the same. Traditions are dynamic, living realities. This is evident in Gadamer's discussion of the productive potential of historical distanciation. This distance is not merely the principle of strangeness, a gulf to be overcome in understanding, but that which allows the true meaning of a classical text to speak. The value of a classic is found precisely in its bearing of a meaning that transcends its originating horizon and can come to life in subsequent moments of tradition. Thus we see that for Gadamer, traditions are dialogues carried out through history insofar as contemporary consciousness is formed within them and, in turn, gives rise to perspectives that challenge what has been handed on. Those meanings that are mere products of their period fade as they fall by the wayside in the stretches of history. The dialogical functioning of tradition keeps past meanings alive and produces new ones.

Gadamer's philosophical perspective provides many resources for a Christian theology of tradition: a hermeneutics of historical retrieval and application, an account of the location of consciousness within particular traditions, and a description of the dynamics of tradition. In order to evaluate the potential of this perspective for a theology of tradition, we will turn to the work of a theologian who has been significantly influenced by Gadamer: Edward Schillebeeckx.

Edward Schillebeeckx's Theology of Tradition

Edward Schillebeeckx is one of several theologians who have productively applied Gadamer's philosophical hermeneutics.[14] Although found most explicitly in his writings on theological hermeneutics, Gadamer's insights have played a significant role throughout Schillebeeckx's theological synthesis since the early 1970s.[15] It informs his christological project, his portrayal of experience, and his articulation of the dynamics of the Christian tradition. These will be explored in turn. Although the role of Gadamer's philosophy will be emphasized, it must be noted that given the fact that Schillebeeckx is an enormously synthetic thinker, many other influences are at work within his thought.[16] This essay will attend as much to the places where Schillebeeckx abandons Gadamer as those where he employs him profitably. Where Gadamer fails him, Schillebeeckx turns to other thinkers. These will be noted but not explored in depth, as the paper will focus on the corrective potential of Foucault, whom Schillebeeckx does not employ.

Schillebeeckx's later work is best known for its christological emphasis and its embrace of historical-critical biblical scholarship. His project in *Jesus*, however, cannot adequately be described as a historical-critical retrieval of the historical Jesus, since he clearly expressed his doubts concerning the possibility of such a task. He preferred to speak of the "phenomenon of Jesus" to which one has access in historical research. The best one can hope for is a historical reconstruction unavoidably marked by the preunderstanding of the contemporary interpreter. For this reason, such a reconstruction could never be done once and for all. It is a task that must be undertaken anew in each age and location. Schillebeeckx's turn to historical reconstruction as an essential moment of theology is clearly informed by Gadamer. He desired to let the historical witnesses to Jesus speak their meanings in a way which can challenge the contemporary Christian community. Although influenced by Metz's notion of "dangerous memory," his description of Jesus as a negative presence has clear affinities with Gadamer's portrayal of the negative moment in dialectical knowledge. This christological dimension of his later theology provides one of the central elements of his theology of tradition. Each new moment of the Christian tradition is held in creative tension with reconstructions of Jesus. Each must be in some way reconcilable to what he said and did.

A second dimension of Schillebeeckx's application of Gadamer to the question of tradition can be found in his theology of experience, a topic with which he became increasingly preoccupied from the late 1970s on.[17] Schillebeeckx's account drew from a variety of thinkers including Theodor Adorno, Ian Barbour, and Karl Popper. The influence of Gadamer is evident in Schillebeeckx's consistent and strongly argued link between tradition and experience. This is especially evident in his later works, where he preferred not to distinguish the two terms, speaking instead of "experiential traditions" or "traditions of experience."[18] As he stated in *Interim Report*, "What was experience for others yesterday is tradition for us today; and what is experience for us today will in turn be tradition for others tomorrow."[19] His description of the handing on of this experience could be drawn directly from *Truth and Method*: "Experience is retained in reminiscence and language: it becomes a living 'deposit,' which is handed on as tradition."[20] All contemporary experience takes place within the interpretive horizon of past traditions. Aware of the tendency for such hermeneutic accounts to legitimate the past and the status quo, and having learned from Jürgen Habermas the role of coercive distortions in communication, Schillebeeckx struggled to find a critical principle from which to question the horizon of tradition.[21] He found this in negative experience. The negative aspect of experience in Gadamer was likely one source of Schillebeeckx's notion of negative, "contrast," or "refractory" experience. Curiously, Schillebeeckx never cited Gadamer's account of negative experience, including his use of Aeschylus' *pathei mathos*, "learning through suffering"; perhaps because of its abstract and individual character.[22] He turned instead to Adorno's *Negative Dialectics*, which provided an ethically charged account of negative experience and a more socially located principle of falsification for traditional meaning.[23] Contemporary experiences of meaningless suffering in which the tradition is actively or passively complicit call the received wisdom into question and provide the impetus for creative innovation.

Schillebeeckx's Gadamerian integration of tradition and experience had consequences for his articulation of the task of theology. It brought about the collapse of his previous understanding of the principle of correlation, which he had understood as taking place between past tradition and contemporary experience. In Schillebeeckx's attempts to reformulate the principle of correlation, we find a sketch of the dynamics of tradition. The contemporary Christian moment is always-already influenced by the Christian past because the tradition forms part of the horizon of contemporary experience. Schillebeeckx's emphasis on the challenge of negative experiences as the inspiration for overcoming suffering led him to describe these elements of the contemporary moment as the ongoing work of God in history, who does not cease to be the "Biblical God."[24] After rehearsing a series of failed reformulations, Schillebeeckx, avoiding the language of correlation, spoke of the "interrelationship" between the cultural forms of the "Christian past and the Christian present."[25] Here he departed from Gadamerian terminology, speaking instead of "semiotic-cultural systems."[26] Christian identity across two semiotic-cultural systems is found not through a comparison of corresponding terms, "but in the corresponding relationships between all the terms involved." He offered an illustration of such identity-in-difference modeled as a series of mathematical proportions.[27] Jesus' message is to his own socio-historical context, as the medieval understanding of faith is to the medieval socio-historical context, as our understanding of faith is to our context. Identity is only present in inculturations, and it is only through these inculturations that humans can encounter the saving mystery bringing salvation about in history. This identity is found in a "fluctuating middle field" between past and present inculturations. It is a moving target that can never be "laid down once and for all."[28] Nevertheless, Schillebeeckx did speak of an "historical identity in what remains, precisely in what gets forgotten and passes away because of its contingency."[29] Compare this with Gadamer's notion of the productive value of historical distanciation: "Only when all their [works of art in this case] relations to the present time have faded away can their real nature appear, so that understanding of what is said in them can claim to be authoritative and universal."[30]

Two strengths of Schillebeeckx's theological application of Gadamer are apparent from this analysis. It addresses well the first problem facing contemporary theological reflection on tradition: tensions caused by the rise of historical consciousness in general and historical-critical biblical scholarship in particular. Schillebeeckx provides a way of both sketching the limits of historical scholarship and positively integrating it into theology and the life of the church. His use of Gadamer is also quite fruitful for addressing the second major problem: the relationship between identity and change in the tradition. By locating experience within tradition and describing tradition as a handing on of experience—a handing on inevitably transformed by the current context—Schillebeeckx is able to portray innovation as being fundamentally in harmony with tradition. The hermeneutics of retrieval, most evident in his Christological writings but also at work within his ecclesiological works, adds to this sense of faithful change. This legitimates his calls for significant changes in the ecclesial status quo.

Nonetheless, Schillebeeckx's need to supplement Gadamer at several points reveals significant weaknesses in the philosopher's position. When dealing with the question of inculturation (the third problem) we noted that Schillebeeckx adopted a more structuralist conception of culture.

Here we encounter a common criticism of Gadamer's position. Does not its emphasis on the value of the meanings borne by traditionary texts tend to reduce the "difference" of each new horizon to the "same" of past tradition?[31] The validity of this criticism is particularly vexing to evaluate in light of Gadamer's description of the fusion of horizons as production of new meanings, not reproduction of past ones. It can be said that, in principle, there is no reason why Gadamer's ideal of historically effected consciousness should be read as a hermeneutics of consent to tradition that elides alterity. Gadamer's conception of tradition is pluralistic and open to encounters with non-Western traditions.[32] His foregrounding of preunderstanding, his notion of the dialectical nature of understanding, and his desire to let strange texts speak in their legitimate alterity remain fruitful for intercultural hermeneutics. What is missing in his position is not openness or a willingness to dialogue with different perspectives, but an awareness of the power dynamics that have excluded much of humankind from the dialogue of traditions in the past, and which constrain dialogue in the present.[33]

This brings us to the fourth problem: idealist ignorance of power. Even while virtually echoing Gadamer's dialectical discussion of suffering and negativity, Schillebeeckx cites not him but the more politically explicit reflections of Adorno. This of course is precisely Habermas's now classic criticism of Gadamer; his position suffers from an "idealism of linguisticality," which cannot adequately address the unavoidable power dynamics in discourse.[34]

Schillebeeckx developed his own sophisticated theoretical synthesis to address these shortcomings, the full analysis of which is beyond the scope of this essay. Instead, we will turn to the thought of Michel Foucault for resources to address the shortcomings of Gadamer.

Michel Foucault

It should be said from the start that this paper is not a proposal for a "theology after Foucault." It will make no attempt to engage Foucault's intellectual project in a comprehensive manner, nor will it follow the more difficult aspects of his position through to their conclusions. The frequent shifts, methodological reorientations (such as archeology, genealogy, problematization), and, above all, the tactical/methodological nature of some of his seemingly ontological assertions would make that impossible in any case.[35] It will focus instead on his description of, and methodological approach to, discourse during his archaeology and genealogy periods in the 1970s, the period which produced *The Archaeology of Knowledge*, *Power/Knowledge*, *Discipline and Punish* and the first volume of *The History of Sexuality*. Foucault provides both a perspective on the workings of tradition which more adequately addresses the location of discourse within institutions and networks of power, and a productive way of conceiving the tactics of the handing on of the Christian tradition.

In a 1976 interview on the topic of "geography," Foucault asserted, "Anyone envisaging the analysis of discourses solely in terms of temporal continuity would inevitably be led to approach and analyze it like the internal transformation of an individual consciousness."[36] This has two consequences for the French theorist. First, temporal models cannot adequately portray the role of power in the formation of discourses. Spatial metaphors better convey the strategic aspect of knowledge, how discourse is "transformed in, through and on, the basis of relations of power."[37] (Hence the title of this essay: "History or Geography?") Second, such overarching portrayals of unified discourse elide alternative knowledges, tending to homogenize all differences into one monolithic tradition.[38] These statements thematize the third and fourth problems facing contemporary theological reflection on the issue of tradition. Before discussing the particular aspects of his thought which address these problems, it is necessary to sketch his overarching intellectual orientation.

Foucault's project is frequently described as "post-structuralist." His relationship with structuralism is complex. Like many French thinkers in the late 1960s, he sought to distance himself from any totalizing thought-form, especially from structuralism, which had dominated French academic discourse for the previous decade. Although Foucault repeatedly challenged portrayals of his project as structuralist, he was clearly indebted to the analytical methods developed by Ferdinand de Saussure and Claude Levi-Strauss.[39] He shared with them an interest in systems of signification, a preferencing of synchronic over historical perspectives, and a de-emphasis of intentionality and authorship. Foucault departed from structuralism (with other post-structuralists) in abandoning any pursuit of fundamental or deep structures in human discourse. Instead he historicized structures or, in his words, "discursive formations." They continue to function as the fields of potential utterances, but they are malleable and fluid, marked with shifts and ruptures.

Foucault outlined an approach to the analysis of discourse in *The Archaeology of Knowledge*. He sought to examine discourse in its "positivity"; on its "exterior" or "surface." Rather than treating utterances as referential by searching within them to retrieve their truth or meaning, or for that matter attempting to unearth the subtext of their hidden, repressed meanings, Foucault would focus on the domain of what is said in any discursive formation. He defined this field by the "principle of rarity." That is, at any given time, of the infinite possible number of utterances, *"everything* is never said," only certain things are.[40] Foucault called this sum of things said and the relations between them the "enunciative domain."[41] This bracketing of meaning and corresponding focus on the positivity of discourse has undeniably been productive in Foucault's various studies. *Discipline and Punish* is exemplary in this regard. There Foucault argued that the rhetoric of increasing humaneness in punishment from the eighteenth to the nineteenth centuries glosses over the expansive deployment of disciplinary technologies throughout the whole of European society. Rather than telling a story of increasing moderation in punishment, Foucault sketched the progressive emergence of a carceral society in which citizens are subject to more, not less, control. A similar dynamic can be observed in his dismissal of the repressive hypothesis in the first volume of *The History of Sexuality*. Rejecting the widely accepted thesis concerning Victorian repression and subsequent sexual freedom, Foucault explored the "discursive explosion" on the topic of sexuality. Refusing to take at face value the assumption that there is a meaning buried within our sexual behaviors, he asked why it is that we are so driven to talk about sex. He located the shift not with Freud or any other modern opponent of Victorian sexuality, but with decrees of the Fourth Lateran Council concerning obligatory confession. Again, attention to the discursive domain tells a very different story: not one of progressive liberation, but of an increasing incitement to discourse.

Foucault explored the dynamics of the persistence of discourse, seeking to understand what keeps some utterances in play and consigns others to oblivion. The various structures involved in the accumulation and propagation of discourse make for a much more complex model than first implied by Foucault's metaphor of the "surface" of discourse. Discourse is supported by various material techniques (books, oral tradition, songs), in relationship to institutions (asylums, clinics, libraries, monasteries, churches, universities, academic societies), disciplinary modalities (commentaries, *summae*, case studies, footnotes) and practices (surveillance, examination, confession), each of which influences discourse and is immersed in the power relationships of human culture. Indeed, if discourse has a surface, it is a deeply textured one. Foucault described these multiple dimensions of discourse as an "archive." These are the focus of his "archaeological" method. "[M]y object is not language but the archive, that is to say, the accumulated existence of discourse. Archaeology, as I intend it, is kin neither to geology (as analysis of the sub-soil), nor to genealogy (as descriptions of beginnings and sequences); it's the analysis of discourse in its modality of archive."[42] Thus archaeology is not the quest for origins, but the analysis of discursive formations. Foucault described them as "historical a-prioris."[43] An archive is a "general system of the formation and transformation of statements."[44] Foucault was careful not to imply that archives necessarily possess any interior logic or coherence; they are not synthetic world-views. They are marked by ruptures, lacunae and incoherences. Nevertheless, the utterances which compose them can be analyzed as *events* in the conditions of their appearance (in terms of the laws governing what can be said in a particular time and place), and as *things* in their range of possible use. Discourse shifts across archives. An utterance which was produced according to the system of formation and transformation of one archive will function quite differently as an object in the particularities of another.[45]

After his shift to a genealogical method, Foucault increasingly emphasized the constitutive role of power in the production of discursive formations, preferring to speak of "discursive régimes" or "régimes of truth" rather than epistemes, formations, or archives. This Nietzschean turn in his thought led him to view meaning in discourse as a comforting distraction from the role of chance and power in the histories of discourses.[46] He asserted that, "The history which bears and determines us has the form of a war rather than a language: relations of power, not relations of meaning."[47] Here we find one of the great strengths of his position. It foregrounds the dependence of discourse on non-discursive practices, technologies, institutions, and power. While for Gadamer utterances become "traditional" because they bear meaning which transcends their originating horizon (that is, they are "classics"), for Foucault discourses perdure because they are kept in play by networks of power.

Foucault provides more than another perspective from which to view discourse. If he describes history as a war, he also offers valuable insights into the strategies and tactics of its battles. An appreciation of Foucault's conception of these tactics requires an understanding of his portrayal of power. His notion of the complex knowledge/

power has been among his most provocative and misunderstood proposals.[48] It is particularly difficult to evaluate because his discussions of the topic often (but not always) appear not in ontological expositions, but in reflections on method. This is the case in the first volume of *The History of Sexuality*. There Foucault's discussions of power are tied to his task of illuminating aspects of the history of sexuality not adequately accounted for by the repressive hypothesis. Thus, he struggled to articulate a notion of power that went beyond sovereign or juridical models that conceive power as something exercised by a subject over a passive object. Portraying power primarily as repression—as the ability to say "no"—this perspective was unable to account for the consent of the dominated and completely missed the positive, productive force of power. Foucault proposed instead a dynamic conception of power dispersed over networks of force inequalities within society.[49] This dispersed network of force functions positively as much as negatively. "What makes power hold good, what makes it accepted, is simply the fact that it doesn't only weigh on us as a force that says no, but that it traverses and produces things, it induces pleasures, forms knowledge, produces discourse."[50]

This productive aspect of power is well illustrated by Foucault's understanding of the constitution of the object domains of academic disciplines. *The History of Sexuality* provides an apt example. The creation of a science of sexuality delimited realms of normalcy and perversion. Rather than discovering a preexisting category (e.g., homosexuality) this discourse created both the object of study as well as a subject location (the homosexual). The productive power of discourse is, however, never stable and monovalent. While régimes of discourse set the boundaries of thought and action, they are fractured and unstable. Foucault spoke of the "tactical polyvalence of discourses." A given discourse "can be both an instrument and an effect of power, but also a hindrance, a stumbling block, a point of resistance and a starting point of the opposite strategy."[51]

The example of the constitution of homosexuality is a case in point. It is both a means of repressive classification of certain individuals in terms of perversion and the principle for a positive discourse of homosexuality which enables claims of legitimacy and naturality.[52] Thus, Foucault's notoriously pessimistic account of power is at the same time significantly optimistic. Wherever power is dispersed, resistance is found along with it. While for him, all truth and knowledge are the embodiments of power, at the same time the fractures and tensions within discursive régimes provide constant occasions for resistance.

Three points of Foucault's thought stand out as particularly relevant for theological reflection on tradition. First, the transmission of discourse is as much an issue of institutions, technologies, and power as it is of meaning. Second, what we are inclined to call "traditions," although they may be unified by some logic or world-view, are subject to fragmented application. That is, while there indeed may be a fundamental logic to the Christian tradition which can be described in some idealist manner, there is no question that its discourses can function in any number of ways, many of which fundamentally contradict what one would hold its meaning to be. As is all too obvious from history, the archive or archives of Christianity can function as much as a support for fascism and chauvinism as they can for justice and liberation. The persistence of discourses of the Christian tradition can be thought of as a kind of palimpsest. In this case, however, the old words are not elided and overwritten by the new. The utterances of the past survive, but are now structured according to, and serving the functions of, the present discursive régime. The words remain the same, but the outline and chapters are reordered.

These two aspects of Foucault's thought help to conceptualize more fully the nature of the Christian tradition by mapping the battleground beneath Gadamer's horizon. Foucault's presentation of the relationship between power and knowledge move us from mapping the battlefield into the tactics of the battle itself. The value of this third point is made clear by the successes of Mary McClintock Fulkerson's analysis of the discourse régime of Pentecostal women. To this we will now turn.

Mary McClintock Fulkerson

In *Changing the Subject: Women's Discourses and Feminist Theology,* Mary McClintock Fulkerson employs Foucault in her attempt to articulate a feminist theology which is not dependent upon liberal, essentialized notions of "women's experience."[53] While crediting this approach with great successes in earlier forms of feminist theology, she faults it for concealing a specific identity: that of white, Western, privileged, academic women.[54] Dependence on this false universal renders feminist theology incapable of respecting difference and unable to value the many forms that women's liberating resistances can take. Fulkerson applies most of what we have just reviewed from Foucault's thought. She is particularly indebted to his genealogical method, which she employs to challenge liberal universal notions of the subject; and to his notion of the relationship between discourse, power and resistance. This latter concept undergirds her analysis of Appalachian Pentecostal women's use of scripture. Her success in valuing the liberating power of these marginal religious practices illustrates the great potential of Foucault's thought for a theology of tradition.

Fulkerson explores the world of Appalachian Pentecostal women, whose biblical hermeneutics would clearly be considered historically, hermeneutically, and politically naive by the canons of the contemporary academic discursive régime, dependent as they are upon notions of literal meaning, inerrancy, and Spirit-inspired interpretation. Their biblical literalism leads these women to embrace biblical texts which subordinate women. Consequently, they actively disavow feminism. Thus, a meaning-centered analysis, which for the purposes of this paper overlaps precisely with Fulkerson's portrayal of liberal feminism, would find little of value in their theology. "The agenda here is not to make Pentecostal women feminists. They simply are not, if feminism is defined in terms of particular ideas. But if our interest is the effects of women's practices in relation to the pertinent discursive formation and the several subject positions it offers, then the practices of Pentecostal women must merit another look."[55] Fulkerson's analysis of their discursive and non-discursive practices reveals great value and sophistication. The Pentecostal emphases on the power of the Spirit and absolute dependence on God create subject positions in which women can exercise significant authority in the community while simultaneously avowing the subordination of women to men. Even as these women employ its rhetoric, their Spirit-grounded exercise of authority transgresses subordination. "The affective transgressions that occur with their performance, from [their] uninhibited bodily display to the way in which women testifiers can take control of a service even when the preacher is a man, signify excesses that belie their descriptions of humility and submission."[56] Their preaching and practices are an example of the tactical polyvalence of discourse. Thus the relationship of discourse to liberating praxis is revealed to be much more complex than the application of an emancipatory meaning.

On the basis of the litmus test of my own feminist theological lexicon about empowerment of women, for example, the submissive-dependence of and self-denegrating language of Pentecostal women looks to be a discourse of utter mysogyny. Read intertextually and as socially graf(ph)ted on their situation however, their practices appear different. For Pentecostal women the pleasures of their canon's reading of the Holy Spirit and the ecstasies afforded in their intimacy with God produce a place of well-being, in stark contrast with the marks of marginalization in their lives. It is not a place immediately compatible with liberationist practices, which are directed toward resisting socioeconomic marginalization, but it is a place of God-sustained integrity. . . . Openings for emancipatory or liberating possibilities are found at the intersection of canonical codes and practices with the suffering and desires of women's social location. These openings can look alien to the ideals of liberation feminism.[57]

The points of rupture within and between discursive régimes provide spaces for liberating practices. Fulkerson's analysis illuminates a very different perspective on the workings of the Christian tradition than one of more Gadamerian inspiration. The legitimacy of a given form of Christianity is not evaluated based on its relationship with the originating meaning of Christianity. Instead it is judged by its ability to provide locations of resistance, empowerment, and liberation that subvert the dominant discursive régime.[58] This entails a fundamentally different perspective on the strangeness encountered in interpretations of biblical texts. Rather than being seen as the negative moment of understanding, as instigation for more careful reading, the tension produced by elements of the Christian archive which seem strange in our contemporary context is not something necessarily to be overcome, but a potential source of productive rupture. Thus Foucault's understanding of discourse provides both a more adequate account of the relationship between the handing on of the Christian tradition and power and, as Fulkerson's application of this analysis to the scriptural discourses of Appalachian Pentecostal women illustrates, a way of valuing the difference of the "periphery" of the tradition without requiring that it be reduced to the terms of the "center." Whatever the merit of criticisms of Gadamer in this regard, Fulkerson's use of discourse analysis contributes something helpful. It provides a way to evaluate Christian identity based not on meaning-based consensus, but on the liberative function of discourses. In so doing, it illuminates the necessity of attending to local histories when engaging in theological reflection on tradition.

Despite these impressive successes, a theological appropriation of Foucault faces serious difficulties. Among these are his notion of the omnipresence of power and his bracketing of meaning. Fulkerson wrestles with what has been called Foucault's "agonistic ontology." She rejects his portrayal of power on the ontological level, but embraces it as a form of analysis which does not succumb to ignorance of its complicity in structures of domination. She further values it for providing a robust account of human fallenness.[59] The role of ontology in Christianity requires comment. There is no question that the foundation of all reality in the gracious, self-giving love of God is among Christianity's most profound beliefs. It is a doctrine which must undergird any adequate Christian ontology. Christian ontological assertions, however, seldom refer to the status quo. The Hebrew and Christian Scriptures generally express such beliefs in the contrary-to-fact form of either protological or eschatological language. Even if this issue of ontology is resolved in this manner, the issue of the enormously pessimistic nature of Foucault's portrayal of the omnipresence of power remains. We have seen that this is accompanied by a corresponding belief in the equally widespread possibility of resistance, and drawn from this a reconception of the tactics of the handing on of the Christian tradition. Regardless of this optimistic element, it should be noted that a tragic sense is not the worst thing for a theology of tradition. Indeed such a perspective is essential for a discussion of tradition where one is not speaking in a protological or eschatological mode, but of the concrete life of the Christian community. There is no small amount of atrocity in the history of the Christian churches and thus a theoretical orientation which can take account of such dynamics is highly desirable.

A second problem with Foucault's theoretical orientation seems less likely to succumb to productive integration. His archeological bracketing of meaning is obviously a profound obstacle for theology. We have seen how his archeological and genealogical methods have much to contribute to providing a fuller understanding of the multiple dimensions of discourse, but in so doing do they rule out taking into account the importance and productivity of the meanings which discourses bear? Foucault's thought is not without *aporiae* in this regard. While his dismissal of meaning in *The Archaeology of Knowledge* can, at times, be read as explicitly nihilistic, his practice of archeology seems to depend on some understanding of meaning in discourse. The mapping of the field of discourse presupposes the ability to distinguish the meanings of utterances, to listen carefully to the contents of the discourse which he aims to treat only in its exteriority.[60] The ethos implicit in the genealogist's desire to unmask the current régime seems to presuppose meaning as well. Why should one care if alternative knowledges are elided? There is the further problem of the status of Foucault's own discourse in this regard. Does it bear a meaning or is it simply a set of utterances which conform to a particular discursive régime? Foucault's methodological bracketing of meaning does not seem to have led him to a completely nihilistic position. In the dialogical conclusion of *The Archaeology of Knowledge* he responded to an imagined interlocutor who criticized him for reserving for his own discourse the freedom he denied others. In his response, Foucault described his task as

> an attempt to reveal discursive practices in their complexity and density; to show that to speak is to do something—something other than to express what one thinks; to translate what one knows, and something other than to play with the structures of language (*langue*); to show that to add a statement to a pre-existing series of statements is to perform a complicated and costly gesture, which involves conditions (and not only a situation, a context and motives), and rules (not the logical and linguistic rules of construction); to show that a change in the order of discourse does not presuppose "new ideas," a little invention and creativity, a different mentality, but transformations in a practice, perhaps also in neighboring practices, and in their common articulation. I have not denied—far from it—the possibility of changing discourse: I have deprived the sovereignty of the subject of the exclusive right to it.[61]

Foucault clearly allows for some (if not much) intentional manipulation of discourse. The speaker is not simply awash in the sea of discursive formations, but can in fact change them. Although he has little good to say about the power of meaning, it is clear that he employs it in his own discursive interventions.[62] This passage supports the application of Foucault's thought for which this essay has argued. It provides a vision of the intransigence of discourse, of the multiple forces that are at work in it in spite of our intended meanings. This is an essential question for a theology of tradition. Is a given utterance a successful, perhaps prophetic rearticulation of the Christian message or is it a domestication which renders the gospel innocuous to the status quo by allowing it to be swept on the tides of the contemporary discursive régime?

Conclusion

This essay has attempted to show that the thought of Michel Foucault provides valuable correctives and supplements to Hans-Georg Gadamer's philosophy of tradition and, for that reason, is of great utility for constructing a contemporary theology of tradition. It is clear that the order of the thinkers could not easily be reversed. One could not begin a theology of tradition with Foucault. His genealogical approach to history precludes any interest in what is handed on in tradition. In attempting to show the complimentarity of these two positions, this paper has framed Foucault with Gadamer in that it has consistently presumed there is a meaning that is handed on in the Christian tradition. Foucault has been employed to provide more complex ways of conceiving the perdurance and corruption of these meanings. Such attending to tradition and meaning are clearly not Foucault's concern, although we have seen the difficulties that he encountered in his attempts to bracket meaning.

The theoretical orientations of Gadamer and Foucault offer a set of mutual strengths and weaknesses for envisioning the dynamics of tradition. Gadamer provides a way of dealing with the problems of historical consciousness and the identity of the Christian community amidst change. If his position can be characterized as a polite ethos of tradition, it does not lack the potential to disrupt. Classic meanings (perhaps undervalued in their own age) remain to disturb long after the constricting prejudices that obscured them fade into oblivion. Yet Gadamer's focus on meaning, if a strength, is at the same time a profound weakness. His portrayal of the fusion of horizons and the historicity of consciousness does not adequately attend to the role of coercion and power in discourse. Foucault's impolite attention to power draws our gaze from the placid horizon to the battlefield that surrounds us. His genealogical discourse analysis provides a deeper portrayal of the historicity of consciousness, sketching out the non-ideational aspects of preunderstanding. In this sense, both thinkers are engaged in a project of thematizing the unthought that is clearly post-Nietzschean in its awareness that historical located knowledge can never be complete.

A theology of tradition that takes into account both perspectives would view the handing on of the Christian message as a function of meaning and power.[63] It would attend to the complexities of receiving a meaning across cultural and historical horizons as well as to the role of power relationships in this handing on—in their ability to corrupt meaning and in their productive ability to keep it in play. Thus, it would have resources to address the obvious institutional and communal dynamics that have been at work in the history of the tradition and continue today. The Christian tradition is not only (or even primarily) a history of texts and their interpreters but also one of communities and their practices and institutions.

More is at stake here, however, than a more or less relatively adequate description of the dynamics of tradition. Tradition is not simply a question of things past but of handing on in the present. These descriptions of tradition bring with them consequences for conceiving the ethos of living in a tradition and of the tactics for handing it on. The Gadamerian approach evokes an ethos of humility and openness to the authority of tradition, of stewardship of meaning and the ongoing productive fusion of horizons and the application of traditional insights. As a practitioner of a tradition, one is engaged in the constant correction of understanding and application.

The Foucaultian perspective implies a clear hermeneutics of suspicion. In this sense it is nothing new. However, its genealogical suspicions go deeper than speculating repressed meanings at work in discourse to question meaning itself as illusory, as merely an effect of the non-discursive elements of discursive régimes. This attention to the non-discursive provides a new focus for the ethos of tradition and the tactics for handing it on. Responsible living of a tradition requires more than clarification of understanding. The example of Christianity and anti-Semitism is illustrative. Attention to the originating horizon of various traditional texts which have legitimated anti-Semitism from the Matthean and Johannine passion narratives to the writings of John

Chrysostom makes clear that these texts were not anti-Semitic in their origins. Their heated polemics emerged in conflicts between relatively small and powerless communities in competition for membership. A proper, open reading of these texts challenges preunderstandings that would use them to legitimate anti-Semitism. Such clarifications of meaning are not however sufficient. It is clear that more than a tragic misunderstanding was involved in the history of Christian anti-Semitism. In contexts where Jews were politically and culturally marginalized, these texts functioned anti-semitically. In such a context, it is hard to imagine a public proclamation of them that would not legitimate anti-Semitism. Thus a Foucaultian perspective suggests an ethos of tradition in which believers are responsible not only for openness to the meanings born within their tradition, but also for the power relationships in broader society that can cause such meanings to have negative effects. To continue with the example, one is obliged not simply to explain how the Christian tradition is not anti-Semitic in its origins and note the various interpretive errors that have marked it in this regard, but also to engage the contemporary discursive régime to address the power imbalances that will continue to cause one's traditional meanings to have unintended, evil effects. This involves a shift from an ethos of participating in liberal civil society speaking for and preserving one's own domain of belief and tolerating others, to actively seeking the political stability of others so that one's own beliefs will not function destructively. A contemporary analogue can perhaps be found in Catholic teaching on homosexuality and the question of civil rights for gays and lesbians.

Corresponding with this ethos is a conception of the tactics of the handing on of traditional meaning. It requires, in addition to engagement with textual witnesses of the tradition and dialogical correction of preunderstanding, attention to the non-discursive aspects of the discursive régime. Our contemporary situation provides an unfortunate example. A central element of the discursive régime of our advanced capitalist culture is extreme commodification. Consumption is a fundamental dimension of our construction as subjects. We consume not simply material goods but cultural ones as well.[64] In this context, any retrieval or rearticulation of the Christian message is likely to be received as just another cultural product to be consumed. Religious beliefs are held in the same hypertrophied part of our consciousness as other cultural commodities—a very different location than was demarcated by the word "creed" in discursive régimes past. The practices associated with this cognitive location are leisure, passive enjoyment and perhaps at its most ethical extreme: sentiment. Consequently, religious beliefs are not easily linked with political and ethical practice. Matters are further complicated by the fact that radical values have become so coopted by Madison Avenue as to render Tom Wolfe's once pointed title, *Radical Chic,* an exercise in redundancy. In this situation, refining one's understanding of the meaning of the gospel will have little impact; for whatever the meaning—no matter how radical or challenging— it will be received as a consumer commodity. To effectively impact the situation, one must tactically engage the discursive régime both on the level of discourse and non-discursive practices. One must engage the structures through which meanings are received. This is much easier said than done given advanced capitalism's seemingly limitless ability to commodify any discourse or practice. If, however, local worshiping communities and their larger denominational structures are thought of not simply as vessels of meaning, but also as discursive régimes themselves, they can be understood as capable of impacting this divide between belief and action in the broader régime of advanced capitalism by providing a location where meaning and action are connected in the community's praxis.

This paper has suggested that Fulkerson's application of Foucault is able to value peripheral forms of Christianity in a way which a more Gadamerian approach cannot. Each perspective resonates with a particular mark of the church. A hermeneutical approach is best equipped to address the question of apostolicity—the adequacy of each inculturation of Christianity to the foundational witnesses of the New Testament. Schillebeeckx's notion of the negative presence of Jesus shows the critical power of such a perspective. Fulkerson's Foucaultian theology seems more amenable to the mark of catholicity in its ability to value the particular liberative potential of diverse forms of Christianity.[65] There is an unavoidable tension between apostolicity and catholicity. Taken alone, each is inadequate. Apostolicity becomes a stifling demand for the repetition of the same; and catholicity becomes centrifugal, fragmenting Christianity into incommensurable local communities. These two marks must be held in tension. The same can be said for the two theoretical perspectives that this paper has explored. Any discussion of the history of the meanings borne by the Christian traditions is naive without a map of the battleground on which history takes place, and this geography of the battlefield is of little interest without the conviction that the message that these traditions bear is meaningful.

Notes

[1] *Tradition and Traditions*, trans. Michael Naseby and Thomas Rainborough (New York: MacMillan Company, 1966). This paper follows Congar in using the singular of tradition to describe the theological reality that is present only in a variety of limited human traditions. In general, the term will be used to describe the active process of handing on the salvation proclaimed by Christianity through various epochs and cultures. Use of the singular is not intended as an essentializing reduction of the plurality of Christian and Catholic traditions.

[2] *Tradition and Traditions*, 308-48.

[3] *Truth and Method*, 2nd rev. ed., trans. Joel Weinsheimer and Donald G. Marshall (New York: Crossroad, 1992), xxvii.

[4] *Truth and Method*, 303.

[5] *Truth and Method*, 306. Emphasis original.

[6] *Truth and Method*, 360-62.

[7] G. B. Madison, "Hermeneutics: Gadamer and Ricoeur," Richard Kearney, ed., *Routledge History of Philosophy*, Vol. VIII: Twentieth-Century Continental Philosophy (New York: Routledge, 1994), 307.

[8] *Truth and Method*, 361.

[9] *Truth and Method*, 389.

[10] *Truth and Method*, 389.

[11] *Truth and Method*, 282.

[12] *Truth and Method*, 279.

[13] *Truth and Method*, 290.

[14] Other significant theological appropriations of Gadamer include that of Ernst Fuchs and Gerhard Ebeling; see the essays collected in James M. Robinson, ed. *The New Hermeneutic* (New York: Harper & Row, 1964); David Tracy, *The Analogical Imagination* (New York: Crossroad, 1984); and Sandra Schneiders, *The Revelatory Text* (San Francisco: HarperSanFrancisco, 1991).

[15] Schillebeeckx's most explicit published reflections on theological hermeneutics are found in the collections *God the Future of Man*, trans. N. D. Smith (New York: Sheed and Ward, 1968), especially the first essay of that collection "Towards a Catholic Use of Hermeneutics," 1-50, and *The Understanding of Faith*, trans. N. D. Smith (New York: Seabury, 1975). An extensive treatment of the topic can be found in an unpublished manuscript of his lectures from Nijmegen, *College Hermeneutik: 1978-1979*, Archief Colleges Schillebeeckx, Theologische Faculteit Nijmegen.

[16] Other important influences include the organic temporal model which he

received from Congar, as well as his appropriation of various Frankfurt critical theorists, which heavily chastened his use of Gadamer in his theological hermeneutics after 1968.

[17] There are lengthy sections devoted to the topic of experience in *Christ*, trans. John Bowden (New York: Crossroad, 1980), (30 pages), *Interim Report*, trans. John Bowden (New York: Crossroad, 1981), (20 pages), and *Church*, trans. John Bowden (New York: Crossroad, 1990), (100 pages). Schillebeeckx also undertook a sustained reflection on the topic "Erfahrung und Glaube" for a German theological encyclopedia, Franz Böckle, Franz-Xavier Kaufmann, Karl Rahner, Bernard Welte, eds., *Christlicher Glaube in moderner Gesellschaft* (Freiburg, Basel, and Vienna, 1980), Vol. XXV, 73-116, and devoted attention to it in his farewell lecture at Nijmegen, *Theologisch Geloofsverstaan Anno 1983* (Baarn: H. Nelissen, 1983).

[18] *Church*, 16

[19] *Interim Report*, 50.

[20] *Christ*, 38.

[21] "Critical Theory and Theological Hermeneutics," *The Understanding of Faith*, 130-131.

[22] *Truth and Method*, 356.

[23] Although Adorno is the theorist most often cited in this context, Schillebeeckx's account of the negative dialectic of tradition seems deeply indebted to Gadamer's appropriation of Hegel, and to Karl Popper's principle of falsification, who is given significant attention in his unpublished *College Hermeneutik*, 84-94.

[24] *Church*, 36.

[25] *Church*, 35.

[26] *Church*, 41.

[27] See *Church*, 42. This illustration was originally offered by Schillebeeckx in *Theologisch Geloofsverstaan Anno 1983*, 15.

[28] *Church*, 42.

[29] *Church*, 36.

[30] *Truth and Method*, 297.

[31] See Elizabeth Schüssler Fiorenza, *Bread Not Stone: The Challenge of Feminist Biblical Interpretation* (Boston: Beacon Press, 1984), 128-40; Francis Schüssler Fiorenza, *Foundational Theology: Jesus and the Church* (New York: Crossroad, 1984), 305; Sheila Briggs, "The Politics of Identity and the Politics of Interpretation," *Union Seminary Quarterly Review* 43:1-4 (1989): 163-80; Mark Kline Taylor, *Remembering Esperanza: A Cultural-Political Theology for North American Praxis* (Maryknoll, N.Y.: Orbis Books, 1990), 67ff.; Robin Schott, "Whose Home Is It Anyway? A Feminist Response to Gadamer's Hermeneutics," in *Gadamer and Hermeneutics*, ed. Hugh J. Silverman, Vol. 4 of Continental Philosophy (New York: Routledge, 1991), 208.

[32] For a response to Gadamer's critics which argues that he has a pluralistic understanding of tradition see Holly L. Wilson, "Gadamer's Alleged Conservatism," in Lenore Langsdorf and Stephen H. Watson, eds., *Phenomenology, Interpretation, and Community* (Albany: SUNY University Press, 1996), 145-58.

[33] Georgia Warnke has responded to these criticisms, arguing that a hermeneutic perspective remains viable if it attends to two circumstances: "First the hermeneutic discussion of meaning through which traditions advance may be not only conditioned but also systematically distorted, by social and economic conditions and relations of power. Second, these conditions may mean that there are interpretive voices that have been repressed or excluded from our hermeneutic debates and from which we have therefore been unable to learn." "Feminism and Hermeneutics," *Hypatia* 8 (1993): 81-98.

[34] "A review of *Truth and Method*," in Fred Dallmayr and Thomas McCarthy, eds., *Understanding and Social Inquiry* (Notre Dame: University of Notre Dame Press, 1977), 361. Habermas's appreciation of Gadamer's position is more obvious when this criticism is read in its context as a chapter of *On the Logic of the Social Sciences*, Shierry Weber Nicholsen and Jerry A. Stark, trans. (Cambridge, Mass.: MIT Press, 1984). For a summary of the debate see Jack Mendelson, "The Habermas-Gadamer Debate," *New German Critique* 18 (1979): 44-73.

[35] For a discussion of the three major methodological orientations in Foucault see Thomas Flynn, "Foucault's Mapping of History," in Gary Gutting, ed., *The Cambridge Companion to Foucault* (Cambridge; New York: Cambridge University Press, 1994), 28-46.

[36] "Questions on Geography," *Power/Knowledge: Selected Interviews and Other Writings 1972-1977*, ed. Colin Gordon (New York: Pantheon, 1980), 69.

[37] "Questions on Geography," 70.

[38] "Two Lectures," *Power/Knowledge*, 81-83.

[39] *The Order of Things: An Archaeology of the Human Sciences* (New York: Random House Vintage, 1973), xiv; *The Archaeology of Knowledge*, trans. A. M. Sheridan Smith (New York: Pantheon, 1972), 199-211. For Foucault's comments on the term "post-structuralism" in terms of Russian Formalism see "Critical Theory/Intellectual History," *Politics, Philosophy, Culture*, ed. Lawrence D. Kritzman (New York: Routledge, 1988), 17-18. For a criticism of the distinction between structuralism and post-structuralism as meaningless see Philip Lews, "The Post-Structuralist Condition," *Diacritics*, 12 (1982): 2-22.

[40] *Archaeology of Knowledge*, 118. Emphasis original.

[41] It is "an anonymous field whose configuration defines the possible position of speaking subjects . . . [that must not be understood as] a great, anonymous voice that must, of necessity, speak through the discourses of everyone; but we must understand by it the totality of things said, the relations, the regularities, and the transformations that may be observed in them, the domain of which certain figures, certain intersections indicate the unique place of a speaking subject and may be giving the name of the author." *Archaeology of Knowledge*, 122.

[42] *Foucault Live: Interviews 1966-1984*, ed. Sylvère Lotringer (New York: Semiotext(e), 1989), 25. Note that this use of "genealogy" differs significantly from his later use of the term.

[43] *Archaeology of Knowledge*, 127. Foucault uses the adjective "historical" to contrast his notion from any transcendental a priori. He plays out this Kantian

reference by describing his project as a "Critical History of Thought" in the tradition of Kant. He describes the fundamental question which drives his project as "subjectivization." The question of "determining what the subject must be, what condition is imposed on it, what status it is to have, and what position it is to occupy in reality or in the imaginary, in order to become the legitimate subject of one type of knowledge or another." Maurice Florence (pseud.), "Foucault, Michel, 1926," in *The Cambridge Companion to Foucault*, 315.

[44] *Archaeology of Knowledge*, 128-30.

[45] Foucault chafed against the label "philosopher of historical discontinuity." He illuminated unseen continuities as often as he shattered ones previously assumed. Nevertheless, his portrayal of discursive formations writes large the location of knowledge. While certain topics of discourse may transcend epistemic shifts, they do not peacefully bear their previous meanings with them. Their function changes in relation to the different discursive formation. One of his overarching goals was to articulate an alternative to a history of ideas approach which would explore the development of a theme across the work of a variety of authors. For Foucault's comments on this issue see "On Power," in *Politics, Philosophy, Culture*, 99-100; and "Truth and Power," *Power/Knowledge*, 111-13. For a succinct account of Foucault's emphasis on discontinuity see Thomas Flynn, "Foucault's Mapping of History," *The Cambridge Companion to Foucault*, 33.

[46] See "Nietzsche, Genealogy, History," in *Language, Counter-Memory, Practice*, ed. Donald Bouchard (Ithaca: Cornell University Press, 1977), 139-64, and his comments concerning "truth" in "The Discourse on Language" appended to *Archaeology of Knowledge*, 215-39. There is an ethos within this method. By exposing the role of chance and caprice in the formation of discursive régimes, Foucault hoped to shatter their seeming necessity and thus create room for alternatives. "I would like to say something about the function of any diagnosis concerning the present. It does not consist in a simple characterization of what we are but, instead—by following lines of fragility in the present—in managing to grasp why and how that-which-is might no longer be that-which-is. In this sense, any description must always be made in accordance with these kinds of virtual fracture which open up the space of freedom, i.e., of possible transformation." "Critical Theory/Intellectual Theory," *Politics, Philosophy, Culture*, 36.

[47] "Truth and Power," 114.

[48] The central, recurring criticism is that by making knowledge co-extensive with and inseparable from power, Foucault leaves no possibility of a non-coercive ideal which can function as a principle of critique. See Jürgen Habermas, "Some Questions Concerning the Theory of Power: Foucault Again," *The Philosophical Discourse of Modernity,* trans. Frederick Lawrence (Cambridge, Mass.: MIT Press, 1987), 266-93; Charles Taylor, "Foucault on Freedom and Truth," in David Hoy, ed., *Foucault: A Critical Reader* (Oxford: Blackwell, 1986), 69-102; Paul Ricoeur, *Main Trends in Philosophy* (New York: Holmes and Meyer, 1979), 369. Foucault attempted to clarify his position in an interview: "when I read . . . the thesis, 'Knowledge is power,' or 'Power is knowledge,' I begin to laugh, since

studying their *relation* is precisely my problem. If they were identical, I would not have to study them and I would be spared a lot of fatigue as a result. The very fact that I pose the question of their relation proves clearly that I do not *identify* them." "Critical Theory/Intellectual History," in *Politics, Philosophy, Culture*, 43. Emphasis original.

⁴⁹ "It seems to me that power must be understood in the first instance as the multiplicity of force relations immanent in the sphere in which they operate and which constitute their own organization; as the process which, through ceaseless struggles and confrontations, transforms, strengthens, or reverses them; as the support which these force relations find in one another, thus forming a chain or a system, or on the contrary, the disjunctions and contradictions which isolate them from one another; and lastly, as the strategies in which they take effect, whose general design or institutional crystallization is embodied in the state apparatus, in the formation of the law, in the various social hegemonies. Power's condition of possibility . . . is the moving substrate of force relations which, by virtue of their inequality, constantly engender states of power, but the latter are always local and unstable." *The History of Sexuality*, Vol. 1: Introduction, trans. Robert Hurley (New York: Vintage, 1978), 92-93.

⁵⁰ "Truth and Power," 119.

⁵¹ *History of Sexuality*, 101.

⁵² Ibid.

⁵³ *Changing the Subject: Women's Discourses and Feminist Theology* (Minneapolis: Fortress, 1994). Fulkerson's position is complex and multifaceted. This paper will only outline the aspects of her position which are applications of Foucault. Her discourse analysis is also significantly influenced by Jacques Derrida, John Frow, and Jane Tomkins, among others. Note that Foucault, while respected, is not uncritically praised by feminist thinkers. Although he explores issues of great concern to feminists, his analyses are criticized for not adequately addressing gender location. See Irene Diamond and Lee Quimby, eds., *Feminism and Foucault: Reflections on Resistance* (Boston: Northeastern University Press, 1988).

⁵⁴ Fulkerson's turn to discourse analysis is an explicit disavowal of Gadamer's phenomenological hermeneutics, which she faults for a similar harboring of the liberal subject. See *Changing the Subject*, 136-40.

⁵⁵ *Changing the Subject*, 285.

⁵⁶ *Changing the Subject*, 289-90.

⁵⁷ *Changing the Subject*, 357.

⁵⁸ Fulkerson's use of Foucault in this regard may presume a more robust notion of agency than Foucault can provide. Although Foucault frequently expressed his desire to explore not only the ways in which power produces human culture, but also the basis of manifold local resistances to power structures, he so stressed the hegemonic function of discursive regimes that the possibility of meaningful resistance at times becomes hard to conceive. The work of Michel De Certeau is a promising supplement in this regard. De Certeau built upon Foucault's notions

of discourse and power, developing an account of the creative agency of cultural consumers. He described them as "unrecognized producers, poets of their own acts, silent discoverers of their own paths in the jungle of functionalist rationality." Their productions "trace out the ruses of other interests and desires that are neither determined nor captured by the system in which they develop." *The Practice of Everyday Life*, Steven F. Rendall, trans. (Berkeley: University of California Press, 1984), xviii.

[59] *Changing the Subject*, 365-66.

[60] Hubert Dreyfus and Paul Rabinow, *Michel Foucault: Beyond Structuralism and Hermeneutics* (Chicago: University of Chicago Press, 1982), 88. This book explores in great detail this aporia in Foucault's thought and the nuances of his attempts to resolve it.

[61] *Archaeology of Knowledge*, 209.

[62] This is only further confirmed by his characterization of his various works as "fictions." "Interview with Lucette Finas," *Michel Foucault: Power, Truth, Strategy,* ed. M. Morris and P. Patton (Sidney: Feral Publications, 1979), 75.

[63] This paper has presumed the complementarity of these two approaches for constituting the object of a theology of tradition. Some have argued for a deeper theoretical reconciliation between phenomenological and structuralist orientations. In addition to the work of Dreyfus and Rabinow already cited, see Hans Herbert Kögler, *The Power of Dialogue: Critical Hermeneutics after Gadamer and Foucault,* trans. Paul Hendrickson (Cambridge, Mass.: MIT Press, 1996); Paul Ricoeur's intellectual project has attempted to mediate between hermeneutic and structuralist perspectives. See *Interpretation Theory: Discourse and the Surplus of Meaning* (Fort Worth: Texas Christian University Press, 1976), and *Hermeneutics and the Human Sciences,* J. B. Thompson, trans. (Cambridge: Cambridge University Press, 1981).

[64] I am drawing here from various Marxist accounts of the subjectivity constituted in advanced capitalism. See Henri Lefebvre, *Everyday Life in the Modern World,* trans. Sacha Rabinovitch (New York: Harper and Row, 1971); Guy Debord, *Society of the Spectacle* (Detroit: Black and Red, 1983); Terry Eagleton, "Capitalism, Modernism and Postmodernism," *New Left Review* 152 (1985): 60-73.

[65] Indeed, Fulkerson's analysis functions well because the traditions she analyzes lack rigid notions of apostolicity. See *Changing the Subject*, 183-90, 239-53.

Part II

NEW READINGS OF OLD TEXTS

Rewriting Early Christian History

Elizabeth A. Clark

The End of "History"?

Some of my fellow historians are sounding the death knell for our discipline. Thus Peter Novick, at the end of his massive book, *That Noble Dream: The "Objectivity Question" and the American Historical Profession*, solemnly proclaims that "[a]s a broad community of discourse, as a community of scholars united by common aims, common standards, and common purposes, the discipline of history" has "ceased to exist."[1] Georg Iggers in his survey, *Historiography in the Twentieth Century*, entitles one chapter, "The 'Linguistic Turn': The End of History as a Scholarly Discipline."[2] Joyce Appleby, Lynn Hunt, and Margaret Jacob, in their more negative assessment of theory's impact on the discipline of history, *Telling the Truth about History*, pronounce that there can be "no postmodern history."[3] What are these solemn obituaries *about*, we may ask?

Peter Novick's *That Noble Dream* provides a good starting point for assessing "the end of history." The phrase "noble dream" in his title refers to the hope that inspired several generations of American historians, copying their German predecessors, that they might attain historical "objectivity."[4] Persisting as a goal for many historians to the present, the creed of historical "objectivity" contained several interrelated propositions. As Novick summarizes them, they are: that the past is real; that historical truth is reached when it corresponds with that reality; that there is a sharp separation between fact and value, the knower and the known, history and fiction; that historical facts exist prior to interpretation, and are "found," not "made"; that "[t]ruth is one, not perspectival"; that although the significance accorded to events might change with the passage of time, the meaning of the events themselves does not change; that historians, as historians, are disinterested judges, not "advocates or propagandists." To be sure, Novick concedes, in recent years historians have nuanced these desiderata and are more likely to claim, for example, that interpretations are tested by facts, not derived from them. Such concessions, however, have required minimal modifications of the objectivist creed.[5]

As is evident, historians had derived their model from early modern and modern notions of scientific "objectivity," and from the philosophical assumption, widely-held since the time of Descartes, that there was "an Archimedean point upon which knowledge could be grounded."[6] With the introduction of the relativity theory in physics early in the twentieth century, the bulwark of foundationalism that historians had sought in the sciences crumbled. Concurrently, avant-garde literary and artistic experiments that employed multiple perspectives and voices shook the intellectual world. Yet, Novick argues, these developments had little effect on the historical profession; no one tried to write history à la James Joyce.[7] The model for historical narrative remained that of the nineteenth-century (not the twentieth) English novel.[8] The unsettling effects of these shifts in scientific (and to a lesser extent, literary) paradigms impressed themselves on the minds of historians much later—for many, not in a decisive way until recent years. To become "professionals," the quest for "objectivity" continued to be central.[9] That "professionalism" in and for itself, "the cult of Research," as historian Moses Finley puts it, *also* constitutes an "ideological stance"[10] remained largely unacknowledged.

"Objectivity," Novick argues, persisted as an agreed-upon ideal only because of the ideological and social homogeneity within the community of historians.[11] Thus the arrival of black and feminist historians in the 1960s and 1970s proved unsettling to the historians' guild—and not just because these newcomers[12] to the field did not "fit" comfortably among an almost exclusively male and white peer group. More important, these scholars brought a different perspective to historical work. As historian Joan Scott expresses it, "women can't just be added on without a fundamental recasting of the terms, standards and assumptions of what has passed for objective, neutral and universal history," for that view of history "included in its very definition of itself the exclusion of women."[13] Black and feminist historians challenged the dominant assumption that the writer of history should be a disinterested judge, that facts were independent of interpretations, that the meaning of events remained unchanging throughout the passage of time. They read Foucault. They read Said. Everybody (in Novick's reconstruction) read Thomas Kuhn on paradigm shifts. "Objectivity" was under attack.[14]

I am glad that historian Peter Novick *himself* concedes that what historians do worst is reflect on epistemology,[15] so that I do not appear too mean-spirited when I criticize my fellow historians on this point. Although all historians now admit that what we have left of the past is fragmentary, that what we can know of it is partial, that all written records ("documents" as well as "literary" productions) are conveyed in language, such considerations seem to have done little to upset the epistemological equanimity of those whom Robert Berkhofer calls the "normal historians." The admission by such "normal historians" that they "cannot capture the fullness of past experience," that "they only have the traces or the residues of the past, and their accounts are necessarily partial"[16] is viewed as sufficient concession to the arguments of the alleged "relativists." The more troubling epistemological questions about "reality" in relation to representation and historians' criteria for assessing "truth" are either not broached or are reduced to the observation that since multiple and varying historical sources witness to past events, more than one story needs to be told.[17] The problem occasioned by historians' fusion of representation and referentiality—what Robert Berkhofer calls the "referential illusion"—is scarcely noted.[18] Historians often still write as if there is a transparency between the past and the reader's mind, as if textual representations have an unmediated relation to a past that is both "real" and "verifiable"—that is, as if a correspondence theory of truth required no argument.

Even though the past no longer exists, even though its traces are often scanty, many historians assumed that their task was to capture at least a part of its fullness. Building up a context—"thick description," in historical guise—would rescue the day. The gaps could be filled in and the story given meaning by the skill of the narrator, i.e., the historian, who would provide the explanation of events, the "because"— and traditional history has indeed focused on cause-and-effect explanation.[19] On this account, the problem facing the historian centered on the relative plentitude or paucity of documents: were there "enough" to tell a story? The task of the historian, it was assumed, was "to make the structure of interpretation appear to be (the same as) the structure of factuality."[20] The epistemological and ontological issues involving "the past" and "facts" in relation to the historian's representation of them remained relatively unexamined.

A "strong" challenge to these claims argues rather that since the past is preserved only as written history, is constituted only in a present-day text, there can be no appeal to a "past" aside from this linguistically constituted record.[21] On this view, it is an illusion of realist historiography to represent what are structures of interpretation as factuality/actuality.[22] Since facts as well as their contexts are interpretive constructs, it is misguided for "objectivist" historians to claim that their interpretations refer to some "actual past realities outside the text"; facts are not already "there" to "coerce" historians' representations.[23]

Likewise, historians' appeal to their discipline's "methodology" and "techniques" of historical research cannot save the day in the philosophers' arena any better. As Robert Berkhofer argues, many "normal historians" believe that if they use the "correct" (i.e., professionally agreed-upon) methods for extracting facts from documents, they could rest assured that their histories were "correct"—as if attentive work in the archives could ensure the "truth" of the product.[24] Here, Roger Chartier's critique is equally sharp: correct documentary procedure does not yield the "true" or the "real." "The pertinent question," he continues, "is what criteria permit us to hold possible the relationship that historical writing institutes between the representing trace and the practice represented."[25] Historians, it appears, have not been able to supply these criteria to the satisfaction of their more philosophically minded colleagues, even those with historians' credentials, such as Chartier.

Issues raised by literary theorists, however, have aroused the greater ire of traditional historians than have the above-mentioned epistemological and ontological challenges. For a profession that struggled to establish itself as a serious "science," the implication that history was basically "like" literature was unwelcome: such an allegation might be made against the "amateurs" who wrote histories for a larger lay public before the late nineteenth century, but could not be leveled against the "professionals" with Ph.D.s who employ the techniques of archival research.[26] Given that nineteenth-century historians struggled to escape literature's marriage to history, its return in the late twentieth century seemed most unwelcome to many historians. As historian David Harlan has expressed it, "after a hundred-year absence, literature has returned to history, unfurling her circus silks of metaphor and allegory, misprision and aporia, trace and sign, demanding that historians accept her mocking presence right at the heart of what they had once insisted was their own autonomous and truly scientific discipline."[27]

Traditional historians' attack on this proposed elision of history and literature centers largely on two points: that events in the world can be read as "texts," and that historical writing differs in no essential way from that of literature. Historians often draw a sharp separation between texts, on the one hand, and actions and practices, on the other: the "world" is not to be swallowed up in "textuality." Moreover, Roland Barthes' claim, adopted by others, that the narrative form employed in historical writing did not substantially differ from the "imaginary narration" of the novel or drama was not well-received by the community of historians.[28] The response of distinguished ancient historian Arnaldo Momigliano to Barthes probably represents the views of many in the profession: history writing, according to Momigliano, is differentiated from other types of literature in "its being submitted as a whole to the control of evidence. History is no epic, history is no novel, history is not propaganda because in these literary genres control of the evidence is optional, not compulsory."[29]

It is noteworthy that historians who embrace an epistemological foundationalism have offered little by way of new arguments to rebut their opponents, a stance suggesting that either they believe that the old appeals to "objectivism" and "realism" are still credible[30]—or they shrink from testing their philosophical skills against those whom they suspect (probably with reason) are more adept than they in theoretical debate.

More frequently, the charge against those who entertain "theory's" challenges to historical writing is simply one of "relativism." The least sophisticated form of this charge is that if post-structuralist claims were seriously entertained, there would be no way to privilege one historical interpretation over another, since every belief would be equally good.[31] Likewise, post-structuralists are labeled by their opponents "deeply disillusioned intellectuals."[32] Even worse, they are lazy: readers of *Telling the Truth about History* learn that whereas those passionate for knowledge (i.e., historical realists) will climb the over-three hundred steps to the Lyon archives, "the relativist might not bother."[33]

Responses to such allegations could be positively sarcastic. Thus historian Robert Berkhofer: "It is a good thing that historians know a fact when they see one in practice," for their efforts to theorize about them might well suggest otherwise.[34] And in mocking tones, anthropologist Clifford Geertz caricatures those defenders of "historical objectivity" who are afraid that reality will disappear unless we believe very hard in it.[35]

How might historians respond to these critiques? Given the two-fold criticism that history was, on the one hand, a low-level intellectual enterprise that simply "told stories" and, on the other, that narrative was ideologically suspect, it was hard to see what a "return to narrative" might accomplish. The critique of narrative from those concerned with ideological issues took a particularly sharp tone. Here, the point is not merely the disciplinary one that history is "like" literature, but that narrative has an underlying political function that runs in a socially (as well as intellectually) conservative direction. According to these critics, narrative works to conceal the contradictions in society by framing a unifying story that emphasizes continuity rather than discontinuity and discord.[36] Narrative is said to serve conservative political ends by justifying "the exercise of power by those who possess it" and attempting "to reconcile others to the fact that they do not."[37] Moreover, as Hayden White argues, narrativity is implicated in fostering notions of individuality and wholeness—the "essentialized self"—that contribute to teaching persons to live "in imaginary relation to their real conditions of existence."[38] In narrative, it is alleged, individual actors are represented as shaping events against a backdrop of unproblematic structures.[39] Moreover, historians themselves could note that there seemed to be a correlation between "objectivist" approaches to history and the use of narrative[40]—so why should "nonobjectivist" historians embrace what appeared to be a tainted category as a prop for their own work? In Joan Scott's view, the "philosophical naivete of this notion of narrative seems to be beside the point; it has become a successful rallying cry for conservative historians."[41] In contrast, theorist and historian Michel de Certeau urges historians to "repoliticize" their history-writing by " ' historicizing' historiography itself."[42] Part of this "historicizing" practice, for de Certeau, will involve the historian's recognition of his or her own specific social placement, a specificity that ideology seeks to erase.[43]

Rewriting Early Christian History

One complaint leveled by scholars who oppose the introduction of "theory" to the study of history is that historians have not actually produced "non-objectivist" historical writing. To the opponents, those most vocal in pressing these theoretical considerations indulge in "an extravagant appeal to new theories and approaches," yet in the end have nothing more to show for their rhetorical efforts than "a new formalism or textual prudence."[44] Even those who applaud the effort "to escape from a baneful positivism" charge that although colleagues aiming to write intellectual history from a post-structuralist perspective "celebrate bold theories," they end by "revel[ing] in cautious truisms."[45] Critics of theoretically influenced historians such as Joan Scott allege that they have not incorporated post-structuralist critique into their actual historical practice,[46] and that their experimentations with "voice" and narrative technique (such as Simon Schama's in *Dead Certainties*) result only in "cacophony" and disturbing disjunctions that confuse the reader.[47] Thus it seems imperative that historians in any field—say, early Christian history—who urge their colleagues to register the claims of twentieth-century theory need to provide examples of how our century's intellectual shifts might affect their own scholarly writing.

Here, I think historians of early Christianity are in a more advantageous position than historians of some later periods who rely heavily on documentary and archival evidence. Scholars of early Christianity, who can be categorized as intellectual historians, work with *texts*—and texts that are very often self-consciously literary and ideological through and through. Why then have scholars of early Christianity been so slow to recognize, much less incorporate, such perspectives? Several answers are possible. On the more generous side, it could be noted that the years required to learn several ancient languages leave little leisure for the exploration of difficult theoretical treatises. Moreover, historians in general are notably inept at philosophy and consider the study of philosophical and theoretical texts "not within their domain." They tend to be trained in a way that emphasizes the quest for "objectivity," for reconstructing past "reality." And it probably *is* easier to reflect on "theory" within the camp of the theorists than to explore its applicability to other fields which have a greater investment in truth claims pertaining to the actuality of the past. As for less generous assessments of why historians of the early church have been slow to respond to the challenges of "theory"—I will leave that to you!

How historians of Christianity might proceed if they viewed their documents as literary texts remains to be seen, because the intellectual

problems disturbing the wider historical discipline seem to have been
little noticed by students of late ancient Christianity. If we adopted
Roger Chartier's arguments that historical work should be an exercise
in analyzing the process of representation,[48] and that historians should
refocus their task to examine the function of ideas in ideological systems,[49] what might our work look like?

Since this paper represents the beginning of a new project, I have
reached no firm position in relation to views such as Chartier's. But I
have made two forays in that direction. My first study appeared in the
March 1998 issue of *Church History* under the title, "The Lady Van-
ishes: Dilemmas of a Feminist Historian after the Linguistic Turn."
There, after surveying some of the problems that literary theory has
posed for feminist historians, I attempted an analysis of texts written
by Gregory of Nyssa about his sister Macrina. Here, I would like to try
my hand at a different set of materials, Augustine's representation of
his mother Monica in the *Confessions* and the Cassiciacum *Dialogues*.
I turn now to this subject.

Augustine and Monica

A half century ago, scholars optimistically mined the *Confessions*
to reconstruct Augustine's chronological and intellectual history. They
built on earlier studies that had traced Augustine's philosophical an-
cestry and had variously charted his "conversion" to Platonism or to
Christianity. Scholars today claim less: it is now conceded there are
many aspects of Augustine's early life about which we learn next to
nothing from the *Confessions* (for instance, we would not guess from
this work that he had at least one sister[50]). If the *Confessions* is removed from the category of autobiographical reportage and viewed
as a literary construct that artfully builds its case through intertextual
allusions to classical literature and Scripture,[51] we doubtless lose what
we may have imagined as "the real Augustine," but we find instead
his literary—and retrospective—self-representation.[52] Augustine the
rhetorician leaves us no avenue by which to secure an "objective"
historical narrative from the literary construction that he here weaves.
Scholars must rather look to "the rhetorical and exegetical strategies
of the *Confessions* themselves,"[53] as James O'Donnell puts it. In his
view—a view with which I concur—the allegedly "narrative" first nine
books of the *Confessions* are "anything but narrative in their construc-

tion; their distinctive feature is not the lively biographical interest they evoke, but rather the complexity of the confessional mode, the allusiveness, and the indirectness of the text's construction."[54]

If such is the case, how are we to assess Augustine's treatment of one of the book's star characters, his mother, Monica? She—or more correctly, Augustine's representation of her—provides a fruitful test case through which to explore the literary constructedness of the *Confessions*. On the surface, we have in the *Confessions* (especially in Book 9) one of the fullest extant portraits of an early Christian woman. The supposition that we have here a "life" of an early Christian woman—so relatively rare in patristic writing—in itself commends the text to us as precious. Can we not gain insight into other early Christian women from examining her story? Perhaps—but probably not in the straightforward way that we might at first assume, for Monica, too, is a literary representation. We can, however, trace in Augustine's representation of Monica some strands of the "theological logic" of the text, how he shaped his story of Monica to bring home moral and theological points that we can detail in his other early writings. Even if we abandon the quest for "the real Monica," we still can identify many significant "Monica-functions."

To begin: the *Confessions*, despite its extended discussion of Augustine's childhood, is not a "family story" in any straightforward sense.[55] That Augustine seems considerably less fond of his father, Patricius, than of his mother, has often been remarked. In the *Confessions*, Augustine does not even note his father's death until, rather casually, two years after the fact[56]—and shortly thereafter in the text addresses God as "Father" in the vocative voice for the first time.[57] Moreover, Augustine reveals to his readers that Monica endeavored to substitute God the Father as a paternal parent for him in place of Patricius.[58] And although throughout the *Confessions* Augustine casts himself as the Prodigal Son who goes astray,[59] he returns not to a human father who welcomes him, as in the biblical parable, but to a divine Father.[60] It strikes me that from the *Confessions* Freud might have derived an interesting example of a "family romance"; here, Augustine's own, inadequate father is replaced with a wondrously adequate substitute.

Yet it is not just Patricius who is "replaceable": more surprising, so is Monica herself. In various subtle ways, Augustine dissociates himself from *both* his parents in the *Confessions*. One theme that suggests this dissociation surfaces in his discussion of human conception. Augustine, we must assume, was not ignorant of "where babies come from" when he claims that it is not parents who produce their children, but God.[61] Humans do not know how they are conceived,[62] he writes, or where the "I" was before it enters earthly life.[63] We simply take it "on faith" that our parents are those who identify themselves as such. Here, Augustine uses children's ignorance of their bodily origin to score the epistemological point that if humans do not believe many things without firm proof, they would "accomplish absolutely nothing in life."[64] We have unassailable knowledge that our origin is from God; confidence that human parents are "ours," by contrast, illustrates a lower-level, "everyday" order of trust that is nonetheless necessary for our bodily sojourn in this world.

Another way in which Augustine delicately effaces Patricius and Monica in their paternal and maternal roles is his claim that they stand as his "brother and sister" in the faith, "fellow citizens" with him in the heavenly Jerusalem. Just as Augustine replaces Patricius with God the Father, so he here substitutes for Monica "our Catholic mother the Church."[65] Later in the *Confessions*, Augustine reaffirms this point: *his* beloved mother is Jerusalem above, the abode of peace.[66] (Augustine here alludes to Paul's allegory of the earthly and heavenly Jerusalems in Galatians 4; that the "Jerusalem above," represented by Sarah, is enjoined in the words of Isaiah 54:1 to "rejoice" as a barren woman, adds further intertextual depth to his displacement of physical maternity.) Such literary dislodgements, I would argue, are not surprising, since Augustine, like other early Christians, seeks to substitute a new spiritual family for his actual physical family. In the new family, he claims, we all equally become "infants in Christ," familial hierarchy—so pronounced in ancient kinship structures—having been erased.[67] The maternal role of Monica is here again occluded.

Likewise, when Lady Continence beckons Augustine to opt for a Christianity marked by sexual renunciation, she is depicted "not as barren but as a fruitful mother of children, of joys born of you, O Lord, her Spouse." She, with the "countless boys and girls surrounding her," lures Augustine to the celibate life, away from the "toys of toys" (*nugae nugarum*) who tempt him to sexual pleasure.[68] Through his portrayal of Lady Continence, Augustine suggests that celibacy is more "fruitful," more "productive" than physical maternity. Motherhood, once again, is of dubious value.

Although literary critic Françoise Lionnet does not pose as an Augustine scholar, she offers some suggestive reflections of "the maternal/the female" in the *Confessions*. Whereas many previous readers of the *Confessions* have been (understandably) puzzled by its structure (what purpose do the final books serve, seemingly "tacked on" to the narrative of Augustine's early life?), Lionnet understands Books 11-13 as integral to the work's structure. In Books 1-9, Augustine focuses on his sinful self, both on his sexual sin and on his sin in "selling words," but Books 11-13 promise a new self which, eventually, will master sin.[69] In her account, Books 11-13 *also* concern the act of self-creation, albeit in allegorical form.[70]

In Lionnet's reading, "woman" represents for Augustine the prime aspect of the sinful self that must be erased[71]—not only his sexual relations as depicted in the first nine books, but also "the female" as represented in his allegory of creation in Book 13. There, "woman" denotes not just Eve, but the "lower" force within the soul (*man's* soul) which must be subject to the reasoning power of the mind,[72] a motif which early Christian writers borrowed from Philo[73] and which Origen made standard.[74] In Lionnet's reading, the unruly passions, coded as female, here represent the negative aspect of the self, the negative "internal other," which needs displacing—and indeed *is* displaced by a "positive self." Augustine explicates this "positive self" in his elaboration of man's creation in "the image of God," i.e., as a rational being. Yet as Lionnet notes, the "feminine" dimension is not simply erased, since Augustine's *God* appropriates attributes of "woman," the "receptive, nurturing, maternal . . . qualities usually coded as feminine in Western culture."[75] It is thus no accident, she concludes, that Augustine associates God with the "place of rest, of absolute peace"—that is, with the maternal.[76]

For Lionnet, it is essential for Augustine to place Monica's death in the *Confessions* in between his recounting of his old sinful self and his vision of the new, saved self. The death of his mother, Lionnet writes, "is the culmination of his narrative of a life of sin and marks his liberation from earthly and bodily connections. It is necessary for his earthly mother to die in order for Augustine to get closer to God. . . ."[77] On this reading, all the necessary "maternal" qualities Augustine assigns to the culminating vision of bliss can be found in God, not in a "real" human woman. Here, "the embodied self, born of an earthly mother," is transfigured and transcended.[78]

If Monica's role as "real mother" of Augustine is so often occluded, what functions does she as a character serve in Augustine's account? What are the "Monica-functions" that Augustine constructs? For one, Monica offers an exemplary paradigm for Augustine's depiction of appropriate wifely behavior. Although Augustine claims that all women, including Monica, bear the sinful legacy of Eve,[79] Monica nonetheless sets a pattern of spousal virtue for other Christian matrons. Her obedience to Patricius, Augustine claims, was in truth obedience to God's law—presumably the "law" of the New Testament Household Codes that enjoins the submission of wives as divinely ordained female behavior.[80] He posits that his mother escaped the beatings that other women suffered from their husbands by never arguing with Patricius when he was angry—and that she reminded her friends that the Roman marriage contract put them in subjugation to their husbands. They were, in Augustine's rendition of Monica's claim, *ancillae*—slave-girls—to their husbands, who stand as lords (*domini*).[81] Monica is, as Kim Power has recently phrased it, "the epitome of obedient subordination."[82] That such a picture of wifehood recommends itself to many of us much less enthusiastically than it did to Augustine goes without saying. His portrayal, it should be noted, is consistent with his approach to women's status elsewhere in his writings.[83]

A second way in which Monica serves a useful purpose for Augustine lies more strictly in the realm of theology and ethics: she is the "faithful servant," indeed, "the handmaid," of God.[84] (That Augustine here uses the word *ancilla* for his mother may well have reminded his readers of another *ancilla Domini*, the Virgin Mary who humbly submits to the angel's announcement of her impending pregnancy [Luke 1:38].) Throughout the *Confessions*, Augustine sounds the theme that God uses people as his servants, even without their knowledge, to bring about the conversion and reformation of others.

Notably, Monica herself plays the role of God's servant in Augustine's conversion, imploring God with her tears and prayers for the rescue of her son. If God had raised *his* own Son from the dead, could not Monica's son be similarly lifted up?[85] Augustine here cites Psalm 144:7, "You sent down your help from above" (a verse that Christians interpreted as referring to the Incarnation) to suggest Monica's role: because of her pious prayers and tears, God had reassured her in a dream that Augustine would come to stand on the same "rule" as she did.[86] Monica is here depicted as playing a semi-salvific role in Augustine's conversion.

Most important, and the "Monica-function" on which I wish to concentrate, Augustine's representation of his mother as "manly" in her faith, despite her "weak women's body," borrows the *topos* of woman-as-wisdom familiar from other early Christian writings, such as Gregory of Nyssa's portrayal of his sister Macrina. Two representations of Monica have often been unproblematically read by those eager to exalt Augustine's depiction of his mother: his accounts of Monica in the Cassiciacum *Dialogues*, and of their discussion at Ostia at the moment of their so-called "vision."[87] These scenes, to certain readers, show that Monica had untapped philosophical potential. I would like to argue for another reading: first, that Augustine's depiction of Monica in the Cassiciacum dialogues serves certain theological purposes; and second, that Augustine's portrayal of Monica at the Ostia "vision" represents a fleshing out of the definition of philosophy he had formulated in those dialogues—philosophy in story form, if you will. Unpacking the "theological logic" of these texts is an enlightening exercise.

In the Cassiciacum dialogues, written shortly after Augustine's conversion, and a decade or more before the *Confessions*, Monica is depicted as present on the country estate at which Augustine and his younger students and friends had gathered for intellectual retreat. In two of these treatises, *De beata vita* and *De ordine*, Monica emerges as more central to the philosophical conversation than we might have expected. She intervenes not only to ask questions, but also to express her opinion. She is represented as arriving at the same definition of happiness as had Cicero in the *Hortensius*.[88] Augustine throughout his treatise *On the Happy Life* praises her astuteness and even claims that she upstaged his argument, beating him to the trenchant point he had reserved for his final triumphant proof.[89] Do we not have here a representation of "woman-as-wisdom"? Yet there is much in these two treatises, *On the Happy Life* and *On Order*, to challenge such a claim.

First of all, Augustine makes clear that Monica is uneducated; he even leaves it doubtful whether she can read or write at all.[90] Augustine himself remarks that despite his praise for his mother, he does not wish to misrepresent the case: Monica, for all her insight, "could not easily acquire a mode of expression that would be free from defect of pronunciation and diction." (Augustine confesses that he himself— the aspiring orator—had been faulted in Italy for his ["North African"?] pronunciation.) Augustine here claims that "the assurance that comes from theory"—men's province—"is one thing," while "that gained by native ability"—such as Monica's—"is quite different."[91] However much Augustine admires Monica's abilities, he himself does not exaggerate her learning.

Interestingly, Augustine in these dialogues does not stress the point we might expect on the basis of his later writings, that the Holy Spirit had infused Monica's heart and mind to enable her to "learn wisdom," a commonplace found in much monastic literature that seeks to explain the theological and moral erudition of the uneducated. Rather, at this early stage in Augustine's theological development, Monica's abilities are described in ways that suggest Augustine here resorts to a type of "natural theology" that he later would imbue with a more distinctively Christian coloration: like the Gentiles of Romans 1, Monica, despite her lack of education, possesses some innate knowledge of God that merely needs drawing out.

Similarly, in *On the Happy Life* and in *On Order*, Augustine offers two examples of uneducated men—uneducated either through their own lack of effort or because they belong to the working classes— with whom observant readers might profitably compare the case of Monica. The first example: Augustine claims that his uneducated male relatives present at Cassiciacum, despite their lack of even elementary literary training, are able to participate in the discussion because of their "common sense"[92]; this concession provides Augustine with the space to imply that Monica, as well, may join the all-male discussants. A second example: Augustine informs the group that there were learned men in the past (read: the *pagan* past), who although shoemakers or workers of similarly low status, were able to achieve wisdom[93]—and so, he seems to suggest, with Monica. Augustine confesses that he will entrust himself to her as a "disciple" in the pursuit of wisdom, so advanced is her understanding.[94] What is the meaning of such a claim?

Here, I accept Kim Power's suggestion that one function of Monica is to provide Augustine with an alternative model of piety to that of educated men. Although Augustine claims that his male friends at Cassiciacum considered Monica as "a great man in their midst,"[95] it seems more likely that Augustine uses Monica to illustrate a second means to faith: not the approach through study that he enjoys, but a way of holiness that simple people of no education can embrace.[96] She represents, in effect, the great mass of untutored Christian laypeople, who nonetheless are sons and daughters of the church. For Augustine, although Monica has not read philosophical books, she nonetheless has access to truth.[97] Although Augustine informs his mother that some women of old did indeed engage in philosophical discussion with men,[98] he assures her that if she steadfastly participates in the "sacred mysteries," that is, in the sacraments, and continues her virtuous mode of life, this lower path will be good enough for her—and for God. There is no need for her to trouble her brain with the problems of theodicy, the origin of evil, or the eternity of the world—these points, Augustine implies, can be reserved as discussion topics for educated men such as himself.[99]

What then does Augustine mean when, instructing Monica on the etymology of the Greek word *philosophia*, he calls her a true "lover of wisdom," that is, a "philosopher"?[100] The Cassiciacum dialogues supply two interrelated answers, both of which, I posit, are given narrative form in Augustine's later description of the "vision" at Ostia in the *Confessions*. A first manifestation of Monica's "wisdom" in the Cassiciacum dialogues is that she does not fear discomfort or death, thus showing that she has achieved (in Augustine's words) "the stoutest stronghold of philosophy."[101] Here, Augustine alludes to Socrates' claim in the *Phaedo* that those who rightly engage in philosophy "study only dying and death."[102] Is this not what Monica is also represented as doing? Can she not be counted as a latter-day "female Socrates"?

Moreover, Augustine claims that true philosophers will experience a vision of Oneness and Beauty, and will be united to the object of their love, the Beautiful. Augustine implies in the dialogue *On Order* that Monica in her own way has found this Beauty, for she has experienced the manifestations of God's order in the world.[103] And these claims lead us back to the *Confessions'* description of the "vision" (perhaps more accurately described as an "audition")[104] at Ostia, the most dramatic portrayal of Monica as a "philosopher" in the entire Augustinian corpus. Here, the two attributes of the true philosopher that Augustine has accorded to Monica in the Cassiciacum dialogues (not fearing death; experiencing Oneness and Beauty) are given narrative form. Yet some problems attend our understanding of Monica as a "philosopher" in this scene as well.

Augustine's rendition of his and Monica's discussion at Ostia, although it appears to cast Monica into a philosophical role similar to Augustine's, is colored through and through with allusions to Plotinus' treatises "On Beauty" and "On the First Three Hypostases," as Paul Henry demonstrated some years ago.[105] These, obviously, are not books that Monica had read—but thanks to the research of twentieth-century scholars, we can claim with some degree of confidence that Augustine had done so.[106] The Ostia "vision" is Augustine's own lightly Christianized version of Plotinian notions of the soul's ascent. However much Monica is represented as joining in the dialogue equally with Augustine, we should not, I think, imagine her as expressing these Plotinian sentiments—and Augustine himself, in describing the scene a decade or so later, concedes that they did not speak in these "exact words."[107]

The Ostia vision seems manifestly linked to the goal of philosophy that Augustine posits in the Cassiciacum treatises *On Order* and *Soliloquies*. The achievement of oneness, the union with what one loves in a vision of Beauty, is the summit of the philosopher's quest, Augustine argues in *De ordine*.[108] In the *Soliloquies*, he asks what lover of wisdom, what philosopher, will be able to gaze on and "embrace Wisdom," with no veil between them—"naked, as it were." To achieve this union with Beauty and Wisdom, the lover must forsake the things of sense. Disengaging the "wings" of his soul from the sticky lime of the body, conceived as a prison, his soul can soar free. Augustine here avers that he does not begrudge this love of Beauty to others. In fact, since those who enjoy this love in common with him will become all the dearer, he urges "many" to share it with him.[109]

At the time he wrote the *Soliloquies*, Augustine claimed that there is more than one road to wisdom, for just as some are able to look at the sun directly, others cannot and need different assistance.[110] Later, in his *Retractions*, written at the end of his life, Augustine worries that from the *Soliloquies* some readers might infer that Christ was *not* the only route to wisdom—an interpretation contradicted by Jesus' pronouncement in John 14:6, "I am the way."[111] In retrospect, Augustine wishes to correct any misimpression he might earlier have given by his phrase, "more than one way to wisdom."[112] Yet at the time Augustine composed the *Soliloquies*, I posit, he may not have been so much pondering whether there can be truth *apart* from Christ, but the dual paths for the educated and the uneducated, the "more than one road" that leads to God's truth. Monica's way, that of the uneducated who nonetheless are faithful Christians, also leads to a heavenly home.

The *Confessions* thus portrays Monica, with all her educational deficiencies, as fully worthy to participate in the experience at Ostia with Augustine. As son and mother here ponder what the eternal life of the saints might be like, they reach out in thought and together touch the eternal wisdom, as Augustine puts it.[113] The scene in the *Confessions* depicting the Ostia "vision" represents in story form the Cassiciacum dialogues' injunction to "embrace Wisdom": here, Monica, despite her lack of education, achieves the summit of the philosopher's quest.

Significantly, the discussion continues with Monica's admission that she no longer clings to the world, that she is ready for death; she does not even care where her body is to be buried, as long as Augustine will remember her "at God's altar." After Monica's death, Augustine's friends report that she had confessed to them at Ostia that she despised life and welcomed death; even if her death were to come while she was on foreign soil, she trusted that God would be able to find her body at the time of the general resurrection.[114] Thus, it seems, the Ostia scene, and Monica's confession, are framed to mirror perfectly the goal of philosophy that Augustine had set out in his Cassiciacum dialogues: her scorning of worldly things, her fearlessness—like Socrates'—in confronting "either discomfort or death."[115] Likewise, Augustine at Cassiciacum had written that when the vision of Beauty appears to the worthy, it will erase from their minds disturbing intellectual problems.[116] In the "vision" at Ostia, Augustine shared that knowledge of Beauty (now more closely identified with God) with his mother, true philosopher at heart.

Yet, as Camille Bennett has suggested, it is not Augustine's old "carnal" mother who is here represented, the mother so eager for her son's worldly success and advancement, but a new "spiritual" mother who emerged in the *Confessions* only after Augustine left her weeping on the shores of North Africa as he sailed away to Italy. Once Monica could renounce her all-too-human desire for long life, and for Augustine to marry and have children (the physical route to immortality), she could become a new, spiritualized mother. She is now fit to share the vision at Ostia with Augustine and to be represented as engaging in philosophical discussions with him and his friends. She has been born to a new life and, more importantly for future readers, she has been granted a new representation.[117]

Is there then no "real" Monica—or for that matter, no "real" Augustine? We are reduced to this option only if we cling to the notion that ancient treatises are transparent to the events and people they depict. But if we abandon that view, and accept, with literary theorists, that there is no such thing as "transparent" literature, we still have a "life" of Monica, but one whose representation is itself molded by literature. This does not, I posit, make it less of a "life"—although, to be sure, it is a "life" of a different sort, a "textualized life," a "life" different from that which we are used to encountering in church history textbooks.

Has then this "lady (Monica) vanished"? If this means, "can we recover her pure and simple from texts?," my answer is "no." But that is not the last word: she leaves her "traces," through whose exploration, as they are imbedded in a larger social-linguistic framework, she lives on. "Afterlife" comes in different forms—or so we should know from the study of Christian history and theology.

Notes

[1] Peter Novick, *That Noble Dream: The "Objectivity Question" and the American Historical Profession* (Cambridge: Cambridge University Press, 1988), 628.

[2] Georg G. Iggers, *Historiography in the Twentieth Century: From Scientific Objectivity to the Postmodern Challenge* (Hanover, N.H./London: Wesleyan University Press, 1997; original German edition, 1993), chap. 10.

[3] Joyce Appleby, Lynn Hunt, and Margaret Jacob, *Telling the Truth about History* (New York/London: W. W. Norton & Co., 1994), 237.

[4] Novick takes the phrase "noble dream," originally derived from Thomas Clarke Smith, as the frontispiece of his book. Clarke Smith's essay, "The Writing of American History in America from 1884 to 1934," *American Historical Review* 40 (1935), was mocked by Charles Beard's response, "That Noble Dream," in the next issue of *American Historical Review* (41 [1935]). Commentators note that the American dream of "objectivity" lacked the Hegelian overtones of Leopold von Ranke's construal of the historian's mission; see, for example, Martin Bunzl, *Real History: Reflections on Historical Practice* (London/New York: Routledge, 1997), 3; Iggers, *Historiography*, 25-26; Leonard Krieger, *Ranke: The Meaning of History* (Chicago/London: University of Chicago Press, 1977), chap. 2.

[5] Novick, *That Noble Dream*, 1-2.

[6] Ibid., chap. 1; 538.

[7] Ibid., 139-44. See also Hannah Arendt, "The Concept of History," in Arendt, *Between Past and Future* (New York: Viking Press, 1961), 50: why do historians hold onto a notion of determinable truth, when philosophers and natural scientists abandoned it long ago; historians seem fixed in practices of an older notion of "science."

[8] Hayden White, "The Burden of History," in White, *Tropics of Discourse: Essays in Cultural Criticism* (Baltimore/London: The Johns Hopkins University Press, 1978; original of this essay, 1966), 43-44.

[9] Novick, *That Noble Dream*, chap. 2, "The Professionalization Project."

[10] M. I. Finley, " 'Progress' in Historiography," *Daedalus* 106 (1977): 137.

[11] Novick, *That Noble Dream*, 61, and chap. 3, "Consensus and Legitimation."

[12] Novick emphasizes, as have many other commentators, that earlier in the century women had been active as historians, but in the post-war years, as home and motherhood became the norm for most women of the middle classes, their numbers in the historical profession dropped off dramatically, to "rebound" only from the late '60s onward (*That Noble Dream*, 366-67, 491-510).

[13] Joan Scott, "Women's History," in *New Perspectives on Historical Writing*, ed. Peter Burke (University Park, Pa.: Pennsylvania State University Press, 1981), 58. Also see Catriona Kelly, "History and Post-Modernism," *Past & Present* 133 (1991): 212: feminist history sometimes advocates reading texts *out* of context, against the grain; "context" may be construed somewhat differently in women's history than in traditional historiography.

[14] In another narrative of "how objectivity came under attack," social historians serve as the agent: by suggesting that there was no one national narrative, they "dug a potentially fatal hole" into which, somewhat later, postmodernists fell. See Appleby, Hunt, and Jacob, *Telling the Truth about History*, 200.

[15] Novick, *That Noble Dream*, 15.

[16] Appleby, Hunt, and Jacob, *Telling the Truth about History*, 234.

[17] Ibid., 256.

[18] Robert E. Berkhofer, Jr., *Beyond the Great Story: History as Text and Discourse* (Cambridge, Mass./London: Belknap Press of Harvard University Press, 1995), 60.

[19] Ibid., 28-38.

[20] Ibid., 60.

[21] Ibid., 14.

[22] Ibid., 63.

[23] Ibid., 70-71.

[24] Ibid., 29; cf. Novick, *That Noble Dream*, 52-53. Also see Paul Ricoeur's formulation of the problem (although Ricoeur offers no critique): for historians, the ontological question about the notion of the "trace" left by the past "is immediately covered over by the epistemological question relating to the document, that is, to its value as a warrant, a basis, a proof in explaining the past" (*Time and Narrative*, Vol. 3, trans. Kathleen Blamey and David Pellauer [Chicago/London: University of Chicago Press, 1988; French original, 1985], 143).

[25] Roger Chartier, *Cultural History: Between Practices and Representations*, trans. Lydia G. Cochrane (Ithaca: Cornell University Press, 1988; French original of this essay, 1987), 65-66.

[26] Novick, *That Noble Dream*, chap. 2, 600; cf. Berkhofer, *Beyond the Great Story*, 63, 135, and chap. 4.

[27] David Harlan, "Intellectual History and the Return of Literature," *American Historical Review* 94 (1989): 581.

[28] Roland Barthes, "The Discourse of History," trans. Stephen Bann, in *Comparative Criticism: A Yearbook*, ed. E. S. Shaffer (Cambridge: Cambridge

University Press, 1981; French original of this essay, 1967), III: 7-20. In Linda Orr's view, the most "consistent critique of history is still performed by the novel: fiction evokes the other history that history refuses to write, preferring its traditional fictions." Yet Orr continues, history performs a highly useful service for fiction in that it establishes "the baseline of verisimilitude so that fiction can take flight with a protective netting underneath" (Linda Orr, "The Revenge of Literature: A History of History," *New Literary History* 18 [1986]: 19).

[29] Arnaldo Momigliano, "The Rhetoric of History and the History of Rhetoric: On Hayden White's Tropics," in *Comparative Criticism*, ed. E. S. Shaffer, III: 261.

[30] Novick, *That Noble Dream*, 567-68.

[31] Thus J. Morgan Kousser, "The Revivalism of Narrative: A Response to Recent Criticisms of Quantitative History," *Social Science History* 8 (1984): 13; cf. David Harlan's construal of the "objectivist" position in his "Response" to David Hollinger, *American Historical Review* 94 (1989): 625; and Clifford Geertz, "Anti Anti-Relativism," *American Anthropologist* 86 (1984): 265.

[32] Appleby, Hunt, and Jacob, *Telling the Truth about History*, 206. The authors admit that they had been instructed on the difference between post-modernism and post-structuralism (202n.4), but they nonetheless have not corrected their nomenclature.

[33] Ibid., 251.

[34] Berkhofer, *Beyond the Great Story*, 53.

[35] See Geertz, "Anti Anti-Relativism," 263-78, discussed by Novick, *That Noble Dream*, 552.

[36] See Philippe Carrard's discussion of Hayden White and Sande Cohen in *Poetics of the New History: French Historical Discourse from Braudel to Chartier* (Baltimore/London: The Johns Hopkins University Press, 1992), 76-77.

[37] John B. Thompson, *Ideology and Modern Culture: Critical Theory in the Era of Mass Communication* (Stanford: Stanford University Press, 1990), 61-62; idem, *Studies in the Theory of Ideology* (Berkeley/Los Angeles: University of California Press, 1984), 11.

[38] For White's writings on narrative and ideology, see, for example, "The Value of Narrativity in the Representation of Reality," *Critical Inquiry* 7 (1980): 1-25; *The Content of the Form: Narrative Discourse and Historical Representation* (Baltimore; London: The Johns Hopkins University Press, 1987), especially his essay on "Droysen's *Historik*: Historical Writing as a Bourgeois Science."

[39] Novick, *That Noble Dream*, 622.

[40] Ibid., 623.

[41] Joan Wallach Scott, "Comment: Agendas for Radical History," *Radical History Review* 36 (1986): 43.

[42] Michel de Certeau, "History: Science and Fiction," in his *Heterologies: Discourse on the Other*, trans. Brian Massumi. Theory and History of Literature 17 (Minneapolis: University of Minnesota Press, 1986; original essay, 1983), 215.

[43] See especially de Certeau's essay, "The Historiographical Operation," in his *The Writing of History*, trans. Tom Conley (New York: Columbia University Press, 1988; original essay, 1974), for a discussion of these themes.

[44] Russell Jacoby, "A New Intellectual History?," *American Historical Review* 97 (1992): 419

[45] Ibid., 424.

[46] A charge directed at Joan Scott's *Gender and the Politics of History* by historian Claudia Koonz in "Post Scripts," *Women's Review of Books* 6 (1989): 19. See now Scott's *Only Paradoxes to Offer: French Feminists and the Rights of Man* (Cambridge, Mass./London: Harvard University Press, 1996).

[47] Cushing Strout, "Border Crossings: History, Fiction, and *Dead Certainties,*" *History and Fiction* 31 (1992): 156-58.

[48] Chartier, *Cultural History*, 13-14.

[49] Ibid., 34.

[50] This we know from Augustine's *ep.* 211, and from Possidius' *Vita Augustini.*

[51] Pierre Courcelle's *Recherches sur les Confessions de Saint Augustine* (Paris: Editions E. de Boccard, 1968; 2nd ed.), with its trenchant analysis of the "literariness" of the *Confessions*, caused an uproar from historians and theologians who believed that Courcelle had erased the "historicity" of the work.

[52] On the problems of understanding Augustine as a "retrospective" self-creation, see the now-classic article by Paula Fredriksen, "Paul and Augustine: Conversion Narratives, Orthodox Traditions, and the Retrospective Self," *Journal of Theological Studies* n.s. 37 (1986): 3-34.

[53] James O'Donnell, *Augustine: Confessions* (Oxford: Clarendon Press, 1992), I: xxi.

[54] Ibid., III: 154.

[55] For a discussion of the late ancient family, using Augustine's as an example, see Brent D. Shaw, "The Family in Antiquity: The Experience of Augustine," *Past and Present* 115 (1987): 3-51.

[56] Augustine, *Confessiones* 3.4.

[57] Augustine, *Confessiones* 3.6.

[58] Augustine, *Confessiones* 1.12.

[59] Augustine, *Confessiones* 1.18, 3.6, 4.16, 8.3.

[60] "The theme of the prodigal son is as much about fathers and estrangement as it is about sons . . .": O'Donnell, *Augustine: Confessions* II: 71.

[61] Augustine, *Confessiones* 1.6.

[62] Augustine, *Confessiones* 9.13.

[63] Augustine, *Confessiones* 1.6.

[64] Augustine, *Confessiones* 6.5. Such a claim echoes Augustine's earlier uneasiness with the Sceptical Academy's position regarding the withholding of assent to sense perceptions; see his *Contra Academicos* for his major discussion of this theme.

[65] Augustine, *Confessiones* 9.13.

[66] Augustine, *Confessiones* 12.16.

[67] Augustine, *Confessiones* 8.2.

[68] Augustine, *Confessiones* 10.11.

[69] For Augustine's reflections on those who "traffic in literature," become "word-merchants," see *Confessiones* 1.13.

[70] Françoise Lionnet, *Autobiographical Voices: Race, Gender, Self-Portraiture* (Ithaca; London: Cornell University Press, 1989), 45, 64. Lionnet is here also concerned to stress that Augustine gives up his old self as writer (and we might add, public orator) to become the consummate "reader" of the "transcendent Other" (56). Exegetic reading becomes "redemption" (39).

[71] Ibid., 32.

[72] Augustine, *Confessiones* 13.32, 13.34.

[73] See Richard A. Baer, Jr., *Philo's Use of the Categories of Male and Female*. Arbeiten zur Literatur und Geschichte des Hellenistischen Judentums 3 (Leiden: E. J. Brill, 1970).

[74] Origen, *Hom. 1 Gen.* 15; *Hom. 10 Exod.* 3; *Comm. Matt.* 12.4; *Hom. 4 Gen.* 4; *Hom. 5 Gen.* 6; *Hom. 2 Exod.* 1; *Hom. 22 Num.* 1.

[75] Lionnet, *Autobiographical Voices*, 32.

[76] Ibid., 44.

[77] Ibid., 56. See likewise Brian Stock, *Augustine the Reader: Meditation, Self-Knowledge, and the Ethics of Interpretation* (Cambridge, Mass./London: The Belknap Press of Harvard University Press, 1996), 121: earlier in the *Confessions* (4.7), the death of Augustine's friend is recounted to illustrate the transitoriness of human life; Monica's death, conversely, concerns eternal life.

[78] Ibid., 65-66.

[79] Augustine, *Confessiones* 5.8.

[80] Augustine, *Confessiones* 1.11.

[81] Augustine, *Confessiones* 9.9.

[82] Kim Power, *Veiled Desire: Augustine on Women* (New York: Continuum, 1996), 76.

[83] Elizabeth A. Clark, "Theory and Practice in Late Ancient Asceticism: Jerome, Chrysostom, and Augustine," *Journal of Feminist Studies in Religion* 5 (1989): 25-46; for a more positive view of Augustine and women, see Gerald Bonner, "Augustine's Attitude to Women and 'Amicitia,'" in *Homo Spiritalis: Festgabe fur Luc Verheijen OSA*, eds. Cornelius Mayer and Karl Heinz Chelius (Würzburg: Augustinus-Verlag, 1987), 259-75.

[84] Augustine, *Confessiones* 2.3.

[85] Augustine, *Confessiones* 9.4; cf. 3.11, 6.1.

[86] Augustine, *Confessiones* 3.11.

[87] The scholarly debates as to whether the experience at Ostia should properly be called "mystical" are summarized by J. Kevin Coyle in "In Praise of Monica: A Note on the Ostia Experience of *Confessions* IX," *Augustinian Studies* 13 (1982): 87-90.

[88] Augustine, *De beata vita* 2.10; Augustine notes that her understanding corresponds with that of Cicero in his (lost) treatise, *Hortensius*.

[89] Augustine, *De beata vita* 4.27.

[90] Augustine, *De ordine* 1.8.26; cf. 1.11.31.

[91] Augustine, *De ordine* 2.17.45.

[92] Augustine, *De beata vita* 1.6.

[93] Augustine, *De ordine* 1.11.31.

[94] Augustine, *De ordine* 1.11.32.

[95] Augustine, *De beata vita* 2.10.

[96] Power, *Veiled Desire*, 88.

[97] Augustine, *De beata vita* 4.27.

[98] Augustine, *De ordine* 1.11.31.

[99] Augustine, *De ordine* 2.17.46. For a discussion of similar themes, see Phillip Cary, "What Licentius Learned: A Narrative Reading of the Cassiciacum Dialogues," *Augustinian Studies* 29 (1998): 160-61.

[100] Augustine, *De ordine* 1.11.32.

[101] Ibid.

[102] Plato, *Phaedo* 9 (64A).

[103] Augustine, *De ordine* 2.19.51-20.52.

[104] O'Donnell, *Augustine: Confessions* III: 133.

[105] Paul Henry, *La Vision d'Ostie. Sa place dans la vie et l'oeuvre de Saint Augustin* (Paris: J. Vrin, 1938); also see discussion in Courcelle, *Recherches*, 222.

[106] See Courcelle, *Recherches*, 156-57.

[107] Augustine, *Confessiones* 9.10.

[108] Augustine, *De ordine* 22.18.48, 2.19.51.

[109] Augustine, *Soliloquia* 1.13.22-1.14.24.

[110] Augustine, *Soliloquia* 1.13.23.

[111] Augustine, *Retractiones* 1.4.3.

[112] We might wonder whether Augustine, in the interim, had read (or learned of from reading Ambrose's rejoinders) the Third *Relatio* of Symmachus, pagan senator and literary afficionado, who had used as one of his arguments for the retention of the Altar of Victory in the senate house that "there is not one road to truth." The *Soliloquies* were written a few years after the conflict over the Altar of Victory, but the event is not reported in Augustine's early writings.

[113] Augustine, *Confessiones* 9.10.

[114] Augustine, *Confessiones* 9.10-11.

[115] Augustine, *De ordine* 1.11.32

[116] Augustine, *De ordine* 2.19.51.

[117] Camille Bennett, "The Conversion of Vergil: The Aeneid in Augustine's Confessions, *Revue des Etudes Augustiniennes* 34 (1988): 63-64.

How the Lion Roars:
Contextualizing the Nine Riddles
in Amos 3:3-8

Barbara Green, O.P.

> *Translating any sentence as a rhetorical question without any clear contextual guidelines, however, is extremely hazardous.*
>
> Shalom Paul
>
> *Riddles of this kind are real brain twisters.*
>
> Francis I. Andersen and David N. Freedman

Not long ago at the funeral of a wonderful gentleman I heard this joke: A man became sick and knew he was about to die. Besides being mortally ill, he was also very rich; and he became frantic to devise a way of taking at least some of his wealth with him when he died. He talked the challenge over with his wife and finally stashed several bags of coins and currency in the attic. Sure enough, he did die not long afterwards. As his wife was meeting shortly thereafter with the family lawyer, she pleaded with him to go up to the attic with her to see what had happened to her husband's readied goods. As they came to the top of the stairs, she saw the bags in place, dusty and clearly still filled with the money her husband had placed in them. She shook her head sadly, saying to the lawyer, "I told him he should have put them in the basement."

Why do we laugh? What do we have to understand for the joke to work? At the very least we need the sense of an afterlife, probably the operative assumption that "you can't take it with you," and the spatial valences on the post-earthly destinations—that one is approached most directly via the attic and one via the basement—and that one trajectory is to be preferred to the other. So the humor of the story is not so much that he tried to take it with him but that he miscalculated his route. Additionally, at what kind of a funeral might such a story work successfully—or rather, since we are needing to be efficient here, where can you imagine that such a story would *not* work at all? That is, at whose obsequies would it not be well received by at least some? Perhaps if the deceased were really a miser, or if he were clearly wicked in some classic and obvious way, or if his death were particularly tragic, or if his wife were at odds with him: in all these situations (and others) it is easy to imagine that the story could not be told comfortably for all hearers. Context makes utterances work.

Another story is told by Mikhail Bakhtin, a Russian philosopher and literary critic, whose insights are also useful for the Amos passage. Bakhtin tells of two people, sitting in a room, both silent until one of them says, "Well." The other does not respond.[1]

He calls the single word spoken, the "well," an utterance. And he goes on to explicate it in terms of context: " 'At the time the colloquy took place, both interlocutors *looked up* at the window and *saw* that it had begun to snow; both *knew* that it was already May and that it was high time for spring to come; finally, *both* were *sick and tired* of the protracted winter and *were looking forward* to spring, and were *bitterly disappointed* by the late snowfall' " (italics as in Clark and Holquist). An utterance, in Bakhtin's sense of it, can be a single word ("Well") or it can be *War and Peace*, or the joke I just told, or for present purposes the nine questions in Amos 3:3-8.

We can make a quick grid of characteristics of an utterance, borrowing from the funeral joke and Bakhtin's story and bringing such insight to bear on the Amos questions. 1) An utterance assumes a dialogue (whether we see it happening or not) between the speaker and some interlocutor(s). The speaker takes into account the likely response even as he or she crafts the utterance. So as I tell my funeral joke, I am framing it specifically in terms of the response I expect to get—responses, actually. I may wish it to be laughed at, or I may wish it to provoke outrage; but as I shape my utterance, I am already responding to what I think will come back to me. 2) An utterance is not abstract but is always particular; there is no sense in taking it outside its context. It might be recontextualized but cannot be context-less. 3) An utterance need not take a particular form or genre, though of course a speaker may select a form for an utterance. We can classify my funeral story as a joke, perhaps as a joke of a particular kind. But form is not the main point. An utterance can select any form and shape and be shaped accordingly. 4) Every utterance is evaluative. Again, my initial example can easily be played out to imagine that a business partner of the dead man might appreciate the shrewdness of the attempt to transfer assets—or perhaps its cluelessness; it would depend on their partnership! The wife of the man might enjoy the notion that she told him so, or she might react to the implication that she was almost as dumb about the afterlife as he was. If the man had enemies, people from whom he withheld generosity, they would likely find the story invigorating; if, on the other hand, the story is told to a group of people who loved the dead man's generosity—as in fact was the case at the funeral where I heard it—then the story will be enjoyed without rancor. The man whom I heard tell the funeral joke, being a dear friend of the man whose funeral we were attending, regretted that he had not been able to share the story with our friend who had died—hence an additional facet of the utterance: we were all invited to consider the enjoyment of the dead man! 5) So, the utterance is constructed with many relation-laden strands and cannot be pinned down to single or final things. 6) The goal of our involvement with an utterance, at least for Bakhtin and the literature he is reading, is self-knowledge and growth in consciousness: to frame our language dialogically, anticipating others' responses and to be affected by what we imagine; and to scrutinize our own responsiveness as we articulate, recognizing our interconnections with others, our own unfinished edges, our inevitable relationality and lack of self-sufficiency and the implications of same.

How can the questions in Amos 3:3-8 be construed utterances in the Bakhtinian sense? Or, to put it differently, how can a sharpening of plausible contexts for the prophetic discourse allow the riddle[2] questions to function more particularly, less vaguely? The threefold strategy I choose to utilize, which aligns this paper with the theme of new histories, can be summarized as follows: First, I assert the need for clear contexts if the language of Amos is to be other than multipurpose, generic, able to be appropriated almost at random. That is, when the quotes are floating above an uncertain context, they are not very useful; someone must claim them and rescue them from a multipurpose existence. Second, though older modes of biblical criticism problematized the process of redaction or editing of written materials, at least some current practice—even historical-critical methodologies such as social-scientific criticism—is content to allow a book like Amos to function primarily in the eighth century and to posit its meaning in terms of that era.[3] The six subcommunities sketched below are plausible in terms of current research on Amos (a case made largely in the notes due to the unusual genre of this paper). And third, the existential issue I have chosen to make focal is the problem of economic class—though the situations of gender and ethnicity might work as well. It is my experience that first-world religious professionals like myself, though uncomfortable with the tag "elite" and preferring to identify with the poor, are in fact much closer to the upper class castigated in Amos than to the more voiceless poor. Seen against almost any comparative sample, the U.S. religious academic is vastly privileged and benefits from that condition constantly.[4] My aim in this paper is to expose somewhat sympathetically that condition against the background of the language of the prophet. If a major purpose of working with utterances is to increase consciousness, it seems a fair move.

A brief note on forms:[5] though all the riddles seem to be questions with the answer "no" implied, they are for all that, still very open-ended in terms of referent as well as amenable to particular circumstances. Let us recall the nine sentences:[6]

a. Do two walk together unless they have made an appointment? (3:3)
b. Does a lion roar in the forest, when it has no prey? (3:4a)
c. Does a young lion cry out from its den, if it has caught nothing? (3:4b)
d. Does a bird fall into a snare on the earth, when there is no trap for it? (3:5a)
e. Does a snare spring up from the ground, when it has taken nothing? (3:5b)
f. Is a trumpet blown in a city, and the people are not afraid? (3:6a)
g. Does disaster befall a city, unless YHWH has done it? (3:6b)[7]
h. The lion has roared; who will not fear? (3:8a)
i. YHWH GOD has spoken; who can but prophesy? (3:8b)[8]

We shall now consider a day in the life of Amos of Tekoa which brings him into dialogue with six groups and which occasions the distribution of questions from chapter 3.[9]

Amos and the elites:[10]

AMOS: "Thus says YHWH: 'For three transgressions of Israel, and for four, I will not revoke the punishment; because they sell the righteous for silver, and the needy for a pair of sandals[11]—they who trample the head of the poor into the dust of the earth, and push the afflicted out of the way . . .' " (2:6-7a).

ELITES: Oh, that again. Tune the harps, please: And a one and a two and . . . : "The one who made the Pleiades and Orion, and turns deep darkness into the morning, and darkens the day into night, who calls for the waters of the sea, and pours them out on the surface of the earth, YHWH is his name! . . . YHWH, GOD of hosts, he who touches the earth and it melts, and all who live in it mourn, and all of it rises like the Nile, and sinks again, like the Nile of Egypt; who builds his upper chambers in the heavens, and founds his vault upon the earth; who calls for the waters of the sea, and pours them out upon the surface of the earth—YHWH is his name" (5:8, 9:5-6).

AMOS: [Shaking his head at their doxological chant:] "Alas for those who lie on beds of ivory, and lounge on their couches, and eat lambs from the flock, and calves from the stall; who sing idle songs to the sound of the harp, and like David improvise on instruments of music; who drink wine from bowls, and anoint themselves with the finest oils, but are not grieved over the ruin of Joseph!" (6:4-6). Do you not feel your own rise and fall as you sing of it, the tipping that awaits the tipsy?[12] You who are not grieved at the prospect will not long avoid the ruin of Joseph, will shortly pay a tax on your consumption, must soon rue the subsidy you are providing for all you enjoy. Trappers trapped as well as trapping. The sandals you market may be your own, the heads under the boot those pates you hold most dear.

ELITES:[13] <We are swift, we are strong, we are mighty. We have bows, we have horses, we are stout of heart> (2:14-16, modified).[14] If we need to move quickly, we can do it. " 'Have we not by our own strength taken Karnaim for ourselves?' " (6:13).[15] Besides, as always, you are not considering *our* situation, the problems with which *we* must cope continually! <Rain withheld when there were still three months until harvest! Rain on some places and not on others! Crops withering in fields where there was no rain, rushing to get access to water wherever we could—never enough, not shared equally! And then blight and mildew, devastating our vineyards

and orchards, locusts eating our figs and olives! Pestilences from
foreign parts, the draft taking our best workers and horses> (4:7-
10, modified).[16] <In all the squares there was wailing; and in all the
streets we moaned, "Alas! alas!"> (5:16).[17] Recognize that we have
more troubles than you grant, O prophet![18] We are caught in a command economy that will squeeze *us* if we do not extract the goods
demanded of us! What you accuse is not *our* fault nor so bad as you
paint it. We must be practical: "When will the new moon be over
so that we may sell grain; and the Sabbath, so that we may offer
wheat for sale? We will make the ephah small and the shekel great
. . ." (8:5-6). It's the economy, *mesuggeh*!

AMOS: How you can chant in a single breath of the water deeds of our
God and of your own flood and drought, with no insight into the
link between them? You acknowledge neither your role as hunters
nor see your identity as quarry. If you feared the latter, you might
delight less in the former. Your denials scare off insight. At the
very moment you swoop to take, you will be taken. Your pending
collapse is not by chance! Your heritage is about to claim you!
"Does a bird fall into a snare on the earth, when there is no trap for
it? Does a snare spring up from the ground when it has taken nothing?" (3:5a5b).[19] The rising and the falling of which you sing is
about to be your own experience!

Amos and his fellow prophets:

AMOS: [Instructing his circle:] "Hear, and testify against the house of
Jacob, says YHWH GOD, the God of hosts: 'On the day I punish
Israel for its transgressions, I will punish the altars of Bethel, and
the horns of the altar shall be cut off and fall to the ground' " (3:13-
14).[20]

THE PROPHETS: <Well, though some of us were raised up to be prophets
. . . they have commanded us prophets, saying, " 'You shall not
prophesy.' They hate the one who reproves in the gate, and they
abhor the one who speaks the truth. Therefore the prudent will keep
silent in such a time; for it is an evil time"> (2:11-12, modified;
5:10,13). Not to mention the scared, who will refrain from faint
and feeble denunciations which are neither politic nor practical.
Besides, father Amos, you have prophesied against the Bethel altar
repeatedly, and still solid it stands, horns to the ready, drawing its
crowd, making its contribution to the economy.[21] It *is* the king's

sanctuary. A lot of decent people go there, and a lot of important ones.[22]

AMOS: To defer prophetic speech is not an option.[23] The political disunity and the cultic obscenity of the Bethel shrine are not offset by the border-securing and the economic pump-priming the place clearly enough accomplishes.[24] Those very people who bring their business to Bethel, for whom you profess concern: your silence is a greater liability for them than it is insurance for you! "But do not seek Bethel, and do not enter into Gilgal or cross over to Beersheba; for Gilgal shall surely go into exile, and Bethel shall come to nothing.[25] Seek YHWH and live, or he will break out against the house of Joseph like fire, and it will devour Bethel, with no one to quench it" (5:5). The time lag you worry about between prophecy and fulfillment, the seeming silence that has followed my indictment feel more prominent here at the shrine than in the heavenly throneroom, yes? Silent, silenced prophets: your temptation to delay announcing what you have been charged with suggests that YHWH reveals to his prophets what he does not plan to accomplish; does he allow them to delay the announcement until the deed has occurred? Whom do you serve: the lion or the lamb? What did you hear: a roar or a squeak? And whom do you serve when you cower at Bethel, meek and mute? "Surely YHWH GOD does nothing, without revealing his secret to his servants the prophets. The lion has roared; who will not fear? YHWH GOD has spoken; who can but prophesy?" (3:7-8a8b).[26]

Amos and the Bethel priests:

BETHEL PRIESTS: [Beckoning to the elites:] "Come to Bethel . . . bring your[27] sacrifices every morning, your tithes every three days; bring a thank offering of leavened bread, and proclaim freewill offerings, publish them; for so <you> love to do, O people of Israel!" <Bring your contributions. Arrange yourselves beside any altar on garments taken in pledge, drink wine bought with fines you have imposed> (4:4-5 abbreviated, 2:8 modified).[28] It's simply a matter of business, yours and ours. You work hard, your laborers don't; you have only what you deserve, and so must we, as you understand.

AMOS: [Interrupting the priestly pitch before the elites can reply:] "Thus says YHWH: 'I hate, I despise your festivals, and I take no delight in your solemn assemblies. Even though you offer me your burnt offerings and grain offerings, I will not accept them; and the offerings of well-being of your fatted animals I will not look upon. Take away from me the noise of your songs; I will not listen to the melody of your harps.[29] But let justice roll down like waters, and righteousness like an ever-flowing stream.[30] Did you bring to me sacrifices and offerings the forty years in the wilderness, O house of Israel?' " (5:21-25).

BETHEL PRIESTS: That was then, this is now! We are not in a position to let you discourage trade like that—horns falling off the altar indeed! We have a living to make, have a ministry to the wealthy as well as to the poor. The king's shrine[31] is expensive to run; and though it may look opulent and powerful to *you*, sir prophet, it is a backwater compared to at least one, as you very well know, coming from Tekoa![32] So we have a case to make for you, a cause you can subscribe to, since your negativity threatens our bottom line. We would beg to line up behind your famous intercessions for the needy, those in trouble, squeezed by voracious predators: You boast: " 'This is what YHWH GOD showed me: he was forming locusts at the time the latter growth began to sprout (it was the latter growth after the king's mowings). When they had finished eating the grass of the land, <*you*> said, "O YHWH GOD, forgive, I beg you! How can Jacob stand? He is so small!" And sure enough, YHWH relented concerning this; "It shall not be," said YHWH. This is what YHWH GOD showed me: YHWH GOD was calling for a shower of fire, and it devoured the great deep and was eating up the land. Then <*you*> said, "O YHWH GOD, cease, I beg you! How can Jacob stand? He is so small!' " (7:1-5).[33] So, prophet, how about being part of the solution instead of just exacerbating the insolvency! We need your intercessions here, our revenues gobbled by locusts and withered by blight! You owe our little Jacob self a helping word.

AMOS: [Angrily shaking his head:] You fail to calculate your own diminishment! " 'I overthrew some of you, as when God overthrew Sodom and Gomorrah, and you were like a brand snatched from the fire; yet you did not return to me,' says YHWH" (4:11). Downsizing is our friend! But not yet familiar enough to you. Let me tell you another one: "This is what he showed me: YHWH was standing beside a wall built with a plumb line, with a plumb line in his hand. And YHWH said to me, 'Amos, what do you see?' And I said, 'A plumb line.' Then YHWH said, 'See, I am setting a plumb line in the midst of my people Israel; I will never again pass them by; the high places of Isaac shall be made desolate, and the sanctuaries of Israel shall be laid waste, and I will rise against the house of Jeroboam with the sword' " (7:7-9). And I made no intercession *that* time! You misread your "need" by a lot to be anticipating a friendly amendment from me! You see poorer fruits tithed, or fewer of them? Let me help you count them: "This is what YHWH GOD showed me—a basket of summer fruit. He said, 'Amos, what do you see?' And I said, 'A basket of summer fruit.' Then YHWH said to me, 'The *end* has come upon my people Israel; I will never again pass them by' " (8:1-2).[34] Little is less than you think. *Qets* closed, plea *keputz*![35] The ink turns red—read—in your ledgers as you struggle with your sums! The lion whose name you bruit as you rake in the lambs is about to brutalize you! Your columns are totaled (9:1),[36] your unease testifies to your disease! "Is a trumpet blown in the city and people are not afraid? Does disaster befall a city, unless YHWH has done it?" (3:6a6b).[37] "Therefore thus I will do to you, O Israel; because I will do this to you, prepare to meet your God, O Israel!" (4:12).[38]

BETHEL PRIEST AMAZIAH: [Losing patience finally:] "O seer, go, flee away to the land of Judah, earn your bread there, and prophesy there; but never again prophesy at Bethel, for it is the king's sanctuary, and it is a temple of the kingdom" (7:12-13).[39] [Aside:] I'd better contact King Jeroboam and tell him what happened here before he hears it from someone else.[40] May it please my lord, it will *not* please my lord: "Amos has conspired against you in the very center of the house of Israel; the land is not able to bear all his words. For thus Amos has said, 'Jeroboam shall die by the sword, and Israel must go into exile away from his land' " (7:10-11).

Amos and the king:

AMOS: [Questioned at court:] That is not quite what I said.[41] But I am not surprised that you finally brought me in to question my recent foray into international diplomacy, those invitations I issued some of our neighbors.[42] You recall: "Proclaim to the strongholds in Ashdod, and to the strongholds in the land of Egypt, and say, 'Assemble yourselves on Mount Samaria, and see what great tumults are within it, and what oppressions are in its midst.' They do not know how to do right . . . those who store up violence and robbery in their strongholds . . . ." It is inevitable: "An adversary shall surround the land, and strip you of your defense; and your strongholds shall be plundered" (3:9-11). And not only you: "So I will send a fire on Judah, and it shall devour the strongholds of Jerusalem" (2:5). "YHWH GOD has sworn by himself (says YHWH, the God of hosts): 'I abhor the pride of Jacob and hate his strongholds; and I will deliver up the city and all that is in it' " (6:8). Your strongholds are your greatest weakness.

KING JEROBOAM: Whoa!! Those visas breach national security, flaunt our royal sovereignty! You can't invite them to inspect my storerooms! Besides, how does the amplitude of my storehouses and the strength of my strongholds promise other than to dazzle our guests? They'll be impressed, even cowed.

AMOS: We shall see who is cowed! "YHWH GOD has sworn by his holiness: 'The time is surely coming upon you, when they shall take you away with hooks, even the last of you with fishhooks. Through breaches in the wall you shall leave, each one straight ahead; and you shall be flung out into Harmon, says YHWH' " (4:1-3).[43]

KING JEROBOAM: <Not likely! I have a winter house and a summer house, a house of ivory and a house of dressed stone> (3:15, modified). Besides, these local toughs will knuckle under as usual when I rattle under their noses the insurance policy we maintain with Assyria; they are thugs, nothing more and nothing less.

AMOS: How did you acquire your several houses? What plans have you for your storehoused grain? "Therefore because you trample on the poor and take from them levies of grain, you have built houses of hewn stone, but you shall not live in them; you have planted pleasant vineyards, but you shall not drink their wine" (5:11). "Hear, and testify against the house of Jacob, says YHWH GOD, the God of hosts: . . . 'I will tear down the winter house as well as the summer house; and the houses of ivory shall perish, and the great houses shall come to an end,' says YHWH" (2:13,15). I am afraid there has been planned an excursionary junket for you as well: "Alas for those who are at ease in Zion, and for those who feel secure on Mount Samaria, the notables of the first of the nations, to whom the house of Israel resorts![44] Cross over to Calneh, and see; from there go to Hamath the great; then go down to Gath of the Philistines.[45]

Are you better than these kingdoms? Or is your territory greater than their territory, O you that put far away the evil day, and bring near a reign of violence?" (6:1-3). Will you still claim "election" when the big boys from the east loom in your wee Samaria? Do you plan to deal with them on your terms alone? You think your fate and those of your neighbors are unconnected? Is their closeness to our midst an accident?[46] Your collusion is heading for our collision; what you have stored up is feeding upon you! Your boasted strength is your greatest weakness, your violent gain is turning in the hand that grabbed it. Admit your responsibility! "Do two walk together unless they have made an appointment?" (3:3).[47]

Amos and the poor:

THE POOR: [Gathered angrily around Amos, who has stopped by their place on his way home:] It *never* works for *us*! God is *not* on our side! We have heard you intercede for *them* when *they* plead victim! Just as we were counting on a disaster to bring them down! [Parodying:] <"When locusts threatened them you said, 'O YHWH GOD, forgive, I beg you! How can Jacob stand? He is so small!' And YHWH relented concerning this; 'It shall not be,' said YHWH. When drought was devouring the land like fire, you said, 'O YHWH GOD, cease, I beg you! How can Jacob stand? He is so small!' And again YHWH relented concerning this; 'This also shall not be,' said YHWH GOD"> (7:2, 3, 5, 6 slightly abbreviated). Only when *they* go *down* can *we* hope to spring *up*.

AMOS: It does not work like that. "Alas for you who desire the day of YHWH! Why do *you* want the day of YHWH?[48] It is darkness, not light! . . . as if someone fled from a lion, and was met by a bear; or went into the house and rested a hand against the wall, and was bitten by a snake. Is not the day of YHWH darkness, not light, and gloom with no brightness in it?" (5:18-20).[49]

THE POOR: <He has *already* given us cleanness of teeth in all our cities, and lack of bread in all our places . . .> (4:6, slightly modified). What is left for us to lose? If "Aram goes back to Kir" (1:5),[50] what is to prevent our reversal too? <Are we not like the Ethiopians to him, people of Israel? Or Philistines, or Arameans?> (9:7, modified). What is the big deal? "See, YHWH commands, and the great house shall be shattered to bits . . ."(6:11).

AMOS: " . . . and the little house to pieces" (6:11). You mistake your position! Your lot is wholly tied in with theirs, and all lots with YHWH. Your loss of confidence in God is their responsibility, a crime for which they must answer; but it does not cease to be yours, for all of that! " 'You only have I known of all the families of the earth; . . . yet you did not return to me, says YHWH . . . therefore I will punish you for all your iniquities' " (3:2, enclosing the refrain of 4:6, 8, 9, 10, 11).[51]

THE POOR: Too late for *us* to pray! We must make *them* pay!

AMOS: What is this no pray? No pray will only lead to you *prey, you* pay! They may think that your lives will be the only ones on the line; but you must not assume that if they are gobbled, you will not be as well. Can you not hear it? The noise is deafening already! "Does a lion roar in the forest when it has taken nothing? Does a young lion cry out from its den if it has caught nothing?" (3:4ab).[52]

Amos and YHWH:

AMOS: [Weary and crumpled at the end of a long day of ministry:] Well, we are launched. "YHWH roars from Zion, and utters his voice from Jerusalem; the pastures of the shepherds wither, and the top of Carmel dries up" (1:2).[53] [He adds meaningfully:] There is no going back. The cat is out of the bag.

YHWH: Some cat! But maybe they have taken your warnings. There may be some hope, a reprieve, a possible rescue. " 'This also shall not be,' said YHWH GOD" (7:3, 6). They are so vulnerable, especially those who have the least sense of it. "Thus says YHWH: 'As the shepherd rescues from the mouth of the lion two legs, or a piece of an ear, so shall the people of Israel who live in Samaria be rescued . . .' " (3:12).[54]

AMOS: Yes! ". . . 'with the corner of a couch and part of a bed' " (3:12). What good will that be for them, or benefit to you, or cost to me?! What of the life of the shepherd, the risk to *me*, having to come between lion and prey? And why do you say they may heed *my* warning? I thought it was *our* warning.

YHWH: [Seeming not to hear:] " 'On that day I will raise up the booth of David that is fallen, and repair its breaches, and raise up its ruins, and rebuild it as in the days of old . . . I will restore the fortunes of my people Israel, and they shall rebuild the ruined cities and inhabit them; they shall plant vineyards and drink their wine, and they shall make gardens and eat their fruit. I will plant them upon

their land, and they shall never again be plucked up out of the land
that I have given them . . .' " (9:11, 14-15).[55]

AMOS: NO!![56] I thought we had an understanding, that I could count on
you once you took me from following the flock to walk with you,
when you said to me, " 'Go prophesy to my people Israel' " (7:15).
"Do two walk together unless they have made an appointment?"
(3:3)? I have many times heard your angry outrage, your anticipa-
tory growl! "Does a lion roar in the forest, when it has no prey?
(3:4a); does a young lion cry out from its den, if it has caught nothing?" (3:4b). Those plans we have worked on are so justifiably
ready to spring—are they all for naught? The greed of the few—
king, priests and gentry—swooping so intently on the paltry goods
of the poor that they do not see what has been planned for them!
And you talk about disabling the snare! "Does a bird fall into a
snare on the earth, when there is no trap for it? (3:5a); does a snare
spring up from the ground, when it has taken nothing?" (3:5b).
They'll never heed me again—none of them will. Just as I get a few
of them attuned to respond to the strains of the shofar, to hear war
rather than worship—as I show them your paw not quite invisible
amidst our local catastrophes? "Is a trumpet blown in a city, and
the people are not afraid?" (3:6a). It wasn't so easy to scare them!
"Does disaster befall a city, unless YHWH has done it?" (3:6b).
Are you a lion or a lamb? Am I a *nabi* or a nob'dy, a *fakir* or a
faker? "The lion has roared; who will not fear? (3:8a). The Lord
GOD has spoken; who can but prophesy?" (3:8b) .

YHWH: Let's make an appointment to go for a walk together, Amos.
There are other secrets I need to show you. [End of the day in the
life of Amos.]

To return, then, to the question of the utterance, and consider whether
or not I have established my contexts responsibly. Utterances are crafted
assuming a response: "my" Amos quotes frequently,[57] asks questions[58]
which—even if "rhetorical"—invite response; his persistent use of
pentads and septads encourages hearers/readers to search for them, to
anticipate them. Utterances always rely heavily upon context: the
riddles all assert, somehow, the relation of cause and effect. The complicated weave of the eight verses catches many features of other Amos
language, with the joins made intricately but not geometrically,[59] trapping the audiences to consider the interlinkage of situations which the

prophet urges insistently. Deeds have results, outcomes have etiologies. There is a crisis looming which is amenable to analysis, whether or not it can still be responsive to repair. I imitated the prophetic language by drawing on economic imagery for wordplay and by using puns somewhat after the manner of Amos. Language choice is not incidental to the content of speech at any level. Utterances need not conform to any genre, though they may well utilize a form, which then becomes influential: the riddles are designed to engage, if not enclose, those to whom they are addressed, appealing to the logic of experience in a way that may seem obvious at the outset (all designed to prompt the answer "no") but actually are considerably more flexible than that. There is no doubt that the imagery of the riddles builds a sense of danger, works to suggest that the hearers are overpowered, caught, paralyzed, unable to escape,[60] but since they are questions, escape is possible; the one asking cannot quite control the contexts from which rejoinders may come. Elites have ways of deflecting critique that seem obvious to others. The language of self-justification is not unfamiliar outside of the eighth century. That Amos has the last word in my reading until the prophet seeks to pin down the deity is a move I chose to make. Utterances are evaluative: The strategy of the prophet seems consistently to prick over-confidence; he suffers that same benefit from the one who utters a riddle back to him at the end of the paper. Utterances are unable to be pinned down, are unfinalizable: this same exercise could be run differently. The utterances should result in some transformation, in self-knowledge: let the reader decide!

Notes

[1] Katerina Clark and Michael Holquist, *Mikhail Bakhtin* (Cambridge: The Belknap Press of Harvard University Press, 1984), 203-4. Further remarks about the nature of utterances (and the links to the huge weave of Bakhtin's thought) are found on the next few pages (to 207 or so). The primary source is V. N. Voloshinov, "Discourse in Life and Discourse in Art" in *Freudianism: A Marxist Critique*, trans. I. R. Titunik (New York: Academic Press, 1976), 97-106. The question of whether or not Bakhtin published under the name of Voloshinov is too complex for discussion here, but the attribution is common among scholars, notably Clark and Holquist.

[2] The questions can be so classified, though perhaps they don't meet contemporary standards for free-standing riddles. They are questions posed, wisdom instruction-style, prompting insight from hearers.

[3] An important issue to flag but one which I choose to sidestep is the possible

redactional layers of the book. Though I have chosen to proceed as though that question were not relevant, I am aware that my reading crosses blithely over various proposed editions of the book. Robert B. Coote, *Amos among the Prophets: Composition and Theology* (Philadelphia: Fortress, 1981), 1-10, proposes three stages (post-Jeroboam II, post-721, post-exilic); Coote recommends that we imagine that the later redactions are not so much a matter of insertion of new material next to older as they are a reworking of older layers with new material added. Hence the B edition includes the A material and the C version re-presents A and B texts. Hans Walter Wolff, *Joel and Amos*, trans. W. Janzen, S. Dean McBride, Jr., and C. A. Muenchow (Philadelphia: Fortress, 1977), 106-13 has six redactional steps. I do not doubt some process of recomposition but have chosen to disregard it in my reading. Shalom Paul, *Amos: A Commentary on the Book of Amos* (Minneapolis: Fortress, 1991), 6, reflects the doubt about ascertaining stages more typical of the most recent scholarship, critiquing Wolff and opining that virtually all of the text is plausible in the eighth century.

[4] Such grids are not difficult to find. For example, Bill McKibben, "A Special Moment in History," *Atlantic Monthly*, May 1998, 57, reminds us vividly that hunter-gatherers consumed some 2500 calories per day to the current average of 31,000 a day (he is counting the consumption of fossil fuel)—with the average modern (North) American using six times that amount. McKibben suggests that whether we wish to avert to it or not, we travel with a large balloon above our collective head, "our hungry shadow selves," which represents our appetites and all that sustains them. He instances, among the many other examples given, a calculation of some Vancouver scientists who suggest that though one million citizens appear to live fairly comfortably on 1.7 million acres, in fact they actually require the produce of 21.5 million acres to sustain their living. While I was reading the article on an airplane, I was angered at a woman next to me who was so obese that she needed half of my seat as well as her own. While rehearsing self-righteous complaints to the airlines, I suddenly realized that my companion had helped me understand the problem of elites very immediately.

[5] Commentators have variant terminology for these phrases in 3:3-8, though in some cases the distinctions seem moot. There is general agreement that they are rhetorical questions, framed so as to generate a response of "No." The key questions, it seems to me, include whether or to what extent and in what manner the specifics of each question are to be read in the contexts of the book. Are the questions generic, able to be used more or less the same in any context? Or are they constructed so as to communicate most specifically and effectively in the presumed historical context of Amos (dated mid-eighth century) and in the literary context set up by the canonical book? I will assume the latter and make my case as I utilize the riddles.

[6] Wolff's detailed discussion of the nine assertions on pp. 179-88 rehearses the general features of the verses raised by commentators: textual variants, meter, form, genre, redactional possibilities, phraseological consistencies, minute differences, likely referents, and plausible intention. Suggesting that the interrogative

sentence is the form and didactic disputation the genre, he posits that passionate controversy and a hope to persuade underlie the sentences. He also opines that we are missing the context that would make full understanding of the text possible. Another set of aspects of the verses is discussed by Francis I. Andersen and David Noel Freedman, *Amos: A New Translation with Introduction and Commentary* (New York: Doubleday, 1989), 383-401: meter, syntax variation, verb tenses, particle patterning, criteria of interlocking symmetry. The best rhetorical study of them is to be found in Yehoshua Gitay, "A Study of Amos's Art of Speech: A Rhetorical Analysis of Amos 3:1-15," *Catholic Biblical Quarterly* 42 (1980): 293-309; he illustrates the use of analogy, repetition, questions, common experience, and the like. David Shapiro, "The Seven Questions of Amos," *Tradition* 20.4 (1982): 327-31 tracks the verses in terms of the wider biblical canon. Shalom Paul comments economically on the passage in "Amos 3:3-8: The Irresistible Sequence of Cause and Effect," *Hebrew Annual Review* 7 (1983): 203-220. (All other references to Paul are drawn from the Amos commentary.) Other specific points will be offered below as germane.

[7] Appended to this riddle is a statement (3:7) which makes an assertion; not in question form, it does not seem to be posing a riddle but rather commenting on a question already posed.

[8] All the direct quotations in this paper come from the NRSV, with the designation YHWH substituted for LORD; there was no sense in trying to avoid the deity's masculine gender. When I have needed to alter the text but wish the Book of Amos quotations to be recognizable, the near-quoted phrases will be set off by <>s rather than enclosed in quotation marks; brackets are used for stage directions.

[9] This is perhaps the best place to indicate an historical setting for Amos. So far as I can tell, the major question is whether we should hear Amos in times of relative prosperity (early to mid-eighth century) or when the slide toward crisis is already underway (from the mid-740s on). The three major commentators I consulted vary a bit but seem to situate Amos prior to the 740s: Wolff ca. 760 (88-89), Andersen and Freedman ca. 765-55 (17), John H. Hayes, *Amos, the Eighth-Century Prophet: His Times and Preaching* (Nashville: Abingdon, 1988), 46-47 ca. 750-48. I must also admit to having been caught by a remark of Philip R. Davies, *In Search of 'Ancient Israel'* (Sheffield: Sheffield Academic Press, 1995), 29: "Consider Amos for a moment. We know very little of the social life of the times in which this hero has his words set. We know only that the eponym and implied author of this book criticized certain practices, and we infer from his criticism that certain things were going on. Had he complimented his society instead, we biblical scholars would be viewing that society in diametrically opposite terms, entirely on his say-so, just as most biblical scholarship accepts his say-so now." Another way to suggest context is offered by Mark Daniel Carroll, *Contexts for Amos: Prophetic Poetics in Latin American Perspective* (Sheffield: Sheffield Academic Press, 1992), 205: "In sum, 3:1-8 raises the issues of conflicting understandings of Yahweh, the divine word, the city, imminent and total judgment, foreign invasion and national pretension, but does not present much detail. Rather that opening section serves to bring these

items to the fore and to set the tone for the information . . . that will begin to fill in the gaps. Stylistically, the main protagonists are set on the textual stage, and its world begins to take shape."

[10] There is vast discussion about the nature of the three hymnic excerpts in Amos (4:13, 5:8, 9:5-6). Typical and useful for an overview are Hayes, 149-50, 160-61, 217-18, who stresses the link between the cosmic and the social; Wolff, 215-17, who is interested in whether the three fragments are plausibly from the same piece or not (conclusion uncertain); and John D. W. Watts, *Vision and Prophecy in Amos* (Macon, Georgia: Mercer, 1977), 9-23, who discusses their specific features at some length. My choice here is to set them as liturgical (Watts, 26) and as both imported into their Bethel context but apt to it, at least in the ears of Amos. Carroll, 248 points out the multiple connections between the deity and water, which is the link I am utilizing here.

[11] Rainer Albertz, *A History of Israelite Religion in the Old Testament Period*, Vol. 1, trans. John Bowden (Louisville: Westminster John Knox, 1994), 159-61, suggests the law of credit is the main culprit in the stratification of the economy; legal means lead to gross impoverishment of the many. The poor are reduced to bartering small items or being bartered for them. Paul, 78-9, takes the sandals as a bribe.

[12] Merold Westphal, Jr., "Questions from the Prophets," in *The Living and Active Word of God: Studies in Honor of Samuel J. Schultz*, ed. Morris Inch and Ronald Youngblood (Winona Lake, Indiana: Eisenbrauns, 1983), 65-70, sums up the prophetic critique as aimed at ingratitude, imperviousness, impiety and injustice.

[13] Coote, 16, urges the possibility of using "elite" as a descriptive term (so non-pejoratively) to indicate the select few, about 1-3% of the population.

[14] Paul, 95-99, observes that the passage (2:14-16) comprises seven highlighted moments of escape, thwarted and resulting in immobility of the one(s) who would flee. He also connects the contrast between the graciousness of YHWH, who assisted a distressed Israel (2:5-8), and the present northern elites, who decline the same favor to those presumably beseeching them (87-88).

[15] Karnaim, in addition to being a place name, offers a wordplay on *karnaim*, the two horns of the altar that YHWH has promised to destroy. "*Karnaim*" thus comes out as an arrogant and empty boast by the elites, who claim as their victory what is more ominously God's destructive deed (Carroll, 269).

[16] Hayes, 146, notes that these disparate items are linked by a refrain.

[17] James G. Williams, "Irony and Lament: Clues to Prophetic Consciousness," *Semeia* 8 (1977): 55, suggests that the Woe oracles of the eighth-century prophets typically lament a present loss rather than future calamity. So here, the lament is for the sickness leading to death, the crisis soon to be compounded into defeat.

[18] The elites multiply their deeds even as they, too, are trashed by the effects of them; their worst problem is refusal to see (Carroll, 49). A similar blindness leading to irony may occur at 4:10, where the death of Israel's young men is paired with the slaying of the firstborn of Egypt (213).

[19] There is some disagreement as to exactly how this hunting scene is to be pictured. Wolff, 180-86, suggests the folded net and a thrown missile; Paul, 100-111, and Andersen and Freedman, 395-97, prefer to see not two actions but one in two stages: a bird, lured by a decoy, swooping down and becoming caught in the trap. Though one may ask about cause and effect, they are nearly simultaneous here.

[20] Carroll, 199-220, roots the certainty of the judgment in the syntax (*ki* asseverative), while Paul, 124, stresses that YHWH will be manipulated neither by worship nor by entitlements of asylum.

[21] Albertz, 164, sketches prophets as financially semi-independent, closer to an upper class context than to the poor, who would have some struggle to distance themselves from their own class interests. Hayes, 202, sees Amos plausibly as part of the royal shepherd establishment.

[22] Carroll, 219, wisely recommends that we envision "a world of religious complexity, where different interests interweave and can feed on an organized cult in any number of ways." He includes popular religion as well as what is usually considered stricter Yahwism.

[23] Wolff, 147, thinks Amos brings forth a "particular kind of speech not previously heard in Israel," linked to the prophet's sense of being compelled to do YHWH's bidding—hence his "unwavering certitude."

[24] Marvin L. Chaney pointed out the multiple purposes served by the Bethel sanctuary in a private communication.

[25] Paul, 163-64, names such wordplays on Bethel and Gilgal "nomen est omen": Gilgal *glh*=Gilgal will go into exile; Beth-el *Beth awon*= house of God is house of nothing.

[26] Paul, 112, and Andersen and Freedman, 390, argue with intricate observations against those more eager to eliminate v. 7 as an interpolation. The prior action (the roaring of the lion) results now in three distinct though related situations: hearers must fear, prophets must speak, and God must follow through. Both Wolff and Paul think that a major strategy of the riddles is to insist on the prophet's need to speak such unpleasant prophecies.

[27] Paul, 140, points out the distancing of the deity from these sacrifices that is accomplished by pronouns: "your sacrifices."

[28] Wolff, 211: 4:4-5 is a parody of the Torah. Coote, connecting the reclining to overconsumption of strong drink, suggests that all the expressions imply wasteful consumption of wine and wheat (36-38). Too much of everything, says Wolff, 276. Hayes, 114, asks whose wine is being enjoyed at the shrine—those consuming it or those from whom it was extracted?

[29] Wolff, 261, describes this passage as the harshest blend of the expressions of revulsion; Paul, 192, observes that the deity's disavowal of cult is expressed anthropomorphically.

[30] Jon L. Berquist, "Dangerous Waters of Justice and Righteousness: Amos 5:18-21," *Biblical Theology Bulletin* 23 (1993): 54-56, identifies that it is YHWH's waters that will be rolling justice down, not small rivulets of human reform. A

statistical note from Wolff (102) may buttress Berquist's point: Wolff says two-thirds of the deeds announced in the book are done by YHWH directly.

[31] Albertz, 128: Bethel is both a public and a royal sanctuary. Carroll analyzes the contribution the shrine would have made to the legitimating of royal authority (200); on 273-77 he sums up the religious world described in the text of Amos.

[32] Watts 33: Tekoa is eleven miles south of Jerusalem.

[33] Paul, 228-30, posits that the first petition asks for an unconditional pardon, with no reference to the deservingness of Jacob, simply to his vulnerability; the second asks YHWH to desist.

[34] Wolff, 91, thinks "imminent end" is a message that will not have been heard before.

[35] Wolff, 319, and others report the wordplay by homonym: *qeyts* from a root *qyts* for summer fruit/ end from *qss*, meaning to bring to an end/chop down.

[36] Wolff, 339-40, sees Bethel as the epicenter of "a big one."

[37] Wolff, 180-86, thinks 6b is bland and incidental; Andersen and Freedman take another tack, 397-98, finding it ominous enough when the trumpet sounds an alarm whose nature is then revealed to be an action of God. No commentator that I found links the shofar's sound to worship as well as to trouble, but it seems plausible in the context set up here.

[38] Carroll sees YHWH and Israel having met previously in cult and in past saving deeds; something new and more ominous is envisioned in this imminent encounter (218).

[39] These verses describing the dialogue between prophet and priest are the most debated in the book. Hayes, 136, reminds us that to attack the royal shrine is to attack the whole monarchical institution. Francisco O. Garcia-Treto, "A Reader-Response Approach to Prophetic Conflict: The Case of Amos 7:10-17," in *The New Literary Criticism and the Hebrew Bible*, ed. J. Cheryl Exum and David J. A. Clines (Valley Forge, Pennsylvania: Trinity Press International, 1993), 119-22 sketches Amaziah as arrogant, rude, and dismissive—all achieved beneath a veneer of careful politeness, use of proper address, double-voicing. Garcia-Treto refers to another facet of Bakhtin's theory, the aspect of double-voicing.

[40] Wolff reports on 310-11 that a responsible official would have to report it; he is also not so sure Amaziah could evict Amos. I cut through the many issues under discussion but refer the reader to a useful discussion of them by Patrick D. Miller, Jr., "The Prophetic Critique of Kings," *Ex Auditu* 2 (1986): 82-85; he notes that prophets and kings feared, needed and threatened each other, with the equation not unchanging. Miller charts the discrepancy in assumption between the two; that is, a conflict of perspectives is being waged, with the priest seeing the king's side (not to mention his own) and Amos arguing for YHWH's side. The contrast involves allegiance to deity or to king, viability of YHWH's will or the king's prerogatives, Amos as an emissary of YHWH or as a disturbance to the king, importance of "thus says YHWH" or "thus said Amos" and so forth.

[41] Hayes confirms, 233, that we did not hear such a thing said.

[42] Hayes, 128, says they are called to be witnesses according to law—an irony,

as Wolff points out, 192. Who exactly these are depends on the historical context, but the best supposition is that they are not likely to be friendly. What exactly they are supposed to see is not clear, given their lack of response (to this hypothetical situation) (Carroll, 193). But their response is not the end point of the prophet's suggestion, in any case. The invitation is actually crafted for the ears of its local addressee, whom I have designated as the king.

[43] Everyone agrees on the difficulties of the terminology and hence the understanding to be gleaned. Hayes, 137-42, and Wolff, 203-7, review the several problems.

[44] Hayes, 183-84: The king and elites are pro-Assyrian, and Amos says that will do no good. Three small kingdoms who presumably relied in a similar way were annexed. Carroll, 257, calls it a dismantling of national hubris by making a comparison with the others. There are other viewpoints on the dating of Amos which would affect the construction of the passage.

[45] Wolff, 274: Calneh and Hamath were conquered in 738, Gath in 734.

[46] Hayes, 16-18: Smaller neighbors will resent Jeroboam II's benefitting from friendliness to Assyria.

[47] Wolff 179-84: This is the only one to lack a parallel, to be peaceful and non-conflicted; it also seems to him vague and begs for more context; he thinks it means two people cannot journey together without first having met. That they are together means that they met—obvious makes it irrefutable. Paul, 109-10, agrees it is peaceful and a bit anonymous; people obviously can bump into each other naturally; he agrees with Wolff. That is, they agree that if together, they met. Andersen and Freedman do not argue against that understanding but pose as well the possibility that this first question is referring not to people but to the propositions which follow: are these items joined pointlessly? they ask (387-88).

[48] Wolff, 255, among many others, comments on Amos' use of "the day of YHWH." The expression is new to our chronological sense of the Bible, though Amos need not have coined it or been the first to use it. Yair Hoffman, "The Day of the Lord as a Concept and a Term in the Prophetic Literature," *Zeitschrift für die Alttestamentliche Wissenschaft* 93 (1981): 42, sensibly suggests that Amos need not be addressing some group, all of whom expect it to be positive for them; certain individuals may have a misconception about it. Most scholars see that the concept is used against outsiders (i.e., foreigners); so my use of it for factions is idiosyncratic. In any case, the sense of my construction here is that the day will not discriminate between the just and unjust, will not fall on only the wealthy and not on the poor. It will be a disaster for all who experience it.

[49] Carroll notes that disaster will bring down everyone, as though the whole nation is guilty, a concept he discusses intermittently (198, 228-29, 239). The system is rotten, and all the interlocking parts of it are doomed. All houses share walls, so to speak (266-68). Momentary escape is illusory (Paul, 186).

[50] Wolff suggests, 157, that Kir is to Aram as Egypt to Israel. The threat is clear. For additional discussion of the implications of Amos' seeming dismissal of tradition see Karel Van der Toorn, *Family Religion in Babylonia, Syria and Israel:*

Continuity and Change in the Forms of Religious Life (Leiden: E. J. Brill, 1996), 291-93.

[51] Wolff, 176-77: election entails commitment, not just deeds. Both Carroll (182-83) and Andersen and Freedman (32) point to 3:1-2 as the most succinct and complete summary of the whole book. That is, the two verses state the content of the book in a single equation.

[52] The YHWH-Lion link exists in Amos (1:2, 3:4, 8) and is ubiquitous elsewhere. This riddle describes two phases of the hunt, whether we envision the lion noisy before the catch or afterwards (Paul, 110). Biblical lions do both, so the difference is small (Andersen and Freedman, 394). The deity roars in Jer 25:30; Job 37:4; Hos 11:10. Wolff, 185, comments on the noise of it—the lion after attacking its prey, to frighten off others; Paul, 110, agrees that stages of the hunt are envisioned and that the lion will be noisy after its prey is taken.

[53] Carmel is the place of the most lush forests; when it dries up, the dessication is serious (Wolff, 125); Paul, 149, and Watts, 55, note that there is significant fire/heat imagery in Amos.

[54] There is ambiguity as to the identity of the shepherd: is it Amos? YHWH? See Hayes, 133-34, for a discussion of the legal particularities of the passage.

[55] Hayes, 221-28, is one who argues that the references to David need not be a later redaction. That is, though they may make excellent sense to post-exilic ears, the statements are general enough to reference other situations as well. He posits that a restoration of the booth of David might be understood as envisioning the reunification of Israel and Judah.

[56] Coote, 129-34, also develops Amos somewhat along the lines of Jonah, though I had forgotten it when I sensed the possibility as well. The reading is a bit different from the view of Carroll, 191, who sums up the deity as "violated, absolutely sovereign, decisive and outraged." David Noel Freedman, "Confrontation in the Book of Amos," *Princeton Seminary Bulletin* 1.4 (1990): 251-52, points out that though it appears from elsewhere in the canon that Amos' prophecy regarding Jeroboam and Amaziah does not materialize, there is no effort to restate or abrogate it.

[57] Wolff, 97, and Paul, 5, between them point out quotations at 2:12, 4:1, 5:14, 6:13, 7:16, 8:5, 9:10. There are undoubtedly other cases to be made.

[58] 2:11; 5:18, 25; 6:12; 8:8.

[59] Andersen and Freedman do the best job of demonstrating the patterns and summarizing them several times on pp. 383-401.

[60] Paul, 106.

Rahner and the "New Histories": Everything Old Is New Again

Ann R. Riggs

The subtitle of this paper comes from a song featured in the film *All That Jazz*. The lyrics of the song reflect a kind of existential ennui: there is no real need to wonder or inquire about what our predecessors have done, because we are doing the same things. For theologians it is a bit different: there is a way of doing the same thing differently, of making everything old new again, without that sense of ennui; we call it retrieval.

The term the "new histories," as the theme of this year's meeting, I understand as referring very broadly to a shift within theology from a methodological paradigm taken from philosophy to one taken from the social sciences. The philosophical paradigm, especially that dominated by the influence of Descartes and Kant, has indeed become old. As someone who came to theology with prior graduate education in philosophy, I sometimes wonder whether I might be one of a dying breed, and so I can perhaps be forgiven if my orientation in the current theological scene reflects an interest in self-preservation: what is the future of a philosophical paradigm in theology? Can it become new again? More particularly, can the theology of Karl Rahner, developed within the categories of that paradigm, be retrieved in an intellectual universe dominated by the new histories?

Of course, the philosophical paradigm itself has not been unaffected by all of this; as part of the *Zeitgeist* critical of a naive universalization of the Enlightenment's faith in human reason and of the atomic social theories and the individualism of classical liberalism, philosophical conversations have also focused on a critical re-evaluation of their own "turn to the subject" and of the various dualisms (appearance/reality, mind/body, self/world, private/public, inner/outer) that have structured much that has appeared in the western European intellectual tradition since the seventeenth century. Descartes and Kant take turns as post-modernity's favorite whipping boys.

Rahner's theological legacy stands in an intersection of these and other intellectual currents. As part of what Herbert Vorgrimler refers to as a second-generation of Catholic scholars who were engaged in efforts to bring the philosophical and theological traditions of the Roman Catholic church into creative dialogue with twentieth-century thought,[1] Rahner was influential behind the scenes in the conversion of magisterial and theological perspectives on the modern world that came out of the Second Vatican Council.[2] One has only to compare Pius X's condemnation of modernism in *Pascendi dominici gregis* with Vatican II's *Gaudium et spes* to realize just what a momentous shift this was. However, Rahner's use of categories and methods borrowed from transcendental philosophy with its emphasis on subjectivity, his concern with individual freedom and conscience, his focus on a personal, existential appropriation of faith and its universal accessibility via the supernatural existential, make for a bit of historical irony: while Rahner (and others) were working so diligently to bring the church into dialogue with the modern world and its liberal agendas, the world itself was moving into what has been called the post-modern era with its emphasis on historical particularity, social location, and the historical formation of consciousness. Thus, to neo-scholastic integralists and contemporary critical theorists alike, Rahner is said to be "too modern," his work too closely allied with modernity's emphasis on subjectivity. Another way in which "everything old is new again."

My work on Rahner takes as its point of departure recent criticisms of Rahner along these lines offered by George Lindbeck,[3] Nicholas Lash,[4] and Fergus Kerr.[5] While Kerr has recently modified his views, citing "a new generation of Rahner readers,"[6] the similarities in the criticisms offered by the three are striking. All of the authors, in one way or another, find the agent of Rahner's philosophical anthropology unacceptably Cartesian: Kerr faults Rahner for his mentalist, individualistic concept of the human person, seeing it incommensurate with his more traditionally social ecclesiology; Lash likewise criticizes Rahner's individualism and regrets that it is exactly the opposite of what Rahner wants to do. Lindbeck's criticism is more subtle: while crediting Rahner (and Lonergan) with an attempt to combine cognitive content and human experience in understanding doctrinal statements, he faults this hybrid approach for its "complicated intellectual gymnastics" and ultimately subsumes it under an experiential-expressivist model, one that emphasizes the universality of (private) religious experience and treats (public) dogmatic formulations as non-cognitive, symbolic expressions of such experiences.[7] All three authors are English-language theologians familiar with the technical problem of the Cartesian ego in twentieth-century Anglo-American philosophy. Finally, all three authors, in different ways, operate in the shadow of Ludwig Wittgenstein, whose critique of the Cartesian ego has become the gold standard in Anglo-American philosophy by which other treatments are measured and to which they are called to respond.

Briefly, the Cartesian ego involves a dualistic anthropology that makes sharp, ontological distinctions between the mental and the physical elements in human nature. The mental element is the stuff of human consciousness and spirituality, of all that makes the human distinctly human. As such it is of a higher order than the material, in which it is encased as if it were some sort of spacesuit; a common phrase is the ghost in the machine. Mechanistic bodies are a kind of prison for individual persons, who are thereby rendered isolated islands of consciousness in a material cosmos, forced to use human language as an inferior means of communication, one that is said to "get in the way" of whatever is imagined to be superior. Mental events are inner, private, and privileged, since only I have access to them and, as the contents of my own consciousness, I cannot doubt them. Epistemology takes these privileged inner events and sets itself the problem of how these isolated islands of consciousness become properly connected with the world and the other conscious islands "out there." Hence the dualisms mentioned above are all taken for granted in a Cartesian view of the human predicament, and the epistemological task is to overcome them. Knowledge proceeds *from* the mental entities, taken as fundamental, *to* claims about the larger world, which, because of their derivative nature, are never quite secure. Cartesian egos are isolated, mentalist, and individualist; ultimately both solipsistic and skeptical.

In a set of variations on a common theme, Lindbeck, Lash, and Kerr all criticize Rahner for his Cartesian approach. However, none of the three gives a sustained, text-based argument for his criticisms; they all rely instead on a few quotes from different works that are given no contextual basis for understanding. There seems to be an interpretive paradigm for Rahner that is taken for granted that, of course, this is how Rahner is generally understood, this is in fact how Rahner *should* be understood. The paradigm stresses the dialectical relationship between the categorical and the transcendental to the point where the distinction becomes a separation. Such a paradigm overlooks the interdependent, mutually determining, hylomorphic form/matter relationship that Rahner uses to develop his distinction between the categorical and the transcendental.[8]

I will argue that this presumption is not warranted, that the issues surrounding the problem of the Cartesian ego are not Rahner's issues and that therefore dealing with those issues requires more attention to Rahner's thought as a whole than Lindbeck, Lash, and Kerr have given. To more accurately trace the issue of the Cartesian ego in Rahner's thought, one needs to define more clearly the questions and issues involved and bring *those* questions to Rahner's texts and see what answers are forthcoming. Warrant for this approach is to be found in the philosophical anthropology of *Spirit in the World*, Rahner's *Erkenntnismetaphysik* of the necessarily embodied finite human spirit, which emphasizes that any knowledge of metaphysical realities, including and especially knowledge of God, requires the "conversion to the phantasms." Rahner reads Thomas in this regard as more radical and more critical than Kant: instead of a distinction between knowledge of sensible realities and knowledge of metaphysical realities (another of the Cartesian dualisms), Rahner argues that for Thomas knowledge of a particular sensible object requires a universal and necessary knowledge of sensible forms that is patently metaphysical. Metaphysical knowledge is not distinct from knowledge of the sensible, but an intrinsic element of it. Hence there is a unity in human knowing that is indicative of the unity of the human person as embodied spirit—and by extension, a socialized, inculturated individual. Rahner's use of transcendental method under this rubric of the unity of the human person and "the one human knowing" therefore is not designed to take him away from the realm of the physical and the historical, but rather to anchor the transcendental more firmly within it.[9] Rahner's emphasis on the integration of the transcendental and the categorical is also evident in some of his theological discussions, e.g. the development of dogma, the unity of the love of neighbor and the love of God, and his theology of the symbol.

Background

Among the interrelated issues involved in the Anglo-American discussions of the problem of the Cartesian ego, the question of epistemological foundations is one of the most important: if a non-physical entity is no longer the basis for the self, then mental entities no longer constitute a privileged point of departure for human knowledge about the world. Integrating the mental and the physical effectively shifts foundational priority to historically mediated patterns of speech and behavior (what Wittgenstein refers to as "language games" and "forms of life") and to foundational images that mediate visions of meaning and value—of the really real and the really important. The culturally mediated nature of these foundations may limit the kinds of claims human beings make for them, but it turns out that it also places pragmatic limits on our skeptical claims. There may be no privileged epistemic states, no universally self-authenticating "clear and distinct ideas," but neither are there any epistemic refuges, so to speak: to be human, to participate in any human activity at all is to operate according to some foundational paradigm or other. All knowledge claims may be perspectival (as post-modern social theorists remind us), but we cannot thereby avoid making them or operating within some perspectival context or other that makes any claims at all possible.[10] These perspectival contexts provide structural limits to doubt and skepticism; can I really doubt, for example, that I am speaking English, that clocks and calendars are by and large accurate, or that the world has existed for many years before I was born? Such limits define our sense of "that's just the way it is" and signal that explanation and justification have come to an end. What would it mean to seriously entertain the possibility that I might be speaking a different language, that all of the world's clocks and calendars are in error, or that the world sprang into being a few days ago? These are not empirical mistakes but challenges to a common sense of what the universe is like and the grounds of my participation in its activities. How do I know that my jacket is *really* red? Not because of a challengeable correlation with a mental sensation, but because I know how to use English color words appropriately: my jacket is a prime example of what we call red.[11]

If knowledge is perspectival and context-dependent, then the per-

spectives and the contexts within which they are embedded circumscribe the contours of the reality which renders those knowledge claims
possible—most of which are far less trivial than those mentioned above.
To doubt that women are equal to men in human dignity, that children
ought to be nurtured, that persons should be treated fairly is to enter a
different universe of moral discourse (or to leave one entirely). As the
necessary conditions for the possibility of human interactions, the foundational images that circumscribe the contours of meaning and value
satisfy the classical definition of the transcendental while also being
historically mediated. In this sense such contours come closer to what
Wittgenstein calls grammar than what Kant calls the transcendental. I
argue that it is possible to read Rahner's use of categories taken from
transcendental philosophy in this way—that what Rahner does with
the concept of transcendental can be better understood as grammar—
and that such a reading maintains the unity and the interdependence of
the transcendental and the categorical that he always insisted upon.
This is because the concept of grammar (i.e., deep grammar, not that
which governs the construction of individual sentences but that which
delineates the range of what is questionable and what is thinkable) is
revelatory not just of the way we think but of our sense of "that's just
the way it is" in the world. Grammar signals the end of justification
and explanation, not because reference to an objective reality fails but
because one is dealing with the defining structures that indicate the
reality within which reference is possible. Grammar is not what we
use instead of metaphysics; it is precisely our understanding of the
grammar of a concept that tells us that we are in the realm of the metaphysical. In Wittgenstein's terms, it is "[t]hought surrounded by a halo,"
an order of possibilities that "must be common to both world and
thought"; it is "*prior* to all experience" and "must run through all experience." It "does not appear as an abstraction; but as something concrete, indeed, as the most concrete, as if it were the *hardest* thing there
is."[12]

Ultimately, this reading also attenuates the recurrent criticism that
Rahner is "too modern," making at least one "old" reading of Rahner—
the one presumed by Lindbeck, Lash, and Kerr—new again. The remainder of my paper will consist in illustrating this reading in more
detail with regard to one issue, that of transcendental experience, since
it is one that is obviously related to the problem of the Cartesian ego.
My goal will be to explicate Rahner's understanding of transcenden-

tal experience in a way that emphasizes the historical particularity of such experiences. My argument will consist of three parts: (1) Rahner's concepts of Absolute Mystery and the universal human experience of God are formal concepts that indicate structural limits of human knowledge and skepticism, qualifying his *Erkenntnismetaphysik* as a nonfoundational epistemology. (2) Rahner's christology supplies the foundational images for understanding his philosophical anthropology and his anthropological methods. Hence, Rahner's so-called fundamental theology is not an apologetic in the sense of an apologetic based on a rationality independent of faith. (3) Rahner's sacramental theology provides the christological paradigm for understanding human transcendence and transcendental experience. If successful, my argument will provide a way of understanding the agent of Rahner's philosophical anthropology as physically embodied, socially embedded, and interpersonally constructed.

Rahner's Concepts of Absolute Mystery and the Universal Experience of God

Rahner's concept of Absolute Mystery is primarily grammatical, not experiential, insofar as it can be understood as a necessary, approachable and recognizable limit to both human knowledge and skepticism. It would be a mistake to read Rahner as substituting a definable, conscious experience of Absolute Mystery (à la Rudolf Otto or William James) for intellectual proofs of God's existence or the arguments from miracles that characterized neo-scholastic fundamental theology. After all, a person need not have any explicit awareness of mystery at all for Rahner to claim that he has had an experience of God.[13] Absolute Mystery is, in Thomas's formulation, the beginning and end of all things, and of rational beings especially; Rahner reworks that as "the whole, not indeed a sum of phenomena to be examined, but the whole in its incomprehensible and ineffable origin and ground which transcends that whole to which we and our experimental knowledge belong."[14] As such, Absolute Mystery is an austerely formal concept (and a theological one), a grammatical marker, not a starting point for a natural theology based on religious experience or even transcendental philosophy.[15]

It is important to note that, for Rahner, Absolute Mystery does not indicate a provisional lack of understanding that will eventually be

made clear; this is to restrict "mystery" to an epistemological category
that implies a real but inaccessible foundation in the cosmos and a
defect in the knowing subject. The so-called mysteries of the universe
are mysteries only in this provisional sense, i.e. they are as a matter of
fact beyond the grasp of the human intellect. In contrast to these provisional mysteries, a mystery *stricte dictum* pertains to that which is
mysterious in itself, and any knowledge of such a mystery can only be
knowledge of its incomprehensibility. This can be truly said of God
alone, the in-itself absolutely incomprehensible mystery that nevertheless underlies and grounds all human striving for meaning. The
foundational end-point of the quest for secure epistemological foundations ends not in clear and distinct ideas, but in a recognition of the
unfathomable reaches of the incomprehensible. Rahner's sense of
Absolute Mystery thereby betokens a nonfoundational epistemology.

The epistemological paradox of grounding human striving in incomprehensible mystery is not lost on Rahner:

> If we raise the question of meaning and attempt to answer it in the
> light of the modern ideal of knowledge, according to which
> knowledge gains its true nature and reaches its goal only when it
> sees through and thus dominates what is known, when it breaks
> down into what for us is unquestionable and obvious, when it
> seeks to work only with clear ideas and seeks to reflect to the very
> last detail the conditions of its own possibility, when as autono-
> mous it seeks itself to decide the limits of what concerns it and
> what does not, when it seeks to be silent about those things on
> which it is impossible to speak clearly, when it is interested only
> in the functional connections of the details of its world of
> experience—in a word, when the modern ideal of knowledge
> prevails as a matter of course and without any need of justifica-
> tion—then any talk of God's incomprehensibility can be under-
> stood only as a sentence of death on the question of meaning and
> how we want to cope with life in face of this prohibition of a
> universal question of meaning is irrelevant.[16]

Rahner's theological sense of Absolute Mystery translates into a
uniquely non-foundational apologetic. As the "bottom line" of all systems of meaning and value, it is revelatory of their limited and provisional character. Rahner associates these limits of human knowledge

with the inevitability of trust and notes its "always already" character; i.e., to confront the absence of secure foundations in the human search for ultimate meaning is to confront the ways in which we have already been molded and shaped by those in whom we could not *not* trust. That which seems so necessary, so undoubtable—the red of my jacket, the language I am speaking, the intrinsic worth of each human being—is nonetheless imbued with a kind of historical contingency: it is because of who I am and of how I have been formed that I think and speak the way I do and value what I value. On the one hand, I need not have come to be like this; on the other hand, given that I have come to be like this, I cannot be otherwise or undo what has been done.

It is important to stress again that Rahner is not offering an experiential fundamental theology based on an unequivocal experience of mystery. Rahner repeatedly emphasizes the implicit and nonthematic nature of the human experience of God as that which shapes our understanding of the really real and the really important.[17] The structural limits to my understanding are operative whether or not I ever become explicitly aware of them as such. He does try to relate his concept of mystery and incomprehensibility to moments of human crisis, involving love, trust, hope, despair, moral choice, etc; but such expositions function more like ostensive definitions than they do epistemological foundations. Somewhat like a teacher using pictures of pies and candy bars to illustrate how fractions work, Rahner is hoping that, if he points out enough such examples (and he uses a variety of them in different writings), sooner or later (perhaps) the reader/listener will "get" what he is talking about: "Aha! *That* is the sort of thing you are talking about. *Now* I understand where you are coming from, where you are going." Rahner's examples help to orient his reader to situations of existential or moral uneasiness; once oriented, the reader who can recognize such situations can better follow his discussion because the terrain now has a familiar look and feel about it. However, his point is grammatical and theological, and not dependent upon such experiences or their particular manifestations.

Rahner's Use of Christology as Foundational Image

Reading Rahner's philosophical anthropology in conjunction with his approach to Absolute Mystery highlights its derivative nature. Rahner's emphasis on the inevitability of trust, of its structural necessity in human life, reflects his theological anthropology and provides an example of a Christian theologian using the content of faith as a foundational image. It is Rahner's christology that provides this foundational image, the grammatical "bottom line" that shapes his approach to the horizon of human understanding and evidences the openness to Absolute Mystery as the *Woraufhin* of human transcendence. Such grammatical "bottom lines," as noted above, are not just acknowledgments of the limitations of human understanding as something detached from and opposed to an objective reality; echoing Maréchal's principle of the affirmation of judgment, we insist that these foundational image lines are about the really real, because to admit that they might *not* be really real is to put them within a context that makes doubt possible—which context then assumes the function of the bottom line. Better phrased, we rarely have the need to insist on the reality of our bottom lines, precisely because they are so robustly real. These bottom lines signal the end of explanation or justification, for we come to the point where the only response to "Why?" or "How do you know?" is "Because that's just the way it is!" This is not to deny that foundational images can be challenged, but to note that, when challenged, they thereby lose their status as foundational, giving way to a broader, more inclusive context that allows for the possibility of being otherwise. Can non-Christians be saved? Does God love persons who are overtly homosexual? Can the church change the way it celebrates mass, understands sacred scripture, or deals with the secular world? Such questions have historically challenged the "bottom lines" of many, prodding them to think the unthinkable. Such challenges are the stuff of which conversions are made.

For Rahner the really real bottom line for the meaning and value in human life is the grace and salvation offered to the world through the Word of God spoken in human history in the life, death, and resurrection of Jesus Christ. This christological hermeneutic is the defining foundation for Christian discourse about the world and the place of our human endeavors within it, and it provides the picture that governs all of his theological reflections. The divine embrace of human reality as privileged mode of revelation justifies for Rahner an anthropological method; the "transcendental-anthropological turn in philosophy since Descartes"[18] itself follows this principle. Note again how this perspective roots Rahner's philosophical reflections in a stance that is ultimately theological. God's ultimate revelation in the life of a particular human being is not an isolated event but a principle of divine activity: the universal scope of the incarnation lies not in a belief that Jesus Christ is the only revelation from God, but in the fact that God's definitive revelation in Jesus provides the warrant for recognizing God's self-communication in human activity, and the human acceptance of that revelation, whenever and wherever it occurs.

Rahner's concepts of anonymous Christianity and the supernatural existential further illustrate how his christology provides the foundational images for his thought as a whole. The one salvation achieved for humanity in the life, death, and resurrection of Jesus Christ as the incarnate Word of God is offered—and accepted or rejected—to all persons in a variety of guises.

No one avoids this offer, because no one avoids making judgments about the meaning and value of human life. This particular application of Rahner's theology of nature and grace finds systematic expression in his thought in a variety of contexts, all reflecting his concept of pure nature as a "remainder concept." For example, secular history is never without traces of God's activity and so includes at least some elements of salvation history, and philosophy's pursuit of truths accessible to human reason will ultimately encounter God, the source of all truth. Extending this structure to transcendental experience leads to an understanding of them as structurally similar to sacramental participation.

Sacramental Participation as a Paradigm of Human Transcendence

Sacramental participation is the most explicit locus for the proclamations and behaviors that demonstrate the Christian "picture" of the God-world relationship; sacramental celebrations constitute the Christian "language game" *par excellence*. This seems to be an operative principle in sacramental theology that is constant no matter how one characterizes that relationship, and Rahner's vision of the sacraments is no exception. For Rahner, the secular life of Jesus of Nazareth is the "clearest manifestation" of the grace/nature relationship, and the anamnestic role of the sacraments makes them a landmark of the grace flowing from that life that permeates all of creation and all of human history.

The world and its history are the terrible and sublime liturgy, breathing of death and sacrifice, which God celebrates and causes to be celebrated in and through human history in its freedom, this being something which he in turn sustains in grace by his sovereign disposition. In the entire length and breadth of this immense history of birth and death, complete superficiality, folly, inadequacy and hatred (all of which "crucify") on the one hand, and silent submission, responsibility even to death in dying and in joyfulness, in attaining the heights and plumbing the depths, on the other, the true liturgy of the world is present— present in such a way that the liturgy which the Son has brought to its absolute fulness on his Cross belongs intrinsically to it, emerges from it, i.e., from the ultimate source of the grace of the world, and constitutes the supreme point of *this* liturgy from which all else draws its life, because everything else is always dependent upon the supreme point as upon its goal and at the same time sustained by it.[19]

Considered as language games (or as clusters of language games[20]) sacramental rituals function something like a multiplication table: they must be learned as customs in their own right, but their fullest appropriation lies in their application to other contexts. It does me little good to rattle off my "timeses" up to twelve or fifteen (an idiot savant might do that better than most) if I cannot use that information to figure out, for example, how to adjust a recipe to feed all of my guests. For Rahner, this "liturgy of the world" remains

veiled to the darkened eyes and the dulled heart of man which fails to understand its own true nature. This liturgy, therefore must, if the individual is really to share in the celebration of it in all freedom and self-commitment even to death, be interpreted, "reflected upon" in its ultimate depths in the celebration of that which we are accustomed to call liturgy in the more usual sense.[21]

Sacramental participation reveals what is "really" going on in the world; it provides the images whereby Christians are to understand the events in their own lives as well as the world at large. This understanding means that one participates in the redemptive power of the grace mediated by the sacraments, we achieve a "genuine enactment" of the liturgical rites, only if we bring to it our enacted "liturgy of faith" that we express in our daily lives. The Christian attending mass (his paradigmatic test case for sacramental participation in general) is envisioned by Rahner as entertaining

> a feeling for the responsibility of statement with their decisions, . . . something of the laughter of children . . . of the tears of hungry children, of the pains of the sick, of the disappointment of love betrayed, of the dedicated realism of scientists in their laboratories, of the dedicated austerities of those who struggle for a liberated humanity—something of all these is in him . . . He knows that those who mourn weep the tears of Jesus, those in prison sit in the cell of the Lord, those who rejoice share in the joy of Jesus, those who are lonely share his lonely nights, and so on.[22]

Rahner is at his poetic best here, not giving a graphic description of anyone's experience of worship, but supplying a veritable cascade of suggestive ostensive definitions of what it might be like to understand the eucharistic liturgy against the liturgy of the world, i.e., as displaying the grammar of world history. So closely does Rahner tie the celebration of the sacraments to an awareness of the liturgy in the world that he is bold enough to suggest that anyone who lacks such an awareness should really not be admitted to the sacraments because such a lack betokens an absence of the requisite faith for a valid reception.[23]

Moments in which this picture becomes an explicit element in an individual Christian's understanding—moments when she understands how to go on by herself, how to use the picture correctly, how to follow the rules of a Christian grammar—are paradigmatic transcendental experiences. They make explicit what has been implicit in a person's understanding, or they mark a shift in a person's understanding by reconfiguring what had heretofore been taken for granted and revealing something previously unknown, or they mark an occasion of renewed enlightenment or commitment in a moral struggle. In whatever form they take, they reveal what is "really real," what the world is ultimately like, and who I am and what I am to do in the light of that reality.

Not every moment of sacramental reception is such an experience, of course, nor are such experiences restricted to times of sacramental reception. However, regardless of the specific occasion of such insights, the practice of sacramental reception remains the practice field (so to speak) for cultivating a picture of Christianity and negotiating "the real world" in terms of that picture. It is a paradigm case of how a revelation from God (one's "take" on the bottom line of what is really real) is mediated within a specific historical, social, and cultural context, insofar as one's picture of church and of one's place therein acquired in the practice of sacramental participation is inseparable from the images of God also acquired in this way.

Sacramental participation construed this way also provides a paradigm for how metaphysical visions in general are tied to the "phantasms" of story, song, gesture, ritual, and material objects. Just as a Christian not need be actually participating in ritual to come to a particular insight about his tradition and its meaning for his own life and/or times, so one not need be a Christian at all to be subject to moments of insight about what is "really" going on in terms of one's own presumed set of meanings and values.

For Rahner, the concept of transcendental experience is primarily about those foundational images that express the presumed bottom line of human meaning and value. Such images may or may not be those portrayed in the narratives, rituals, and doctrinal formulations of the Christian tradition, but some such foundational images are always operative in human functioning. This is to return to the discussion above about the structural limits to skepticism. One may or may not be able to articulate one's own foundational images, or the images that one articulates may or may not be those that are operative in one's actions and choices. Personal awareness is not the issue in the functioning of these images; that is why Rahner can claim that everyone has had an experience of God whether or not he or she recognizes it.[24]

In Rahner's scheme of thought, transcendental experiences are to Christian sacramental participation (or sacramental experiences) what secular history is to salvation history, what philosophy is to theology. This approach to human transcendence does justice to Rahner's insistence that the transcendental and the historical are intimately conjoined, mutually determining, like the hylomorphism of form and matter and like the distinction-without-separation that characterizes his theology of nature and grace. This approach to human transcendence also sees the individual as physically embodied and socially embedded, simultaneously subject to the determining factors of his or her personal history and yet capable of moments of critical insight and distancing. For human beings are never mere functions of their social location; what would it be like to encounter creatures with bodies that look human but who never sense the limitations or ask the questions presented by their systems of meaning and value and who therefore never encounter the concurrent possibilities of transcendence? Transcendence is not only, nor even primarily, the stuff of Otto's *mysterium tremendum et fascinans*; it is also (like the sacramental life as a whole) the stuff of everyday life. And this is so because the *mysterium*, the Absolute Mystery that has graced our natural, very ordinary lives, is not on the other side of a Cartesian divide between the self and the world, between the inner and the outer, between what is private and what is public. It is the incomprehensible against which our humanity reveals itself as simultaneously limited and transcendent; it is the mystery within which we live and move and have our being.

Notes

[1] Herbert Vorgrimler, *Understanding Karl Rahner: An Introduction to His Life and Work* (New York: Crossroad, 1986), 55-56.

[2] Vorgrimler, *Understanding Karl Rahner*, 94-101, and "Karl Rahner: The Theologian's Contribution," in Alberic Stacpoole, ed., *Vatican II Revisited: By Those Who Were There* (Minneapolis: Winston Press, 1986), 32-46.

[3] George Lindbeck, *The Nature of Doctrine: Religion and Theology in a Postliberal Age* (Philadelphia: Westminster Press, 1984).

[4] Nicholas Lash, *Easter in Ordinary: Reflections on Human Experience and the Knowledge of God* (Notre Dame, Ind.: University of Notre Dame Press, 1990).

[5] Fergus Kerr, *Theology after Wittgenstein* (Oxford and New York: Basil Blackwell, 1986).

[6] Fergus Kerr, *Immortal Longings: Versions of Transcending Humanity* (Notre Dame, Ind.: University of Notre Dame Press, 1997), 181. Works cited by Kerr include Karen Kilby, "The *Vorgriff auf esse*: A Study in the Relation of Philosophy to Theology in the Thought of Karl Rahner" (Ph.D. diss., Yale University, 1994); Michael Purcell, "Mystery and Method: The Mystery of the Other, and Its Reduction in Rahner and Levinas" (Ph.D. diss., University of Edinburgh, 1996); Nicholas Healy, "Indirect Methods in Theology: Karl Rahner as an Ad Hoc Apologist," *The Thomist* 56 (1992): 613-34; and Russell [R. R.] Reno, *The Ordinary Transformed: Karl Rahner and the Christian Vision of Transcendence* (Grand Rapids, Mich: Eerdmans Publishing, 1995).

[7] Lindbeck, *The Nature of Doctrines*, 17.

[8] This understanding of Rahner is not unique to those who are critical of him. Mary Hines, in *The Transformation of Dogma: An Introduction to Karl Rahner on Doctrine* (New York: Paulist Press, 1989); Roger Haight, in *Dynamics of Theology*

(New York: Paulist Press, 1990) and *The Experience and Language of Grace* (New York: Paulist Press, 1979); and Anne Carr (to a lesser extent), in *The Theological Method of Karl Rahner* (Missoula, Mont.: Scholars Press, 1977), all seem to share it also.

⁹ Karl Rahner, *Spirit in the World*, 2ⁿᵈ ed, trans. William Dych (New York: Crossroad Continuum, 1994, 1968), 75-77 and *passim*.

¹⁰ The self-referential nature of this claim, and how the problems and paradoxes of self-reference impact a proper understanding of its apparent universal and timeless scope, have not, to my knowledge, received any critical attention.

¹¹ The doubting examples are based on Ludwig Wittgenstein's *Über Gewißheit/ On Certainty*, trans. by Denis Paul and G. E. M. Anscombe, ed. G. E. M. Anscombe and G. H. von Wright (New York: Harper & Row, 1972). Regarding my treatment of the color red, see Ludwig Wittgenstein's, *Philosophische Untersuchungen/ Philosophical Investigations*, 3ʳᵈ ed., trans. G. E. M. Anscombe (New York: Macmillan, 1958), §381. Hereafter cited as *PI*.

¹² Wittgenstein, *PI* §97.

¹³ Karl Rahner, "The Experience of God Today," *Theological Investigations* (hereafter *TI*) IV, 154 and *passim*.

¹⁴ Karl Rahner, *Grace in Freedom* (New York: Herder and Herder, 1969), 191.

¹⁵ While other treatments of Rahner also see his dogmatic theological principles driving his putative natural theology, R. Reno's discussion in *The Ordinary Transformed* is the most self-conscious in defending Rahner against criticisms of its inappropriate philosophical foundations (in this case, those of Fergus Kerr). Reno's argument proceeds from Rahner's treatment of nature as a remainder concept to his theologically driven appropriation of philosophical categories; see *The Ordinary Transformed*, esp. 176-95.

¹⁶ Rahner, "The Human Question of Meaning in Face of the Absolute Mystery of God," *TI* XVIII, 95-96.

¹⁷ See, e.g., Rahner's essay, "The Experience of God Today."

¹⁸ Rahner, "Theology and Anthropology," *TI* IX, 38.

¹⁹ Rahner, "Considerations on the Active Role of the Person in the Sacramental Event," *TI* XIV, 169-70. After the word "sacrifice" Rahner inserts a footnote that refers the reader to the work of Teilhard de Chardin, citing as an example his *Hymn of the Universe* (London and Glasgow: Collins, 1965).

²⁰ Nicholas Lash, "How Large Is a Language Game?" *Theology*, 87 (1984): 19-28. I agree with Lash that Wittgenstein images language games at the micro level, so to speak (giving orders, obeying them, praying, providing an ostensive definition), rather than at the level of a universe of discourse. I am less convinced of Lash's own image of a language game as "the linguistic component of a type of behaviour or 'form of life' " (24), because it seems to me that one of Wittgenstein's main points is that linguistic components (words, phrases, etc.) are *not* separable from the behaviors in which they are embedded—gestures, facial expressions, vocal inflections, etc. My own impression (and the way I use the terms here) is that a particular *Lebensform* is shaped by a characteristic clustering and prioritizing of

different language games. So going to communion, genuflecting at the altar, and asking for forgiveness might be among the language games in which many Christians participate as defining elements of their participation in a Christian *Lebensform.*

[21] Rahner, "The Active Role of the Person," 174.

[22] Ibid., 170-71.

[23] Ibid., 171.

[24] Rahner, "The Experience of God Today," 150-53.

Meaning and Praxis in History: Lonerganian Perspectives

Donna Teevan

Introduction

History and meaning are closely related in the thought of Bernard Lonergan. For him, history is an expression of meaning that is open to growth in authentic living or to decline into inauthenticity. We have a living relationship with meaning that makes changes in meaning and in the institutions it constitutes an ever-present possibility. To the extent that shared meanings are authentic, they promote progress and create the conditions for the continued enhancement of human well-being. Conversely, inauthentic meanings effect decline, as the evils of indifference and malice eat away at the heart of human community. One way of understanding social conflicts is to see them as clashes in the meanings that consciously or not so consciously guide the lives of those involved. To bring about significant changes in history would seem, then, to demand the transformation of the meanings that people unconsciously assume, verbally espouse, and actually embody.[1]

Drawing on Lonergan's approach to meaning and praxis, I will argue that historical change—be it progress, decline, or redemption—may be understood as a transformation of the meanings that constitute personal and social self-understanding and action.[2] Authentic praxis, in this view, consists in the mediation of meanings that are in accord (as much as possible) with the Reign of God. Although I am using the ideas of Bernard Lonergan, I am sometimes going beyond the connections that he explicitly made; hence, I have subtitled this essay "Lonerganian" rather than "Lonergan's" perspectives on meaning and praxis.[3]

History: Progress, Decline, and Redemption

Historical Process

Lonergan argues that there is no blueprint for history, and that the goal of historical process, in an empirical sense, is simply whatever becomes determinate in the process itself. A key feature of that determination is human initiative and responsibility for the making of history. As historical experience dramatically illustrates, such initiative may be in the service of either good or evil, of either the flourishing or destruction of life. Individual and collective responsibility for world constitution, then, implies the possibility of either social progress or social decline, of either developments or breakdowns in the human good. Historical process, for Lonergan, is fundamentally a compound of progress, decline, and redemption.[4]

Another way in which Lonergan presents historical process is in relation to meaning. Discussing the challenge of historical investigation in *Method in Theology*, he notes that the individual and group action examined by historians has both a conscious and an unconscious side. Normally, he argues, the conscious flow, which he describes as constituted by intentional acts of meaning, controls human action.[5] Historical action is meaningful action.

Decline

In *Insight* Lonergan discusses two types of decline that reflect a distorted dialectic of community, a destructive negotiation of the relationship between human intersubjectivity and practical common sense.[6] The first of these kinds of decline is what he calls the shorter cycle of decline, a cycle of decline that stems from group bias. In the grip of such bias, the self-interest of a group will lead its members to champion only those ideas that help justify its existence or its dominance in relation to other groups. Such selectivity, with its disregard of possibly vital insights, breeds a deterioration of the social situation. Although Lonergan did not cast his discussion of this issue in these terms in *Insight*, one way to describe this dynamic is in relation to questions of meaning; one might say that group bias involves a distortion of the *meanings* that constitute a social situation.[7] The dominant group's constitutive meaning enjoys a hegemony as it subjugates understandings that challenge the story it tells.

There is a longer cycle of decline, as well. The culprit in this case is what Lonergan calls general bias, with its overvaluation of common sense and its penchant for short-term benefits at the cost of long-term gains. In brief, the general bias of common sense is unequal to thinking on the level of history because it rejects the scientific and philosophic insights born of long-term perspectives and committed to long-term, sustained results. The longer cycle's aversion to acknowledging complexity and its repeated neglect of the ideas offered by critical intelligence leads to ever more restricted viewpoints and to a cumulative deterioration of the social situation.[8] Here, too, we may interpret the distortions wrought by bias as meanings missed or misconstrued.

Lonergan suggests that the means of reversing the longer cycle of decline lies in a direct countering of its weakness. Fundamentally, what is needed to reverse this slide is not some new idea in technology, economics, or politics but a change in persons and in their understanding of historical responsibility.[9] From this rise in personal integrity and growth in historical vision will flow the policies, programs, actions, and attitudes that make for a sound technological, economic, and political life. The ecological crisis, to use an example that Lonergan did not invoke, stems from centuries of short-term thinking bolstered either by distorted philosophic and scientific analyses or by the rejection of any theoretical analysis in the name of "practicality." Meeting this crisis, ecological theologians point out, necessitates a change in the way in which many of us understand our place in the cosmos and our relationship to all forms of life.[10] Specific plans of action will tend to be band-aid measures inconsistently applied without the fuller understanding that comes with the collaboration of critical intelligence and mature, integrated feelings.

Progress

Although Lonergan uses the terms progress and decline as social analogues to the developments and breakdowns of individuals, social progress depends on the development of the individuals who constitute the social situation (and, similarly, social decline results from the intellectual, moral, religious, and affective breakdowns of persons). Progress, he argues, "proceeds from originating value, from subjects being their true selves by observing the transcendental precepts, Be attentive, Be intelligent, Be reasonable, Be responsible."[11] It is the sustained observance of the transcendental precepts that engenders the series of improvements that make for progress.

Redemption

This flow of improvements is ever precarious, however. Examples of continual advances in integrity and justice in history are difficult to locate. Lonergan contends that there is a radical problem, a fundamental impediment to sustained progress, that cannot be solved by a correct philosophy, ethics, or human science.[12] This problem consists in the human "incapacity for sustained development," and its ultimate solution lies only in the grace of God that enables human beings to cooperate with God in the divinely originated solution to the problem of evil.[13] Acknowledging that efforts to overcome decline and to promote progress present a staggering challenge, Lonergan discerns an important function of religion in relation to the social situation. He argues that "a religion that promotes self-transcendence to the point, not merely of justice, but of self-sacrificing love, will have a redemptive role in human society inasmuch as such love can undo the mischief of decline and restore the cumulative process of progress."[14] Later in this essay, I will explore how this process of redemption may be understood as the transformation of meaning effected by the gift of God's love. At this point, I want only to note that I do not interpret the self-sacrificing love advocated by Lonergan as an invitation to self-annihilation, a ploy historically aimed particularly at the oppressed; rather, I would suggest that, historically, fidelity to one's partnership with God in the work of love and justice often entails self-sacrifice. Lonergan seems to recognize that persons and communities acting as agents of redemptive love encounter evil in very tangible ways that often result in intense suffering and perhaps even death. Still, he urges people to persist in their efforts for justice, for only the willingness to meet evil with love can end cycles of violence, hatred, and revenge.

Meaning

Incarnate Meaning

In his discussion of the functions of meaning in particular, Lonergan stresses that human beings are born into traditions and communities that are constituted by meaning. He delineates five carriers of meaning: intersubjectivity, art, symbols, language, and persons. It is the last carrier, the lives and deeds of persons, i.e., incarnate meaning, that I wish to consider here. Incarnate meaning is embodied in a person, in her way of life, her words, or her deeds. It may involve many or all of the other carriers of meaning in that intersubjectivity, art, symbols, and language are all created and embodied by human lives and deeds. The meaning incarnate in a person may be that person's meaning for just one other person or for an entire national, social, cultural, or religious tradition.[15] Incarnate meaning, moreover, is not just individual but may be found in the achievements of groups as well. Obviously, the incarnation of meaning in community has been a powerful force in human history.

A community is not, according to Lonergan's use of the term, just any aggregate of individuals living near each other geographically but "an achievement of common meaning," an achievement that may be linguistic, religious, cultural, social, political, or domestic.[16] Community arises from the conjunction of the constitutive and communicative functions of meaning. Its boundaries are marked by the common experiences, understandings, judgments, and commitments that together actualize common meaning. Lonergan's notion of community should not be mistaken for a disembodied collection of meanings and values, however. He insists that "the primordial basis of [human] community is not the discovery of an idea but a spontaneous intersubjectivity."[17]

Lonergan's emphasis on shared experience, understandings, judgments, and commitments can give rise to the suspicion that he wishes to suppress difference. While I do believe that Lonergan's formulations of the notion of community do not adequately address issues of diversity, especially cultural diversity, I would still suggest that his ideas on community may be appropriated in ways that are helpful in thinking through these issues. First, Lonergan's emphasis on the fact that communities are achievements and not givens calls attention to the need to build or, to use a different metaphor, to cultivate communities conscientiously. Second, this achievement of community may best be understood as an exercise of solidarity, as M. Shawn Copeland's development of a Christian feminist theology of solidarity has shown.[18] With Lonergan's work among her sources, Copeland has articulated her own understanding of community as a project, a struggle for solidarity that respects concrete human personhood differentiated by the complex of gender, race, social class, and ethnic-cultural heritage.[19]

Since community is an achievement of common meaning, in Lonergan's view, it should not be surprising that community, like meaning itself, is never a fixed and permanent achievement. While meaning may enjoy the refinements that come with genuine development, it does not escape the effects of the bias generative of decline. The ongoing coherence and progress of any community is not to be taken for granted. Bias may have taken hold of a community's life, or new challenges may have arisen as conditions changed. The meanings that once charged the group's vitality may now seem lifeless. The community may be forced to reassess and possibly change its core meanings. Lonergan claims that to transform the meaning of an institution is to alter its concrete reality. He illustrates his point with this example: "The state can be changed by rewriting its constitution. More subtly but no less effectively it can be changed by reinterpreting the constitution or, again, by working on men's minds and hearts to change the objects that command their respect, hold their allegiance, fire their loyalty."[20]

Communities, then, are constituted by meaning and are the incarnation of meanings that may serve to promote good or evil. Communal life is not fixed, however, and within the community persons mediate meanings that reshape their lives together. Furthermore, the community itself mediates meanings to other communities.

The Mediation of Meaning

A lecture called "The Mediation of Christ in Prayer" offers us some ideas on mediation that will allow us to connect meaning and praxis.[21] In this talk, Lonergan generalizes the Aristotelian notion of the immediate and the mediated to say that a factor, quality, property, feature, or aspect is immediate in its source, origin, ground, or basis and is mediated in its consequences, effects, derivatives, outcome, field of influence, radiation, expansion, expression, manifestation, and revelation.[22] Of particular interest for the purposes of this essay is Lonergan's development of the concepts of self-mediation and mutual self-mediation.

One form of self-mediation, according to Lonergan, is self-consciousness. Growth in self-consciousness is an adventure in self-discovery and a call to decision about what one is to make of one's life. Self-consciousness invites us to step out of the pack of "drifters" who simply follow what everyone else is doing. Although this description may seem focused on individual decision, Lonergan points out that this process of self-discovery and decision takes place within the community we share with families, other human beings, and God. Again we see Lonergan argue that community is more than just any group of human beings. Formally, it is an intentional reality that is sustained, if not initially formed, by the decisions and commitments of its members. In brief, "the community is what people mean it to be."[23]

The life of a community is a dynamic one that is not restricted to the received idea of its identity. Lonergan stresses that a change in the community's normative meaning, in its understanding of what it ought to be, opens up new possibilities for its future.[24] The self-mediation of a community, its revelation of itself to itself, occurs in its living, in the way it revises its common meanings, values, and commitments in response to challenges and opportunities for growth. Written history offers a reflection on that process; thus it, too, serves as a self-mediation of the community.

Lonergan extends this analysis of self-mediation to the individual within the community. She reveals herself to herself and others in her living. The community offers her concrete possibilities and constraints, but it is her own living that manifests the existential decisions she has made in regard to her situation. Self-mediation, then, is the manifestation or revelation of a community or of an individual. Recognizing that communities and individuals are dynamic and interactive, Lonergan introduces his notion of mutual self-mediation, a process of mutual influence and transformation. Mutual self-mediation, he suggests, occurs in romantic love, education, family relationships, friendships, and collegiality in the workplace.

I would propose that Lonergan's notion of mutual self-mediation be conceived as an exercise of praxis. What becomes manifest in the process of mutual self-mediation is the meaning incarnate in a person or a community. The mediation of this meaning in reflective action and communication is potentially transformative of a person, community, or situation.

Praxis

From his explanation of the Aristotelian notion of praxis in the first paragraphs of a 1977 paper "Theology and Praxis," Lonergan goes on to "arrive at a conception of theology as basically a praxis."[25] Distinguishing praxis from *techne*, he states that praxis concerns our doing or conduct under the guidance of *phronesis*, whereas *techne* concerns the making of a product under the direction of skill or technical know-how. The making of a product differs greatly from the fashioning of a life that is praxis. A product is an object that once crafted passes beyond the control of its maker, but praxis is an ongoing exercise of responsible freedom that results to a greater or lesser degree from our own deliberation and choice.

Lonergan defines praxis as "a compound of theoretical and practical judgments of value"[26] which have as their criterion the authenticity or lack of authenticity in the subject's being.[27] Judgments of value are determinations of whether something is truly or only apparently good. They may also involve comparisons between truly good courses of action to determine if one approach is better, more important, or more urgent.[28] Lonergan's use of the term sometimes connects praxis not just with any choice but with actions that are consistent with the norms immanent in conscious intentionality, with what is in harmony with attentiveness, intelligence, reasonableness, and responsibility. Such usage is not consistent but it does occur clearly at times, as in this description of "the cardinal point of method as praxis": "it discerns a radically distorted situation; it retreats from spontaneous to critical intelligence; it begins from above on the level of evaluations and decisions; and it moves from concord and cooperation towards the development of mutual understanding and more effective communication."[29] Lonergan's notion of theology as praxis begins with something like what Edward Schillebeeckx describes as a negative contrast experience, the lived sense that life in a particular situation is not as it should be and that human failures to love and live justly are to blame.[30]

Although Lonergan would see working for more just social, cultural, economic, and political conditions as absolutely necessary, he does not reduce praxis to an effort to gain measurable material results. Praxis, in his analysis, demands more than concern for practical results; it calls for the fullness of human subjectivity. The human subject, he insists, "is not just an intellect or just a will. Though concerned with results, he or she is more basically concerned with himself or herself as becoming good or evil and so is to be named, not a practical subject, but an existential subject."[31] What Lonergan is suggesting here is not that responsible human beings ought to be concerned with their own goodness as if it were some kind of possession, but that their interest in practicality is rooted in their awareness that they contribute to both the goodness and evil at work in the world.

Healing and Creating in History: The Remaking of Meaning

Historical experience horrifyingly illustrates how difficult authentic cognitive and existential praxis is to achieve. Rather than recounting Lonergan's argument for the solution to the problem of evil in *Insight* or his discussion of the Law of the Cross in *De Verbo Incarnato*,[32] I would like to build on his conviction that the love of God can bring a healing and reshaping of the meanings that constitute our lives.[33]

Imagining and implementing changes in meaning demand a certain openness of the human spirit. As developed by Lonergan in a very brief paper, "Openness and Religious Experience," a consideration of the topic involves distinctions among openness as a fact, an achievement, and a gift.[34] What I wish to do here is to take his comments as a starting point for reflections on the role of grace in the making and remaking of meaning in historical experience.

First, Lonergan states that openness as a fact is the pure desire to know, the self as the "ground of all higher aspiration"; it is wonder as a "primordial fact" and as a principle of possible achievement.[35] Openness as a fact is what Lonergan calls "the pure question," i.e., "the primordial 'Why?'," "the spirit of inquiry," "the drive to know." The primordiality of the pure question is no guarantee that it will operate unfettered in the lives of individuals or communities. Although Lonergan speaks of openness as "a fact," he is not claiming that in fact, in actuality a situation of open and undistorted communication prevails—quite the opposite, he would argue. Still, for him openness is indeed a fact in the sense that there is an openness to human intentionality that is so integral to full human personhood that its frustration or distortion constitutes a violation of human dignity.

There is also a sense in which openness is not just a given—since it can be blocked—but is something to be achieved, which brings us to the second aspect of openness that we must consider. As Lonergan conceives it, openness as an achievement is "the self in its self-appropriation and self-realization."[36] The achievement of openness that comes with self-realization is reached when one's actual orientation coincides with the exigencies of the unrestricted desire for the true and the real, the good, and transcendent mystery.

But it is clear as well that some openness is the requisite condition for this achievement: without some degree of openness how can greater openness be achieved? There arises, then, the question of how openness can be attained if for some reason the questions and desires that would drive us toward integrity have been blocked or distorted by bias. Lonergan recognizes this problem and identifies it as our incapacity for sustained development, a problem that can be remedied only by the grace of God.

The recognition of this need brings us to the third aspect of openness, that it is a gift effected by divine grace. He maintains that besides the openness made possible through a natural growth in consciousness there is also an openness that is beyond the capacity of finite consciousness to achieve on its own and is given as a gift from God. In *Insight* Lonergan speaks of the gift of universal willingness, the antecedent willingness "to learn all there is to be learnt about willing and learning and about the enlargement of one's freedom from external constraints and psychoneural interferences."[37]

Although openness as a gift must be distinguished from openness as an achievement, there is an intricate connection between the two, a connection that can be made with some help from Lonergan's later remarks on human development. In a paper entitled "Healing and Creating in History," he presents human development in terms of two vectors that he calls the healing and creating vectors.[38] He describes the creative process as a progression of insights coalescing, correcting, and complementing each other; the creating vector moves "from below upwards," from experiencing, through understanding, on to judgment, and finally to action.

Bias and decline can creep in to undermine this movement, however, and so there is also the need for a healing process, one that moves "from above downwards." The healing vector of human development begins from the point of transformative love and moves "downward" to heal the biases that afflict all levels of consciousness. The healing and creating processes work together for the human good, and Lonergan argues that neither can suffice without the other.

To return to the topic of openness and to go beyond Lonergan's own comments on this point, I would suggest that "openness as an achievement" reflects the operation of the creating vector and "openness as a gift" results from the work of the healing vector. The gift of God's love promotes a healing that allows human creativity to operate with an openness that unhealed biases had previously hindered. Openness is *given* in an act of healing, which in turn promotes the *achievement* of a greater openness as one's life-giving and world-building potential becomes more fully realized.[39]

The process of redemption in history is thus not simply a matter of human courage and imagination but also of divine grace. Praxis, as the mutual self-mediation of authentic meanings, is founded in and sustained by the love of God. The analysis offered here suggests that, given the ubiquitous and often insidious nature of evil, healing is required if human beings are to mediate to each other meanings truly consistent with God's Reign.

To explore the practical implications of Lonergan's thought, we might consider how progress and redemption in history require solidarity with the poor and oppressed. Conversion to the oppressed, solidarity with them in their struggle, is a risky affair for the privileged. Conversion to themselves as actors in the world is a risky affair for the oppressed. As Brazilian educator Paulo Freire's argument for the development of critical consciousness indicates, authentic social transformation demands a change in how the people perceive the meaning of their lives and their world.[40] His description of the oppressed person's struggle to overthrow the oppressor housed in their own psyche chillingly reminds us of the invasiveness of bias and of the need for a healing and conversion that reaches into the depths of the psyche. Without conversion, without some change in the meaning incarnated, enacted in the lives of people, there will be no thoroughgoing, radical change in the meaning that constitutes the situation.

Certainly, one can see here the relevance not only of Lonergan's description of intellectual, moral, religious, and affective conversions, but also of Robert Doran's notion of psychic conversion.[41] The latter, endorsed by Lonergan as a complement to his work, is the reorientation of the censorship exercised over images and affects from a repressive to a constructive functioning in one's own development. It allows for the admission into consciousness of images needed for fuller insight into reality. It seems to me that this transformation of the human psyche, when understood in the context of Freire's work, can be an important factor in the process of history as it frees persons to be agents of progress rather than victims and/or perpetrators of decline.

Conclusion

Lonergan's work reminds us that historical action is meaning-full, embodied action and that historical progress and decline are fundamentally changes of meaning mediated by persons in community. I must remark, however, that Lonergan has been criticized for his focus on the role of the individual in this process. Analyzing Lonergan's concept of praxis, Charles Davis, for one, has contended that his "analysis of the human condition is intellectualist and individualist."[42] I do see how Lonergan's project may be construed in this fashion, but I am persuaded that certain aspects of his work—his notion of community and his analysis of bias, to name two—would prohibit conceiving human persons apart from their social, economic, and political context.[43]

My point in this paper has not been to defend Lonergan on this broader issue but to explore how his understanding of the meaning incarnate in persons and communities, mediated in human living, provides a notion of praxis that can contribute to the building up of the Reign of God in history. From a Lonerganian perspective, praxis is the mutual self-mediation of the meaning incarnate in persons and community. When authentic, praxis is ultimately the mediation of the love of God.

Notes

[1] Lonergan himself makes these connections between historical change and the transformation of meaning. See, for example, his "Natural Right and Historical Mindedness," in *A Third Collection: Papers by Bernard J. F. Lonergan, S. J.*, ed. Frederick E. Crowe (New York: Paulist Press, 1985), 169-83. Lonergan also connects his interest in history with his concern for the good. He states, for instance, that "my notion of the human good is interconvertible with my notion of the structure of history." *Collected Works of Bernard Lonergan*, ed. Frederick E. Crowe and Robert M. Doran, vol. 10, *Topics in Education: The Cincinnati Lectures of 1959 on the Philosophy of Education* (Toronto: University of Toronto Press, 1993), 24.

[2] In focusing on meaning, I do not wish to neglect the issue of values and disvalues. My approach here is to see value as an aspect of meaning. In *Insight* Lonergan defines the notion of being as the all-inclusive term of meaning. *Collected Works of Bernard Lonergan*, ed. Frederick E. Crowe and Robert M. Doran, vol. 3, *Insight: A Study of Human Understanding* (1957; Toronto: University of Toronto Press, 1992), 381-83. *Method in Theology* (New York: The Seabury

Press, 1972) presents a distinct notion of value, however, that goes beyond the centrality of the notion of being in *Insight*. Robert Doran has argued that in *Method* "even when the function of meaning that predominates is the cognitive function, the intention of being is an intention of what is valued as the true." He suggests, then, that "the intention of value, sublating the intention of being, is in effect the core of meaning (though this expression is not used)." Robert M. Doran, *Theology and the Dialectics of History* (Toronto: University of Toronto Press, 1990), 575-76.

³ Much scholarly work has been done to examine or to develop further the implications of Lonergan's understanding of historical process. I can offer only a few citations of these efforts here. On the development of Lonergan's thinking on the topic of history, see Michael Shute, *Origins of Lonergan's Notion of the Dialectic of History: A Study of Lonergan's Early Writings on History* (Lanham, Md.: University Press of America, 1993) and Frederick Crowe, *Lonergan* (Collegeville, Minn.: The Liturgical Press, 1992). For scholarship that builds on Lonergan's approach to history, see Doran, *Theology and the Dialectics of History*; Matthew Lamb, "The Social and Political Dimensions of Lonergan's Theology, in *Desires of the Human Heart*, ed. Vernon Gregson (New York: Paulist Press, 1988), 255-84; Lamb, *Solidarity with Victims: Toward a Theology of Social Transformation* (New York: Crossroad, 1982); Lamb, "Wilhelm Dilthey's Critique of Historical Reason and Bernard Lonergan's Meta-Methodology," in *Language Truth and Meaning*, ed. Philip McShane (Notre Dame, Ind.: University of Notre Dame Press, 1972),115-66; Frederick Lawrence, "Self-knowledge in History in Gadamer and Lonergan," in *Language Truth and Meaning*, 167-217.

⁴ Bernard Lonergan, "The Transition from a Classicist World-View to Historical-Mindedness," in *A Second Collection: Papers by Bernard J. F. Lonergan, S.J.*, ed. William F. J. Ryan and Bernard Tyrrell (London: Darton, Longman, & Todd, 1974), 8-10. In this essay, Lonergan states that "there is in my book *Insight* a general analysis of the dynamic structure of human history, as in my mimeographed text *De Verbo Incarnato* a thesis on the *lex crucis* that provides its strictly theological complement. The analysis distinguishes three components: progress, decline, and redemption," 7.

⁵ Lonergan, *Method in Theology*, 178.

⁶ On the dialectic of community, see Lonergan, *Insight*, 242-44. Interpretations of this idea vary. Matthew Lamb distinguishes the positive dynamism of "the radical tension of community" (i.e., the tension between spontaneous intersubjectivity and practical intelligence) from "the dialectic of community," which he describes as a tension that has become repressive, "alienating intersubjectivity and thwarting practical intelligence." Lamb, "The Social and Political Dimensions of Lonergan's Theology," *Desires of the Human Heart*, 268. On my reading, Robert Doran would include both types of tension within his understanding of Lonergan's "dialectic of community." The former represents what Doran understands as an "integral" dialectic and the latter a "distorted" one. See Doran, *Theology and the Dialectics of History*, 364-65.

[7] I am using the phrase "social situation" in a broader sense than Lonergan uses it in *Insight* or even in *Method*. In *Method* Lonergan identifies vital, social, cultural, personal, and religious values, 31-32. He defines social values as those related to the good of order which provides for the vital values (health, for example) of the whole community. Cultural values are those meanings and values that animate human living. At this point in the article, I am referring to "the social situation" as one that encompasses vital, social, and cultural values. I will go on to explore how personal value (that of the self-transcendent person as an originator of value) and religious value (the love of God) are key elements in the transformation of the social situation broadly conceived.

[8] Lonergan, *Insight*, 254-57.

[9] Ibid., 258.

[10] See, for instance, the work of Sallie McFague, especially *The Body of God: An Ecological Theology* (Minneapolis: Fortress Press, 1993) and *Super, Natural Christians* (Minneapolis: Fortress Press, 1997).

[11] Lonergan, *Method*, 53.

[12] Lonergan, *Insight*, 654.

[13] See Lonergan's discussion of the problem of liberation in *Insight*, 653-56, and his approach to the problem of evil in that same volume, 709-51.

[14] Lonergan, *Method*, 55.

[15] Ibid., 73. See also his remarks on this topic in two earlier writings, "Time and Meaning" (1962) and "The Analogy of Meaning" (1963) in *Collected Works of Bernard Lonergan*, ed. Robert C. Croken, Frederick E. Crowe, and Robert M. Doran, vol. 6, *Philosophical and Theological Papers 1958-1964* (Toronto: University of Toronto Press, 1996), 94-121 and 183-213, respectively.

[16] Lonergan, *Method*, 79.

[17] Lonergan, *Insight*, 237.

[18] M. Shawn Copeland, "Toward a Critical Christian Feminist Theology of Solidarity," in *Women and Theology*, ed. Mary Ann Hinsdale and Phyllis H. Kaminski (Maryknoll, N.Y.: Orbis Books, 1995), 3-38.

[19] See especially ibid., 27-33.

[20] Lonergan, *Method*, 78.

[21] For the use of Lonergan's ideas to develop an understanding of communication in relation to the human good, see Francisco Sierra-Gutierrez, "Communication: Mutual Self-Mediation in Context," *Communication and Lonergan* (Kansas City: Sheed & Ward, 1993), 269-93.

[22] Lonergan, "The Mediation of Christ in Prayer," *Philosophical and Theological Papers 1958-1964*, 162-63.

[23] Ibid., 172.

[24] Ibid.

[25] Lonergan, "Theology and Praxis," in *A Third Collection*, 196.

[26] Lonergan, "Third Lecture [on Religious Studies and Theology]: The Ongoing Genesis of Methods," in *A Third Collection*, 161.

[27] Lonergan, *Method*, 37.

[28] Ibid., 36.

[29] Lonergan, "Third Lecture [on Religious Studies and Theology]," in *A Third Collection*, 163.

[30] Edward Schillebeeckx, *Christ: The Experience of Jesus as Lord*, trans. John Bowden (New York: Crossroad, 1988), 817-21.

[31] Lonergan, "The Subject," in *A Second Collection*, 84.

[32] Bernard Lonergan, *De Verbo Incarnato* (Rome: Gregorian University, 1964).

[33] On Lonergan's Law of the Cross, see the work of William Loewe, such as "Toward a Responsible Contemporary Soteriology," in *Creativity and Method*, ed. Matthew Lamb (Milwaukee: Marquette University Press, 1981) and "Jesus, the Son of God," in *Desires of the Human Heart*, 182-200.

[34] Bernard Lonergan, "Openness and Religious Experience," in *Collected Works of Bernard Lonergan*, ed. Frederick E. Crowe and Robert M. Doran, vol. 4, *Collection* (Toronto: University of Toronto Press, 1988), 186.

[35] Ibid., 186-87.

[36] Ibid., 187.

[37] Lonergan, *Insight*, 647.

[38] Lonergan, "Healing and Creating in History," in *A Third Collection*, 100-109.

[39] This is not to say that grace is not operative in the creating vector as well.

[40] Paulo Freire, *Pedagogy of the Oppressed*, rev. ed., trans. Myra Bergman Ramos (New York: Continuum, 1993/1st English edition 1970). For connections between Freire and Lonergan see Doran, *Theology and the Dialectics of History*, 38-40.

[41] For a discussion of intellectual, moral, and religious conversion, see Lonergan's *Method*. On affective conversion, see Lonergan, "Natural Right and Historical Mindedness," in *A Third Collection*, 179. On psychic conversion, see Robert M. Doran, *Psychic Conversion and Theological Foundations: Toward a Reorientation of the Human Sciences* (Chico, Calif: Scholars Press, 1981) and his *Theology and the Dialectics of History*.

[42] Charles Davis, "Lonergan's Appropriation of the Concept of Praxis," *New Blackfriars* 62 (March 1981): 119.

[43] There have been quite a few studies in defense of the politically and socially engaged character and implications of Lonergan's work, but I will suggest here just a sampling. In addition to the work of Copeland, Doran, and Lamb already cited: Nancy Ring, "Sin and Transformation from a Systematic Perspective," *Chicago Studies* 23 (1984): 303-19; Frederick Lawrence, "Lonergan as a Political Theologian," in *Religion in Context*, ed. Timothy Fallon and Philip Boo Riley (Lanham, Md.: University Press of America, 1988); Frederick E. Crowe, "Bernard Lonergan and Liberation Theology," *Appropriating the Lonergan Idea*, ed. Michael Vertin (Washington, D.C.: The Catholic University of America Press, 1989), 116-26.

Part III

NEW SOURCES

The Priest in the Movie:
On the Waterfront as Historical Theology

James T. Fisher

In 1997 I published a book that opened with a verse from an 1860s' folk ballad, "Tom Dooley," a song that was revived to sudden and unexpected hit status by the Kingston Trio in 1958 and quickly became misidentified with a real-life Tom Dooley, the Irish-American Catholic folk hero also known as the jungle doctor of Laos. Scores of people had asked me in the course of my research on this other Tom Dooley: "Wasn't there a song about him?" In conflating my Dooley with the North Carolinian Confederate Army veteran and desperado immortalized in the ballad, they confirmed the centrality of popular culture artifacts to the modern American consciousness. Eventually I realized that the question—far from offering a humorous sidelight to the project—provided a central theme of the work itself, as it evolved into a study of celebrity sainthood, collective memory, and ethnoreligious politics.[1]

From "the man in the song" we turn now to "the priest in the movie," as my current work focuses on the efforts of John Corridan, a New York Jesuit and labor priest, to expose and topple the corrupt leadership of the International Longshoreman's Association (ILA), a union dominated in the early and middle years of the twentieth century by Irish and, in their separate sphere of influence, Italian American Catholics. The leadership of the ILA—in particular Joseph P. Ryan, the union's "President-for-life"—enjoyed very close ties with religious and political leaders in a region we will designate the "Catholic metropolis," a territory surrounding New York Harbor that included Staten Island, the coastal portions of Brooklyn, the West Side of Manhattan, and Hudson County, New Jersey, communities whose densely packed, heavily Catholic neighborhoods (over three-quarters of the inhabitants of Hudson County, for example, were Catholic) supplied the bulk of the ILA's rank and file. In the early and middle decades of the twentieth century, more than 90 percent of the union's members were Roman Catholic.[2]

In 1948 John Corridan launched a crusade to reform the ILA, which also, inevitably, challenged the time-honored ethos of the Catholic metropolis, an elaborate mosaic of ethnic communities that had been evolving since the middle of the nineteenth century. Father Corridan launched his mission armed mainly with a Jesuit mandate to bring Christian education to industrial workers, but he quickly expanded his apostolate, as we shall see, relying increasingly on vital contacts with secular reformers, investigative journalists, and even Hollywood film makers.[3]

For if the priest is John Corridan, the movie is, of course, *On the Waterfront*, winner of eight Academy Awards, including Best Picture for 1954. Father Corridan is portrayed in the film by Karl Malden, whose preparation for the role included frequent sojourns with the Jesuit to such waterfront establishments as Billy the Oysterman's, located not far from the Xavier Labor School on West 16th Street in Manhattan, where Corridan served as assistant director. Malden even wore Corridan's hat and coat during filming on the docks and streets of Hoboken in the cold late autumn of 1953. With the approval of his provincial, Corridan sold the rights to his story to Columbia Pictures and served as technical adviser on the film. He also obtained permission for shooting on the Hoboken docks from his friend Austin Tobin, the director of the New York Port Authority, and he enlisted the aid of other influential supporters of his ministry.[4]

John Corridan's role in the making of *On the Waterfront* extended far beyond mere logistical support. The film in fact originated in a collaboration between the Jesuit labor priest, a Protestant journalist, and a Jewish screenwriter. *On the Waterfront* represents a theological occasion, or captures a theological moment, if you prefer, whose meaning is embedded in a collaborative process that is less unlikely than we might normally imagine.

Historians often tend to view films simply as reflections of some empirical social reality that is more concretely real than the version presented on celluloid. In this sense a religious historian might approach a film—or any work of art—as a projection of some theological issue, say, that is always more authentically experienced in its original, unmediated version. It is my contention that the theological occasions enshrined in *On the Waterfront*, however, are products of the same kinds of relationships, conflicts, and tensions that also generate theological reflections in a pluralist society. At the same time, other elements in the film—peripheral to its creator's main concerns—invite us to re-examine some underlying historical and religious issues, specifically, the enduring resistance within the Catholic metropolis to threats of change emanating from both within and without its scrupulously observed boundaries.

On the Waterfront was directed by Elia Kazan from a script by Budd Schulberg, a novelist best known for his 1941 best-seller, *What Makes Sammy Run?* Schulberg first met John Corridan in 1950 in the course of gathering material for a screenplay he hoped to write on "some phase of the New York waterfront dock scandals." Schulberg had read "Crime on the Waterfront," Malcolm Johnson's Pulitzer-Prize winning 1948 series of exposés for the tabloid *New York Sun*, but only later did he learn that most of Johnson's material came from the voluminous files on waterfront corruption that John Corridan had compiled beginning in 1946, when he was assigned to the St. Francis Xavier Labor School in Manhattan.[5]

In 1936 the New York Jesuits had created an Institute of Social Science at Xavier High School designed to provide adult education in labor-management relations to a largely working-class local constituency. Under the directorship of a young Jesuit, Philip Carey, by 1941, the renamed Xavier Labor School was strategically located near the West Side docks and various manufacturing and wholesaling operations, and was not far from Union Square, a hotbed of socialist and communist fulminations against both capitalism and the church, which allegedly failed to speak out against economic and social injustice. According to Jesuit historian Joseph M. McShane, in the 1930s the order recognized the need for

> lay agents to bring about "the ultimate Christian reconstruction of [industrial] society." Therefore, through the labor schools they hoped to train leaders who, filled with "enthusiasm for Christ, and . . . unselfish zeal," and speaking "in the tongue of their fellows" could effectively infiltrate the labor movement and "bring Catholic doctrines and principles to bear" on union activities. In other words, the Jesuits felt that the primary goal of

their labor schools was the creation of an apostolic "fifth column" that could work within the labor movement to Christianize all of industrial society.[6]

The Jesuits were also armed with the landmark social encyclicals *Rerum Novarum* (1891) and *Quadregesimo Anno* (1931), and the growing American tradition of Catholic social action embodied in such groups as the Catholic Worker movement and the Association of Catholic Trade Unionists (ACTU), many of whose members worked very closely with Jesuit labor priests in New York and other industrial cities. The Jesuit labor schools, concludes Joseph M. McShane, were driven primarily by a religious mission to instill an "action-oriented" spirituality within the urban Catholic working class.[7]

Perhaps the best-known labor priest, John Corridan, was born in 1911 and grew up on Manhattan's Upper West Side. Like Phil Carey, whose father was a subway motorman, Corridan came from a working-class, Irish immigrant family. After his father, a New York policeman, died in 1921, Corridan worked to help support his mother and brothers while being educated at Ascension Parochial school and at the Jesuit's Regis High School. Corridan then went to work as a Wall Street office boy while attending NYU at night, but in 1931, after reading Rene Fullop Miller's *The Power and Secret of the Jesuits,* he applied and was accepted for admission into the Society of Jesus. Following studies in the novitiate at St. Andrew's-on-Hudson in New York, Corridan studied philosophy and economics at Saint Louis University, taught at Canisius College in Buffalo, and worked in the Crown Heights Labor School in Brooklyn before embarking on a four-year course in theology leading to his ordination in 1944.[8]

Shortly after Corridan was assigned to the Xavier School in 1946, Father Phil Carey placed him in charge of an apostolate to longshoremen. Corridan was not the first priest to grow deeply disturbed by the inhumane working conditions and union racketeering that pervaded the waterfront: Father John Monaghan of St. Mary's Church in Staten Island, the first ACTU chaplain, was a veteran advocate of dockworkers, while Msgr. Edward E. Swanstrom of the Brooklyn Diocesan Commission for Catholic Charities had exposed the plight of longshoremen in his 1938 study, *The Waterfront Labor Problem.* John Corridan was unique, however, in his role as a labor advocate who cultivated links to secular journalists and reformers, the key allies of his campaign.[9]

John Corridan first emerged as a public champion of waterfront insurgents in November, 1948, when he supported a wildcat strike of ILA members that coincided with the publication of Malcolm Johnson's spectacular exposés of waterfront corruption, of which Corridan was an ardent if unacknowledged collaborator. In a signed article appearing that same month in a more conventional vehicle, the Jesuit weekly *America*, Corridan condemned the "joint criminal neglect" of both the New York Shipping Association and the ILA leadership, against which elements of the rank and file were in more or less permanent rebellion. "The heart of the matter is the system of hiring along the waterfront," Corridan wrote of the notorious if time-honored "shapeup," whereby longshoremen were obliged to appear several times each day on a given dock, in hopes of being chosen for work by a hiring boss, an individual who—though technically employed by shippers—was generally a handpicked agent of union bosses. "Men are hired as if they were beasts of burden, part of the slave market of a pagan era," Corridan charged.[10]

Corridan's unpublicized but highly active collaboration with the Protestant journalist Malcolm Johnson resulted in his first meeting with Budd Schulberg in 1950 and led directly to the making of *On the Waterfront*. Johnson recalled that "after I'd talked to Father Corridan he got me emotionally involved in the plight of the longshoremen . . . He did the same thing to Budd Schulberg. He used both of us to accomplish his purpose—to clean up the waterfront." Schulberg later explained that Johnson had urged him to "go down to Xavier's and see Father John. He really knows the score." "Out of that meeting," by Corridan's recollection, "the movie *On the Waterfront* was born." Schulberg, noted Corridan, was fascinated by the story of a priest "acting as a protagonist for rank and file longshoremen rebelling against a corrupt social system. 'Budd,' I said, 'you can do a "Going My Way" with substance.' "[11]

Over many subsequent lunches at Billy the Oysterman's, Schulberg recalled, Corridan spoke

in vivid detail of the various mobs controlling different sections of the harbor, and of their multiple angles for illicit gain through control of the piers. . . . But I think his moral indignation was most aroused when he described the complicity of the stevedore and shipping companies who bribed and openly encouraged the underworld elements, and the compliance of the city politicians who were often in league with the dock bosses and their "respectable" protectors. "What hurts me," Father Corridan says, "is that some of these fellers profess to be Catholics and assume they can remain in good standing just by showing up for Mass every Sunday. And yet they think nothing of treating their fellow human beings like dirt every day in the week. They seem to forget that every man is precious in the eyes of our Lord and that He died for all of us, as brothers in Jesus Christ, and not just for the privileged few."[12]

The son of a prominent Hollywood film producer, Schulberg may have been Corridan's most devoted student. Schulberg later recalled that "Father Pete, as he was known, swore like the longshoremen and drank with them, but he gave me feelings about Christ that I never had before." "I listened intently to Father John, whose speech was a unique blend of Hell's Kitchen, baseball slang, an encyclopedic grasp of waterfront economics and an attack on man's inhumanity to man, based on the teachings of Christ as brought up to date in the papal encyclicals on the reconstruction of the social order. Long before I was ready to write either a novel or a film, Father Corridan and his rebel disciples in the mob-controlled International Longshoremen's Association had begun to obsess me." In a 1988 profile of Schulberg, a journalist reported: "For someone whose background is, by his own definition, Jewish humanist, Schulberg displays an unusual understanding of Catholic teachings. Some people . . . thought he was converting to Catholicism when he wrote the screenplay and novel, he said." He did not, but he speaks with authority on the church's social teachings. By his own admission Schulberg became "a kind of mouthpiece" for Corridan and the ILA insurgents, "describing their struggle in the *New York Times Magazine*, the *Saturday Evening Post* and *Commonweal*. The film project became a potential weapon on the side of social justice."[13]

As Corridan later wrote, of his collaboration with Johnson and Schulberg, "the triangle was complete but not the movie." Renowned director Elia Kazan shared Schulberg's enthusiasm for the film, but the project was repeatedly turned down by major studios before independent producer S. P. Eagle (Sam Spiegel) finally made a deal with Columbia Pictures; shooting commenced in Hoboken late in 1953. "*On the Waterfront* was a movie born of laughter and anguish,"

Corridan recalled, for all the collaborators "are friends of mine in the real waterfront struggle." *On the Waterfront* traces the moral transformation of ex-prizefighter and sometime-longshoreman "Terry Malloy," played by Marlon Brando. Terry's brother, "Charlie the Gent" (played by Rod Steiger), is the brainy top lieutenant of "John Skelly," better known as Johnny Friendly (Lee J. Cobb), a ruthless gangster who controls a powerful local branch of an unnamed longshoreman's union.[14]

As the film opens Friendly dispatches Terry Malloy to coax a dissident longshoreman, Joey Doyle, to the roof of his apartment building, from whence he is promptly hurled to his death by mob enforcers. Though Terry had believed Joey—who shared his passion for pigeon racing—was merely to be worked over by the thugs, his pangs of conscience are readily salved by Johnny Friendly, who promises Terry a coveted and largely phantom job in the loft of a dockside warehouse. In a pivotal scene, Joey Doyle's sister, Edie (Eva Marie Saint), desperately seeking the identity of her brother's murderers, appears on a dock controlled by Johnny Friendly just as a shapeup is being called. She is soon joined by Father Pete Barry (Corridan's nickname in the Society was "Pete"), whom Edie had assailed on the previous night after the priest performed the last rites over her brother's body. When Father Barry told Edie he'd be in the church if she needed him, she had cried out: "Was there ever a saint who hid in the church?"[15]

Prompted by Edie's challenge, Father Barry had come down to the waterfront "to take a good look for myself" at his true parish. The two watch in dismay as dozens of longshoremen grimly face another shapeup in which only a small number of their peers are chosen for work (the shapeup depicted in this scene ends in a melee when the hiring boss, frightened by the crush of desperate men, tosses a handful of metal tokens in the air: the precious "tabs" indicating a longshoreman has been hired for the day). Father Barry then approaches a small group of dejected men to ask why they accept such inhumane treatment. On being informed that the union local is controlled by gangsters, and there is no safe haven for dissidents to air their grievances, Father Barry offers the "bottom of the church" to the incredulous workers.[16]

This scene truly represents a theological moment, as a product of the collaboration between John Corridan, Malcolm Johnson, Budd Schulberg, and, of course, director Elia Kazan, the latter three non-Catholics. Along with subsequent scenes in the film, it represents the most effective depiction of Father John Corridan's ministry ever produced. The film is more powerful than accounts of Corridan's work found in Catholic publications, and presents the priest's views more effectively than did Corridan himself, who struggled for years to win converts to his reform crusade at the parish and neighborhood level.

The scene is framed by Father Pete Barry's proclamation, "This is my parish," and his pledge that the beleaguered longshoremen would find a safe haven in "the bottom of the church" to air their grievances against the corrupt union leadership. In claiming the entire waterfront as his parish, Father Barry invoked the desires for an integral Catholicism, for a faith without boundaries, themes so pervasive in the Catholic revival and myriad apostolates of Catholic Action from the 1930s through the 1950s. In offering the "bottom of the church" to the oppressed workers, Father Barry implicitly turned the customary architecture of religious authority on its head, as if in anticipation of a looming "preferential option" for the poor and dispossessed. (This meeting scene was shot at Sts. Peter and Paul Church, located at Third and River Streets in Hoboken. The Hoboken locations were highly effective in presenting to viewers an unfamiliar urban landscape: since the New York skyline was visible in several scenes, the film was clearly set somewhere else; in an indeterminate urban space that evoked the "strangeness" of the Catholic metropolis).[17]

In 1989 Budd Schulberg made explicit his intentions for the film and presumably those of Corridan, who had died in 1984. "Today it's called liberation theology," he remarked, in paying tribute to his fallen Jesuit ally and inspiration. "The waterfront priests were the forerunners." *On the Waterfront* clearly invites a reading that focuses primarily on Father Barry's struggle to introduce the tenets of Catholic social justice to the waterfront, along with the "action-oriented," working-class spirituality fostered by the Jesuit labor priests. At the same time, however, one need not be in thrall to the methods of cultural studies to observe that elements in the scene we viewed together undermine the desires of Father Barry—and his creators—for an integral Catholicism on the waterfront. For example, in the shapeup scene Pop Doyle, Edie's longshoreman father, doffs his cap to Father Barry before reproaching the priest: "I'm surprised with you, Father, if you don't mind my sayin' so. Lettin' her see things ain't fit for the eyes of a decent girl." While Pop Doyle's gesture conveys the deference accorded to priests in the Catholic metropolis, his words reinforce the clear boundaries separating the rank and file from the clergy.[18]

Although this tension may ultimately be resolved in the film, on the waterfront of history Father John Corridan was faced with the much more daunting challenge of converting the entire culture of the Catholic metropolis, of redrawing its boundaries and replacing the codes of immigrant devotional Catholicism with those drawn from a comparatively modern idiom of Catholic social justice. This struggle is the subject of my larger study, "Covering the Waterfront: Culture and Ideology in the Catholic Metropolis, 1936-1960." The Xavier Labor School Papers at Fordham University, the main archival source for this work, contain substantial evidence that many rank-and-file Catholics along the waterfront resisted Corridan's challenge to the time-honored code of waterfront life, including its separation of religious life from labor politics.

In the scene described above, Father Pete Barry asks the downtrodden longshoremen, "What about your union?" As though in anticipation of the labor priest's desire to intervene, a correspondent calling himself "the son of a longshoreman" wrote to Corridan in May, 1953:

> "My father was a longshoreman and raised seven (7) children and in Catholic schools. We did not starve, we were well brought up, my father worked under the shapeup system and things were not as bad as in the papers. I see no reason for making such a big time over the I.L.A. affairs. J. P. Ryan may have overstepped a bit— all the fellows do when they get a bit of power . . . Father for your information Politics and Labor have always had their "bad boys" and strange to say a great many of them have been Roman Catholics . . . Please now for the benefit of all of us who try to follow in the teaching of our religion back out of this gracefully. A great many members of our I.L.A. are good living Catholics and I think it is a disgrace to have Mr. Connolly [Patrick "Packy" Connolly was executive vice-president of the ILA] challenging you or you challenging him.[19]

Another Catholic critic urged Corridan to "1. Confine yourself to the Church of God and what it represents. 2. Teach the law of God, that's what you went to the seminary for. 3. Immediately abolish your self-appointment as the waterfront Priest, and savior of the waterfront." Yet another correspondent wrote: "All I can say as a Catholic why don't you confine your duties to the Church what a laugh the Reds must have got out of you. You a Priest trying to hurt a man (Ryan) who goes to Mass and also pays many a Bill for the Guardian Angel Church."[20]

To be sure, Corridan was deeply admired, even revered, by a small cadre of union insurgents, including Arthur "Brownie" Browne and Johnny Dwyer, a World War Two veteran who led a reform movement in ILA Local 895 on Manhattan's Lower West Side. But Corridan's mentor, Father Phil Carey, acknowledged in 1984 that Corridan was "betrayed by some of the dockers he trusted . . . only Arthur Browne came back to thank him for all that he had done" [after Corridan was removed from his waterfront apostolate in 1957].[21]

The sources of Corridan's ultimate disappointment are beyond the scope of this paper, but there were numerous reasons why many waterfront Catholics viewed his crusade with suspicion—some involving union politics narrowly construed, others rooted in the ILA leadership's appeal to fear and its willingness to employ tactics of intimidation—but the fundamental issue concerned the threat of changes imposed from outside the boundaries of the Catholic metropolis. At the height of a 1951 wildcat strike by longshoremen, Corridan had made a dramatic appearance at ILA Local 791 in Chelsea, offering a brief and simple prayer: "God grant that our government may order us back to work in honor. May God protect and preserve us this day." Three years later, shortly after the ILA was expelled from the American Federation of Labor over its corrupt practices, Corridan addressed a group of longshoremen at a Manhattan hotel, in hopes of winning their support for a new union under the auspices of the AFL.[22]

"Why as a priest have I been interested in seeing you get a New Deal?" asked Corridan, who went on to explain: "The New Deal that I have sought for you comes closer to the Christian ideal. It will give you a better opportunity to live reasonably happy and secure both within your family and on your job at the docks. It will give you a better chance to save your souls." Corridan's invocation of the New Deal was sure to arouse a strong reaction in the early 1950s. While voters in the Catholic metropolis—like Catholic voters nationwide—had strongly backed Franklin D. Roosevelt in his four successful presidential campaigns—they opposed programs that threatened to impose governmental control over their family lives and, to at least some extent, the workplace. The intense Catholic opposition to a proposed constitutional amendment banning child labor in the late 1930s symbolized these concerns. The Catholic press was "overwhelmingly against the amendment," while all eight of New York State's bishops came out against the measure in 1937. Now, in the early 1950s, the popularity of Senator Joe McCarthy's anti-communist crusade rekindled suspicions that the New Deal had been socialist in orientation; moreover, the emerging social justice tradition that closely linked such figures as Msgr. John A. Ryan to Roosevelt's New Deal had always co-existed uneasily with Hudson County's Hague machine and other Catholic-dominated political organizations along the waterfront.[23]

For all of these reasons, John Corridan faced a tremendous challenge in seeking to close the gap between Catholic social theory and waterfront practice. "The two most important things in your lives are your families and your jobs," he told longshoremen in 1954. "The two places where you will save or lose your souls," he concluded, echoing Pius XI's *Quadragesimo Anno*, "are within the family and on the job." In the weeks leading up to the election between the AFL and the ILA for control of the longshoremen's union, Corridan "was actively on the stump . . . campaigning for an A.F. of L. triumph." The ILA narrowly won re-certification after a bitter struggle. *On the Waterfront* opened in New York theaters several weeks after the May 26, 1954, election. John Corridan always believed that had the movie been released before the election, the outcome would have been different, a view echoed by Charles R. Morris, who wrote in *American Catholic*: "Longshoremen thronged to see the movie, and it almost certainly would have swung the election against the I.L.A." Others have noted, however, that many dockworkers were none too pleased to see their trade depicted as a cesspool of corruption and gangland violence. *On the Waterfront* did not resolve the conflict between Catholic reformers and the waterfront's old guard; it simply provided moviegoers across the nation with a fleeting glimpse of a largely alien world.[24]

In his tireless effort to transform the ethos of the Catholic metropolis, John Corridan seemingly enjoyed the great advantage of being himself a product of the "old neighborhood," unlike secular reformers and many prominent Catholic exponents of social justice, including Dorothy Day. Yet the collaborative process of constructing the Father Pete Barry character for *On the Waterfront* revealed the vulnerable nature of Corridan's role and recalls the broader Catholic struggle for cultural authority in postwar America. The actor Karl Malden recalled that Corridan "begged me, 'Karl, don't play me like a priest, play me like a man.' Here was a tough, hard-boiled individual who told me, 'I was born in this neighborhood. When I was growing up there were two ways to go. Become a priest or a hood.' " Malden concluded, "He had become the one, although in many ways, he had the personality of the other, and he had stayed in the neighborhood to try to bring the two forces together by teaching." Yet we need to carefully interrogate the sources of Father Barry's persona, to determine the ways in which his character was shaped to fit various expectations of just how a waterfront priest would look.[25]

For openers, most residents of Corridan's Upper West Side neighborhood had become neither hoods nor priests but were hard-working members of the urban working class. Corridan's plea to Malden may have reflected a personal concern, but it also evoked longstanding ambiguities in the representation of the American priesthood, ambiguities often generated by Catholics—as in Corridan's case— as well as by others. Screenwriter Budd Schulberg later confessed to his own reservations over scripting a priestly character. "I was approaching the phenomenon of waterfront priests with a certain blindness. You might even call it prejudice . . . Isn't there always the danger of religious demagoguery such as clouded the career of Father Coughlin?" Whenever Catholic figures—and Catholic themes—engage the discourse of American popular culture these kinds of uneasy relationships almost always ensue, as though in the very act of collaboration with secular media a new cultural form is generated, albeit one that mirrors the wider relationship of Catholicism and American society.[26]

Corridan's dilemma was further complicated by the existence of a rival waterfront priest, Msgr. John J. O'Donnell, the pastor of Guardian Angel Church, the Shrine Church of the Sea, located at Tenth Avenue and Twenty-First Street in Manhattan, nearer to the actual waterfront than St. Xavier's location several blocks to the southeast. Msgr. O'Donnell, who was widely known as "Taxi Jack" by priests of the archdiocese, was the chaplain of the Port of New York and a close associate of his parishioner, ILA President Joseph P. Ryan. In an authorized history of the union published in 1966, author Maud Russell sharply criticized John Corridan, claiming that "he admitted that he had never seen the hold of a ship, nor suffered any jeers from dock gangsters" (contrary to the depiction of Pete Barry in *On the Waterfront* who, in a celebrated scene, is assaulted by thugs while delivering his "Christ is in the shapeup" speech over the body of a dissident long-shoremen killed by union gangsters). " 'I viewed the waterfront very infrequently," Russell quotes Corridan, "except for shooting some publicity photos on the dock." In sharp contrast to Father Corridan, Russell continued, "We must look at the record of the Right Rev. Msgr. John J. O'Donnell ... If any man can be called the waterfront priest, the title must go to Msgr. O'Donnell. His unceasing efforts have brought him nothing but respect and loyalty from longshoremen, their families and neighbors."[27]

"I have a deep and abiding affection," declared Msgr. O'Donnell, "for men who labor because, once upon a time, I labored and paid my way through college and seminary, by really the sweat of my brow and I am proud of it. I have always had the firm conviction that problems of labor should be settled by those who know how, by experienced labor men, by men who have come up the hard way and through learned experience." When Joseph P. Ryan was indicted for misappropriation of union funds in 1953, Msgr. O'Donnell responded that Ryan was a personal friend and added: "He keeps his hands off the spiritual things of my church and I keep my hands out of his business."[28]

Msgr. O'Donnell especially enjoyed hosting communion breakfasts that brought together leading figures from labor and political circles. John Corridan astutely recognized that these seemingly benign ritual gatherings served to reaffirm the symbiotic relationship between the leadership of the ILA, Democratic Party bosses, and prominent clerics within the New York archdiocese. In his sharp critique of this traditional institution, Corridan cited the admonition of Pius XI: "For there are some who, while exteriorly faithful to the practice of their religion, yet in the field of labor and industry, in the professions, trade, and business, permit a deplorable cleavage in their conscience and live a life too little in conformity with the clear principles of justice and Christian charity. Such lives are a scandal to the weak, and to the malicious a pretext to discredit the church." "If religion is on the decline as a moral influence in the lives of many people," Corridan concluded, "breakfasts such as these, as much as the corrupt conditions on the waterfront, are a cause."[29]

Corridan's opponents found him an elusive adversary, given his neighborhood credentials and his stature as a Jesuit. While ILA historian Maud Russell branded him a publicity hound who never saw a

real pier, Msgr. John J. O'Donnell, at the height of the 1951 wildcat
strike, reported to archdiocesan officials that Corridan "had been working every other day along the waterfront, frequently as a longshoreman, discarding his clerical garb, and while there had engaged in fisti-
cuffs with various characters." It was further alleged that Corridan
had started the 1951 strike! Corridan believed that the charges had
been instigated by Joseph P. Ryan and William J. "Big Bill"
McCormack, a self-made waterfront entrepreneur and prominent
Catholic layman recently publicly identified by Corridan as the "Mr.
Big" who allegedly controlled numerous waterfront rackets from behind the scenes of his trucking and stevedoring firms. The charges
against Corridan, from whatever source, resulted in a November 1951
meeting between Corridan, his provincial, and New York's Francis
Cardinal Spellman, who was apparently persuaded of the falsity of
O'Donnell's charges, though rumors quickly spread along the waterfront that Corridan had been silenced by the cardinal.[30]

If Corridan's Catholic enemies were unable to locate properly his
role on the waterfront, his non-Catholic allies and collaborators
struggled in their own way with the "foreignness" of the Catholic
metropolis. In the scene discussed above, when Father Pete Barry asks
the longshoremen why they accept such inhumane treatment, one man
explains: "The waterfront's tougher, father—like it ain't part of
America." But if the waterfront was not part of America, then neither
was the whole of the Catholic metropolis, a charge that had been made
implicitly for decades not just by nativists but by reformist critics of
the Hague machine, of Tammany Hall, and indeed of the ILA. Crusading journalists and reformers often used such terms as "feudal"
and "medieval" to describe the ethnopolitical geography of the communities ringing the waterfront.[31]

If the waterfront was non-American, then so too was the elabo-
rately devotional Catholicism that had flourished there for generations.
In 1951 the renowned journalist Joseph Mitchell wrote of Italian-
American baymen laying nets in New York Harbor: "Some of them
tack saints' pictures and miraculous medals and scapular medals and
little evil-eye amulets on the walls of their pilothouses." While the
spirituality of Italian-Americans on the waterfront differed in many
respects from that of the Irish-Americans, these groups, like so many
American Catholics, shared a deeply Marian piety. Yet the Jesuit historian Joseph McShane acknowledged that labor priests "focused their

energies almost exclusively on the development of devotions to St. Joseph and the holy family as a family unit. In light of the fact that Mary played such an important role in the devotional lives of most Catholics, it is surprising that she received so little attention from the labor priests."[32]

Father John Corridan's involvement in the production of *On the Waterfront* did not extend far into matters of characterization, with the exception, naturally, of Father Pete Barry, who is transformed during the course of the film into a fearless advocate of a democratic union that can only be achieved by recourse to external judicial authority. The film's creators were not concerned with the representation of working-class Catholic spirituality: the film reprises standard notions about ethnicity (Italian-Americans are portrayed as union goons, while the Irish—apart from the ruthless Johnny Friendly and the upwardly mobile Charlie "the Gent" Malloy, Terry's older brother—are depicted as hapless and docile when they are not talking about whiskey) and the gendered character of religiosity (Pop Doyle continually attempts to send his college-student daughter Edie "back to the Sisters where you belong").

Father Pete Barry, like his inspiration, John Corridan, invests his faith in secular elites as the vehicle for bringing social justice to the waterfront. Corridan hoped that through his cooperation not just with film makers but with reform-minded columnists like Murray Kempton, social critics such as Daniel Bell, and officials of the Waterfront Commission of the Port of New York—a watchdog agency created in 1953—a rationalized, regulated, and efficient waterfront would result, to the benefit of tens of thousands of longshoremen and their families. This ideological posture is reflected in Father Pete Barry's "Christ is in the shape-up" speech in *On the Waterfront*, which was adapted from a talk Corridan had given not to dockworkers but to members of a Jersey City chapter of the Knights of Columbus ("it was a tactical move oblique to outsiders and observers unfamiliar with the intricate social organization of Roman Catholicism" wrote New York journalist Joe Doyle in an obituary of Corridan. "The speech was a signal for longshoremen who were fed up to start coming around Xavier Labor School for strategy sessions").[33]

"Some people think the Crucifixion only took place on Calvary," intones Father Barry in *On the Waterfront*, while longshoremen and union leaders look on in varying poses of awe and disdain. "They better wise up. Taking Joey Doyle's life to stop him from testifying is a crucifixion—Dropping a sling on Kayo Dugan because he was ready to spill his guts tomorrow—that's a crucifixion. Every time the mob puts the crusher on a good man—tries to stop him from doing his duty as a citizen—it's a crucifixion."[34]

Barry/Corridan's "Christ of the shapeup" speech—with its clear focus on specific reforms—recalls in some respects the Protestant Social Gospel movement of the early twentieth century, but the speech is also thoroughly grounded in the christology of the social encyclicals and the emerging tradition of the Jesuit labor schools. It is not the speech but the reaction to it that is so jarring in *On the Waterfront*: in the midst of his peroration Barry is splattered with fruit, then bloodied by a can tossed by one of Johnny Friendly's henchmen as the more sympathetic workers passively look on. Maud Russell, in her otherwise unreliably partisan history of the ILA, plausibly claimed that "those who know the temper of New York's Catholic longshoremen found this scene ludicrous" (her contention that they also found "the whole film preposterous," while debatable, is not wholly unfounded).[35]

The "Christ is in the shapeup" scene from *On the Waterfront* offers the most powerful representation of modern Catholic social teaching ever presented to a national audience, but the film simultaneously features stereotypical portrayals of ethnic, working-class Catholicism. Although John Corridan was the central mediator between the world of the waterfront and the film world, his own tenuous stature within the Catholic metropolis was far too complex an issue to be captured on celluloid. In light of the Jesuits' post-conciliar stress on "enculturation" in dealing with "non-Western" peoples (a notion clearly rooted in the oldest traditions of the Society) it is perhaps ironic that Corridan's cultural dilemma was wholly embedded in his relationship with the most complex and extensive Roman Catholic community ever witnessed in North America. As a product of that community who had developed a counter-cultural ideological stance, Corridan, in his collaborations with reformers, film makers, and longshoremen alike, naturally overlooked the cultural contradictions inherent in his own insurgent posture.

On the Waterfront was a remarkably successful film: in 1997 the American Film Institute ranked it eighth on its list of the one hundred greatest American movies. It also made a deep impact; as one of the film's harshest critics acknowledged: "the public took it seriously."

The film was lauded in both the secular and Catholic press, with critics for the latter duly noting its dramatic spiritual as well as esthetic power. Before long, however, the film's legacy became mired in recriminations directed at director Kazan and screenwriter Schulberg, both of whom had "named names" as friendly witnesses testifying before the House Un-American Activities Committee. The film's historical context—especially John Corridan's role as a crusading labor priest—has been largely neglected by scholars.[36]

Yet as Budd Schulberg has insisted for decades, Corridan "was the inspiration for our film of *On the Waterfront*, every word spoken by his prototype in that picture came straight from the mouth of this straight-talking waterfront priest whose contribution to Christian service through social justice must never be forgotten." Approaching certain films and the products of other relevant cultural forms not as mere artifacts but—as in the case of *On the Waterfront*—embodiments of theological desire, we might help open paths to collective remembering.[37]

Notes

[1] James T. Fisher, *Dr. America: The Lives of Thomas A. Dooley, 1927-1961* (Amherst : University of Massachusetts Press, 1997).

[2] For one illustration of the pervasiveness of Catholicism on the waterfront, see Bill Farrell, S.J., to "Pete" Corridan, Box 10, folder 2, Xavier Institute of Industrial Relations Papers, Fordham University Archives. Father Farrell discusses with Corridan recent requests by tugboat workers of the Moran fleet that he celebrate a mass aboard a tug.

[3] The most detailed treatment of Corridan's work is Allen Raymond, *Waterfront Priest* (New York: Holt, 1955), essentially a collaboration between Corridan and Raymond, a veteran New York journalist. The best historical overview of labor issues along the New Jersey-New York waterfront is Vernon H. Jensen, *Strife on the Waterfront: The Port of New York Since 1945* (Ithaca: Cornell University Press, 1974).

[4] Raymond, *Waterfront Priest*, 136.

[5] Malcolm Johnson's "Crime on the Waterfront" series ran for twenty-four installments in the *New York Sun* between November 8, and December 10, 1948.

[6] Joseph M. McShane, S.J., " 'The Church Is Not for the Cells and the Caves': The Working Class Spirituality of the Jesuit Labor Priests," *U. S. Catholic Historian* 9 (Summer, 1990): 289-90.

[7] McShane, "The Church Is Not for the Cells and the Caves," 290; for an alternative interpretation of the labor schools see Peter McDonough, *Men Astutely Trained: A History of the Jesuits in the American Century* (New York: Free Press;

Toronto: Maxwell Macmillan Canada; New York: Maxwell Macmillan International, 1992), 98-118, 309-13.

[8] Raymond, *Waterfront Priest*, 4-5.

[9] Edward E. Swanstrom, *The Waterfront Labor Problem: A Study in Decasualization and Unemployment Insurance* (New York: Fordham University Press, 1938); see also "Priests on the Waterfront," Chapter Sixteen in Malcolm Johnson, *Crime on the Labor Front* (New York: McGraw-Hill, 1950).

[10] John M. Corridan, "Longshoremen's Case," *America* 80 (November 20, 1948): 176-78.

[11] Malcolm Johnson quoted in a British newspaper, the *Catholic Herald* (August 6, 1954); Budd Schulberg, "Introduction" to Raymond, *Waterfront Priest*, x; John M. Corridan, unpublished manuscript, Box 11, folder 41, XIIR Papers, Fordham.

[12] Schulberg, "Introduction" to *Waterfront Priest*, xi-xii.

[13] Budd Schulberg, *On the Waterfront: The Final Shooting Script* (Hollywood: S. French, 1980), 143; *New York Times*, April 26, 1987; *Newsday*, October 25, 1988; *New York Times*, September 14, 1994.

[14] Corridan, unpublished manuscript, Box 11, folder 41, XIIR Papers, Fordham.

[15] Schulberg, *On the Waterfront*, 12; the published script is not identical with the filmed version of Schulberg's screenplay: a comparison reveals numerous alterations made by the performers in the film. I have chosen to cite the published version both because it is readily accessible and because it represents an earlier stage of development of the project and thus may reflect more directly on John Corridan's tutelage of Budd Schulberg.

[16] Schulberg, *On the Waterfront*, 29-36.

[17] For accounts of the making of *On the Waterfront*, see Karl Malden, *When Do I Start?* (New York: Simon & Schuster, 1997), 236-46; Elia Kazan, *A Life* (New York: Knopf, 1988), 514-29.

[18] *Los Angeles Times*, December 30, 1988; Schulberg, *On the Waterfront*, 34.

[19] "The Son of a Longshoreman" to Rev. John M. Corridan, Box 11, folder 1, XIIR Papers, Fordham.

[20] Unsigned letters to John M. Corridan, n.d., Box 11, folder 3, and Box 11, folder 1, XIIR Papers, Fordham.

[21] Philip Carey, S.J., to Msgr. George Higgins, July 27, 1984, Box 12, folder 4, XIIR Papers, Fordham.

[22] Raymond, *Waterfront Priest*, 149.

[23] John M. Corridan, typescript of speech, February 1, 1954, Box 11, folder 30, XIIR Papers, Fordham; George Q. Flynn, *American Catholics and the Roosevelt Presidency, 1932-1936* (Lexington, Ky: University of Kentucky Press, 1968), 108-117.

[24] Corridan speech, February 1, 1954; Raymond, *Waterfront Priest*, 250; Charles R. Morris, *American Catholic: The Saints and Sinners Who Built America's Most Powerful Church* (New York: Times Books, 1997), 217.

[25] Malden, *When Do I Start?*, 241.

[26] Schulberg, "Introduction" to *Waterfront Priest*, x.

[27] Maud Russell, *Men along the Shore* (New York: Brussel & Brussel, 1966), 138-39.

[28] Ibid.; John C. Carey to Editor, *New York World-Telegram and Sun*, May 2, 1953, manuscript in Box 11, folder 3, XIIR Papers, Fordham.

[29] Raymond, *Waterfront Priest*, 46-49.

[30] Ibid.; cf. John J. McMahon, S.J. to John M. Corridan, S.J., November 6, 1951, Box 10, folder 1, XIIR Papers, Fordham.

[31] Schulberg, *On the Waterfront*, 36.

[32] Joseph Mitchell, *Up in the Old Hotel and Other Stories* (New York: Vintage Books, 1993), 473-74; McShane, "The Church Is Not for the Cells and the Caves," 296.

[33] Joe Doyle, Obituary of John M. Corridan in *Chelsea-Clinton News*, July 26, 1984. For a partial listing of the journalists with whom Corridan shared information on the ILA and waterfront crime, see Raymond, *Waterfront Priest*, 136. For the Waterfront Commission, see Peter B. Levy, "The Waterfront Crime Commission of the Port of New York: A History and Appraisal," *Industrial and Labor Relations Review* 42 (July, 1989): 508-22.

[34] Schulberg, *On the Waterfront*, 79.

[35] Russell, *Men along the Shore*, 138.

[36] Ibid; for the standard analysis linking *On the Waterfront* to Kazan and Schulberg's decision to testify, see Victor Navasky, *Naming Names* (New York: Viking Press, 1980), 199-222, 239-46; many critics have noted the religious symbolism in the film, while ignoring the substantive influence of Catholic social teaching. Peter Biskind, *Seeing Is Believing: How Hollywood Taught Us to Stop Worrying and Love the Fifties* (New York: Pantheon Books, 1983), 174-76, characterizes Father Pete Barry as a manipulative, "ruthless crusader" serving the ends of a "corporate liberal" social order. David Shipman, in *The Story of Cinema: A Complete Narrative History from the Beginnings to the Present* (New York: St. Martin Press, 1982), 876, refers simply to "a rather dotty Karl Malden as the local priest."

[37] Budd Schulberg to Norman Weissman, October 4, 1984, Box 12, folder 4, XIIR Papers, Fordham.

Revealing Resistance: Luise Rinser's Celebration and Suffering

Pamela Kirk

"Today I know that there is no future which can be severed from the past to be rendered independent. I even know that strictly speaking the past does not exist. The past is locked into and inseparably united with the present."[1]

Veterans revisit the beaches of Normandy. Anne Frank's Dutch friend, Miep Gies, publishes her memoir about helping the family in hiding. Swiss banks agree to offer restitution to descendants of Holocaust victims of money deposited during the Third Reich. At an exhibit of the Boston Museum, a Monet "Waterlily" is discovered to be the confiscated property of a Jewish collector. Each of these incidents testifies to the intersection of past and present. Each points to the unresolved nature of conflicts resulting from the Nazi past. The Vatican has recently demonstrated an awareness of the ghosts of the Third Reich and the necessity of exorcizing them. In March of 1998 in an accompanying letter to "We Remember: A Reflection on the 'Shoah',", John Paul II wrote of his "fervent hope" that the document would "help to heal the wounds of past misunderstandings and injustices" and "enable memory to play its necessary part of shaping a future in which the unspeakable iniquity of the Shoah will never again be possible."[2] The report itself calls for a "moral and religious memory" and appeals to Christians to be aware of the "tormented" history of relations between the Christians and the Jews. It admits that "the balance of these relations over 2,000 years has been quite negative." This relatively short document was the final culmination of meetings between Vatican officials and Jewish leaders that began in 1987 and were interrupted after "tensions developed" upon Pope John Paul II's meeting with Austrian President Kurt Waldheim, known to have been a Nazi officer.[3] The response of the Jewish members of the Catholic-Jewish Liaison Committee to the report was less than enthusiastic.[4] However, as an indication of the desire for the two communities to work together they issued a short joint statement, "Care for the Environment: A Religious Act."[5]

It is hard not to be struck by the tentative nature of the exchange just described, when contrasted with the millennial framework in which the Pope had placed the pronouncements, and before which the church "encourages her sons and daughters to purify their hearts through repentance of past errors and infidelities." The contrast is even more striking in the official admission by the French episcopate about the response of the Catholic church in France during the Nazi occupation:

> For the most part, those in authority in the church, caught up in a loyalism and docility which went far beyond the obedience traditionally accorded civil authorities, remained stuck in conformity, prudence and abstention. This was dictated in part by their fear of reprisals against the church's activities and youth movements. They failed to realize that the church, called at that moment to play the role of defender within a social body that was falling apart, did in fact have considerable power and influence, and that in the face of the silence of other institutions, its voice could have echoed loudly by taking a definitive stand against the irreparable.[6]

Along with the Vatican's recent call for reflection and penance in conjunction with the behavior of Christians during the Nazi era has come the celebration of men and women who suffered heroically for their resistance to the Nazis. The Vatican has beatified the Franciscan Pater Maximilian Kolbe, who volunteered to go to the Hungerbunker and starve to death, replacing a man with children. It has beatified Franz Jaegerstaetter, a pacifist farmer. Some of the people singled out in themselves represent aspects of the problematic and unsolved nature of the issues raised by the Third Reich's ideology. The recent canonization of Edith Stein is a case in point. Stein, a converted Jew, philosopher, and Carmelite nun fled to Holland with her sister, where the two of them were eventually arrested and deported to the gas chambers at Auschwitz. Jews have questioned whether she is a Christian martyr or a martyred Jew. More controversial still is the recent beatification of Croatian Cardinal Archbishop of Zabgreb, Alojzije Stepanic, who was known to have been a Nazi sympathizer at the beginning of the Nazi occupation.[7]

It would be unfair and untruthful to ignore examples of resistance out of a misplaced skepticism or even cynicism about the resilience of Christian faith and the human spirit.[8] Coming as they do alongside the less than adequate response of the Vatican hierarchy to the institutional church's relationship to Nazi laws and policies, these commemorations raise questions: Do they represent a capitulation to the temptation to create an idealized view of individual Catholics under the peculiar stress of the Nazi totalitarian regime? Do they mean to imply that the heroic virtue of a few mitigate the failure of the institution in a time of crisis? Furthermore, do we know to what extent the resistance of the individuals in question was shaped by their Catholicism?

From another perspective, the current focus on Catholic resisters can also be viewed as symptomatic of the need to break open and explore the memories and histories of those who have resisted. What was the nature of their resistance to a totalitarian regime with its glorification of a pagan Germanic past, with its systematic plan to eliminate "inferior" races? If David Goldhagen's book *Hitler's Willing Executioners* has raised in a provocative way the issue of compliance with the persecutions of the Jews at the level of ordinary people, can we not speak meaningfully of a level of non-compliance or resistance in the daily lives of individuals?[9] Though an examination of German novelist and essayist Luise Rinser's life and work during the Third Reich will not provide an answer to all of the above questions, it will provide a living example of the life of an "ordinary" person who consistently refused to assent to the demands of the Nazi legal system.

Rinser (b. 1911) was first brought to my attention in 1995 because of the publication of her letters to Karl Rahner, which revealed Rahner's passionate attachment to her.[10] My subsequent research has found her a fascinating and controversial Catholic writer. Her novels of the fifties and sixties that dealt with religious themes in the context of Catholic Bavaria led her to be classified as a moralizing Catholic novelist by the left, while her leftist public political engagement for peace and nuclear disarmament made her too far to the left for many of the Catholic establishment. In the letters Rinser wrote to Rahner in the 1960s she complains that she has never been invited to read in her "hometown," Catholic Munich. Because she was intent on developing her own novelistic style while remaining in the framework of traditional narrative, rather than participating in the radical experiments with form of many of her contemporaries, Rinser was not taken seriously as a novelist by literary critics. Because she did not fit into conventional categories used to classify contemporary German literature she was rarely included in histories of German literature.[11] The general reading public was more appreciative and a half dozen of Rinser's novels have made the best-seller lists. It has been her "*zeitkritische*" essays and diaries published in the 1970s and 1980s that have won her critical acclaim, causing her to be compared to the acknowledged master of the form, Max Frisch. In 1984 she was the candidate of the Green Party for president of the Bundes Republik. The ambiguous place Rinser holds in post-war German literary and political circles may explain why—although her first novel *Die gläsernen Ringe* (The Glass Rings) is acclaimed as "a female *bildungsroman*" occupying "a unique position in the German literature of the Nazi period,"[12] and her *Prison Diaries* is acknowledged as "one of the few narratives of women's (WW II) war experiences from a woman's perspective"[13] and although she was under death sentence when the Allied troops liberated her— she is not mentioned in books on resistance.

Historians still struggle to define "resistance" in the Third Reich. One historian has developed "two qualities by which we may judge resistance: whether the behaviour in question was public, and whether it challenged Nazi power."[14] Another describes resisters as people who believed only the defeat of Nazi rule could save Germany.[15] Luise Rinser not only exemplifies the first three characterizations of resistance, but also fits a broader definition "that includes the less heroic cases" that take into account "the fragility of resistance and the inconsistency of human bravery," which one historian has argued "may in the end inspire a greater intellectual and moral sensitivity toward the subject than a definition that includes only the exceptional greatness of heroic martyrdom."[16] Furthermore, her work offers various levels of reflection on her experiences in the Third Reich, as well as a critique of Nazi ideology that contains a religious component.

> I had a normal Catholic upbringing. I am thankful that Bavarian Catholicism (in as far as it wasn't political) was beautiful, colorful, and musical. It was a baroque heaven with ringing of bells, the fluttering of flags and the Corpus Christi procession. It

smelled of incense and wax candles and wilting birch and antique
gold embroidered mass vestments. I am often asked, why I don't
leave the Catholic church, which would seem to be a logical
consequence of my critical attitude. Well, even if I left the church
I would still remain a Catholic who has left the church. That has
nothing to do with the institutional structure of the church nor the
power politics of the churches and their Christian political
parties. It goes much deeper. It belongs to the magical and
mystical regions.[17]

Beginning with her own family, Rinser was a member of an
anti-Nazi subculture before Hitler's rise to power, which though never
organized, existed and formed a fragile support network. Even after
Hitler's assumption of dictatorial powers Rinser's parents did not join
the Nazi party, and suffered loss of jobs as a result. Her father, an
elementary school teacher, church organist, and accomplished singer,
took early retirement rather than teach under a Nazi regime. Her mother,
Rinser writes, was "instinctively" against Hitler.[18] Rinser herself finished her studies, likewise in elementary education, under the Nazi
regime. Because the Nazi government was especially sensitive to the
importance of the indoctrination of children and youth, and would not
tolerate alternative views in areas of education, Rinser soon had to
leave her teaching position because of her refusal to join the Nazi
party.

Shortly after leaving teaching she married the young composer
and conductor Horst Guenther Schnell. Their interest in music and
art brought them into contact with "undesirable" artists. Schnell had
studied under Paul Hindesmith in 1937, the last year he taught in
Berlin before he was designated as undesirable and artistically decadent. Rinser recounts visiting the exhibit of "Decadent" Art in Munich
when she had burst into tears of rage and, sobbing, had railed against
the exhibition, attracting the notice of other visitors and the guards.
Horst Guenther, "more reasonable," Rinser says, quickly spirited
her out of the exhibit before she was arrested. Such uncontrollable
outbursts of rage and indignation get Rinser in trouble later in prison,
but they also intimidate others and give her psychological space.
Later the young couple visited the apartment of Emil Nolde, one of
the artists held up for ridicule in the exhibition. She asks: "What did
we expect to do by visiting Nolde? I'm not sure any more. I pre-

sume that it was an act of moral restitution by proxy."[19]

When her husband had a position as conductor of the orchestra of the state theater of Braunschweig, he was not allowed to conduct because both of them were known anti-fascists. This is where Rinser would write her first novel, *Die gläsernen Ringe*. In 1979 she began the first volume of her memoirs on the fortieth anniversary of the day she began writing the first chapter, September 1, 1939, the day Germany declared war on Poland. Remembering, she writes of herself in the third person: a young woman four months pregnant goes up to the rooftops of the northern German town to hang up the wash. Then she goes downstairs to her second floor apartment:

> What does the young woman do now? She does something unexpected, which surprises her totally: she sits down with her apron still damp and with cold hands, red and wrinkled from washing the clothes. She sits down at her desk and immediately begins to write, as if pursued. She writes and writes as if her life depended on it, and truly, her life does depend on it. She has to save herself. The rabid dog is after her. He is panting and has Hitler's eyes and Hitler's voice. He had declared war on Poland, and on the world and on Life. She has to save herself, for the sake of the child and there is only one way to save herself: she must write. What does she write?[20]

The Glass Rings opens when a child sees the coming of the gray river of soldiers flowing through the town. "The child was afraid of what she did not know and what the adults called 'war.' "[21]

Die gläsernen Ringe was published in 1940 when the German war effort was in full swing. It is both a coming of age novel and an expression of almost unbearable longing and nostalgia for peace.

> I was a five year old child and lived in a small quiet town, and my childhood was even quieter than the town itself. One day, however a gray stream began to flood through the streets, and Mother said: "Look, our soldiers! How bravely they march along." The gray flood of soldiers continued for many hours and many days. The town was suddenly filled with the stamping of feet, and rough singing. Even the nights were robbed of their silence. Columns of trucks rattled through the streets, and shouts

pierced the darkness. The child, lying alone in her room sensed
the fever and the uncertainty in the air . . . One day Father left
with them, and then Mother left the town with me.[22]

Mother and daughter go into the country to stay with the mother's
uncle, who is the chaplain for an old convent in a village. The world
Rinser evokes with dreamlike intensity through the eyes of the girl is
at once profoundly German and profoundly Christian or Catholic.
Plants and especially flowers are lovingly described as is the shape of
the landscapes. The festivals that are the high points of village life are
evoked. The first is Corpus Christi, when everyone gets dressed up
and goes out into the village to celebrate through columns of freshly
cut birch branches.

German monastic architecture and art is explored through the won-
dering eyes of the girl. Her first morning in her new home she wan-
ders through the run-down, but still beautiful building and discovers a
room filled with mysterious draped objects. When she lifts the cloth
covering them, she discovers baroque statues of the saints, some of
whom she recognizes. The saints are veiled and hidden and can only
be discovered by a child. By creating this idyll within a profoundly
Christian framework, she destroys the Nazi image of the "true Germany" as pre-Christian by evoking the best that was Christian Germany with a poignancy that is painful.

The world into which she ventures contains faces that are not ap-
preciated in Nazi Germany and that teach her about life. She feels the
pull of the wild life of the gypsy boy she encounters at the edge of the
monastery property. She learns compassion from her aunt's treatment
of an old beggar, possibly a Jew, who years ago immigrated from
Russia and Poland, two countries that at the time of the book's publication were at war with Germany.

In the midst of this idyll the girl confronts and battles the demonic
in herself. She discovers within herself the desire to destroy beautiful
things—a beautiful lily her mother has cut for her to wear in the Corpus Christi procession, which she destroys because of the ridicule of
the other children. On another occasion she finds a mysterious well,
which according to legend sprang up in connection with a saint passing through. She throws a huge stone into it in order to destroy its
stillness.

At the end of the novel the girl describes last leave-takings as she and her mother prepare to rejoin her father, who has been a prisoner of war for several years. The girl, now ten years old, feels strengthened by what she has learned and enters the world of returning soldiers and prisoners of war. In *The Glass Rings* Rinser has created two worlds: the lost idyllic world that is childhood, and a certain German past gone forever. The Nazis denied the book a second printing undoubtedly because they sensed the power of the picture Rinser created.[23]

In the autumn of 1941 Rinser and Schnell moved to Rostock where their second son Stefan was born. In the autumn of 1942 Schell was drafted. By Christmas he was dead. Because of the heavy Allied bombing of northern German cities, Rinser and her sons were evacuated east to Silesia and later went south to her parents' home in Bavaria. She describes traveling in the darkened train, in third class, with many stops in open country: "Bombs fell around us. Sirens screamed, Nuremberg was in flames."[24] Once in Bavaria she lived in a run-down little hut out in the country. One of her aunts had a radio and listened to the BBC nightly, a "crime" for which some people incurred death sentences. Her daughter, Rinser's young cousin, brought her the news of Allied troop movements stuffed in the toes of her stockings. Rinser then spread the news.[25]

Another act of resistance that had profound consequences for her personal life was her marriage to a gay writer, Klaus, in the summer of 1943. Klaus was also a communist and pacifist whom Rinser had met when she was a refugee in Silesia. He sought her out in Bavaria because the Gestapo was looking for him in Berlin. When his Berlin apartment was bombed his mother came and lived with them and the tiny house became very crowded. When a letter from the Gestapo came for him, he went underground in Berlin and later came back to her. After he had done this several times he convinced her that marriage was the only way he could avoid arrest and the camps.[26] The marriage would mitigate suspicions of his homosexuality and allow him to be registered in Bavaria where he was less known. They were married in the cathedral in Salzburg in 1943.

In October of 1944 the thirty-three-year-old Rinser was arrested, betrayed by a neighbor and childhood friend. By that time the Gestapo had a long list of complaints against her. (All of which Rinser says were true.) They bear listing because they reveal the public nature of her resistance and also indicate the degree and scope of control and paranoia of a totalitarian government. She was accused of having made discouraging remarks about the course of the war to soldiers on leave from the front and advising them to desert. She corresponded with enemies of the people who lived abroad (Herman Hesse). She was accused of giving solace to Polish women prisoners of war and of having brought them shoes and soap. She regularly threw cigarettes to the Russian prisoners who were doing construction work in Salzburg. She had refused to join the Nazi party or any of their organizations. She had refused to work in a munitions factory to serve the German people. But the immediate cause of her arrest was that the husband of her childhood friend denounced her for speaking disrespectfully about Hitler and for encouraging her to tell her husband to desert since the war would soon be over.[27]

Rinser's prison diaries are one of a very few from World War II written by a woman. They cover the period from her arrest on October 12, 1944, to December 21, 1944.[28] At this point she had not yet had her last interrogation (February 1945) and had not yet been sentenced to death (April 1945).[29] Their mood is in stark contrast to the ecstatic and celebratory tone of *Die gläsernen Ringe* and represents a transformation of Rinser's previous spirituality. Like Dorothy Day, Rinser had felt the presence of God in life from early childhood.[30] "My definition of Faith is trust. That is the center. That foundational trust which was given to me with life itself. Disbelief was never a temptation for me."[31] The teachings of the medieval mystics attracted her because they corresponded to her basic religious sensibility. Nicolaus of Cusa's *coincidentia oppositorum* particularly fascinated her: "The coincidence of all opposites in God . . . there are no opposites in the World, there are no contradictions. We are the ones who make them; there are only polarities. Day is not day if there is no night. Life is not life if there is no death. One is enfolded in the other, becomes the other. Everything changes. The only thing permanent is change."[32] This mysticism, based on a sensitivity to the symbolic representation of divine life in and through the world, made it possible for Rinser to rise above the kitsch of some religious imagery to deeper theological meaning. She writes that once while celebrating mass with Karl Rahner in Innsbruck she suddenly understood the depth of the traditional piety of the Sacred Heart of Jesus as she was looking at a baroque painting in which Christ passionately offered his heart as if he had just ripped it from his body. "Suddenly I grasped it: this is the representation of the most extreme despair over the senselessness of the Sacrifice. No one wants this heart.

No one accepts the offer of eternal love, no one answers the cry of the Lord of the earth, no one answers the cry of the earth itself. The sudden burning pity with this loving one, with this love of God become human, forced me to my knees."[33]

Revealing a time of despair and bitterness, the prison diaries have almost no explicit religious referents except in the figure of a priest who comes to visit the women, ostensibly to counsel and comfort them, to hear their confessions. Rinser discovers that he is using his position as chaplain as a way to get sexual favors from them in exchange for his contacting people outside. In her introduction to a re-edition of the *Diaries* (1963) she explains that the struggle between herself and God went on at a level too deep to be described.[34] In the first volume of her memoirs written in 1979, she writes:

> Did I think about God during these months? Did I pray to him for liberation or did I seek comfort with him? Did I pray that he protect my children? Not at all. God was not present to my consciousness. I experienced that I had to be able to live without God, without metaphysical forces and help. I was totally left to my own devices. Now pull whatever you can out of yourself! Now show who you are with no assistance from outside or from above! I didn't wrestle with my fate, or with God either. I was only full of rage at the Nazis, who had forced this fate upon me and millions of others. I was reduced to a part of myself, to the political. What had happened to my religiosity? Did it simply crumble silently in the face of danger? Was religion only a superstructure that did not hold up under duress? Perhaps I was not a religious person, but a political one. God for his part did absolutely nothing to make himself noticed. Did he exist? Did I need him? I was strong enough to stand alone. So it is possible to exist without God. One can live in the wilderness. Only when I later experienced what it is to live with God, did I recognize how it is to be without him. There in the prison God had tested me. He looked at me from afar to see how I stood up under the stress. Nothing came to help me. Nothing except my own vitality. I became a compact bundle of the will to survive.[35]

If she did not wrestle with God she wrestled with herself and came to humbling conclusions: "Sometimes I see myself here as never before. I see myself with my lower instincts, with false opinions of honor, morality, class consciousness and all these nice acquired, conventional ideas. In the end there was nothing left of me but an animal that wanted to eat, sleep, that is afraid of being beaten, and that wants to escape into freedom. Outside prison we merely disguise these things with many words."[36]

In contrast to Rinser's feeling forgotten by God are the Jehovah's Witnesses who are her cellmates for awhile.[37] They are confident, calm in their faith, that their suffering for Jehovah is a presage to the end times.[38] There are fifteen of them in the prison with Rinser. The oldest is eighty-five.[39] Rinser describes her early conversations with them:

> "I reproach them that you can't expect political salvation from a supernatural source, that would be too comfortable. We need to work ourselves for social reform. I try to explain the principles of socialism to them. They shake their head in embarrassment. 'That is all nonsense. Only the Lord will save us' . . . I am not able to understand their doctrine. It seems to me that they don't have any ideas other than hatred for the powers of oppression and hope in Christ."[40]

At another point they tell her about Jehovah's Witnesses being driven through the city in open trucks to the prison where executions were held. "They recount all this without complaining. It seems natural for them to suffer for their faith. Nearly every sentence beginning with 'The Bible says.' 'The Bible says, that the just must suffer.' Without calling on the Bible, I have to agree with them."[41]

Rinser was conscious that writing functioned as a survival mechanism for her even before her imprisonment, as she began to write *The Glass Rings* the day after Germany invaded Poland. "I wrote to save myself, not in order to become a writer."[42] She began her writing in prison on a bit of paper she found in a mattress in her cell, the legacy of another's attempt to write. She continued on bits of packing paper she found, and finally on the available "toilet paper," newspaper where she could write in the margins, or preferably "old lists of prisoners" that had the back and the margins free.[43]

Rinser, the professional writer, is not the only writer in prison. She encounters the writings of others on the walls of the prison cells. They are the pathetic attempts of prisoners to leave a trace of their existence for those who will follow them into the experience of the prison cell. They range from obscenities to prayers to "calendars" that count the days spent in prison. One heart-wrenching example is love letters that Rinser sees on the walls of a cell being used as an air-raid shelter. A French laborer is convinced his lover has betrayed him. The truth is that she has been imprisoned for fraternizing with him and is inconsolable because of the separation. Rinser breaks down when she reads the letters.

At one point the prisoners in Rinser's cell each get a book to read. One of her cellmates tosses Tolstoy's *Resurrection* aside and Rinser picks it up. As she leafs through it she notices that someone had underlined in red and written in the margin. "All the passages which were about the injustice of the legal system, about corruption and about tyranny were underscored. Often the same words: 'Ugh, just like in the Third Reich. Just like Hitler.' " It is at this point that Rinser notices that she has "forgotten how to read." "It made me tired. I forgot what I had read on the previous page. I was distracted and could hardly understand what I was reading."[44]

Though Brenner identifies writing with "self-introspection" as a mode of resistance and comments that "life narratives affirm individuality and personhood under the rule of terror that sought their dehumanization,"[45] Rinser herself characterizes her own description of her prison experience as lacking in introspection. She "had experienced more and at a deeper level and with more passion" than she was able to describe. She stresses that in the immediate postwar year (*The Diaries* were first published in 1946), she was concerned to record the facts, and was not really capable of reworking the notes scribbled on bits of paper into an in-depth reflection on her experience, consumed as she was by the struggle to survive in the devastated landscape of the defeated Germany. "I wanted to create a totally accurate picture of life in prison, like a photograph, not a confession of my inner, subjective experiences."[46]

This purpose has as its unintended result the creation of community, at least for the reader, through the stories of the lives of the other prisoners that Rinser narrates as she draws us into the lives of the law breakers in the Nazi prison. These include women who have had affairs with the French, former allies, now "enemies" and wives of SS officers. She shows us women who have had abortions, as well as those who have performed them. Nazi law was strict on this, not because of a sense of the sacredness of life, but because of the necessity of replenishing desirable racial stock. Listening to other prisoners, she recounts, "I learned some new things, eight different ways of aborting. I keep having to overcome my bourgeois prejudices. I have never seen Life the way I get to see it here: naked, ugly, hard, but unvarnished and real. If I ever get back into normal life I will be a different person."[47] We meet black-marketeers, as well as lost souls who have wandered from camp to camp, from prison to prison.[48] One young woman, a Communist Party member who was liberated from Auschwitz, was rearrested when she came back to Germany. She is on her way to Dachau when Rinser meets her.[49] Rinser experiences the collective "we" of the prisoners, a community full of tension and dissension, yet nonetheless which understands itself as unified when confronted with the "non-prisoner" world.

Prison Diaries does not end with the day in April of 1945 when Rinser leaves the prison with a group of prisoners who try to wander homeward through a war-ravaged landscape. The last day's entry is December 21, 1944. It is a painful time because of the news that the Allied advance has been stopped in the Battle of the Bulge, but also because she is having to face Christmas without her two little sons. It is a dark time also because her appeal has not come back from Berlin.

It is not possible to explore in greater detail other dimensions of Rinser's experience as a resister, but a basic pattern emerges. If we consider her experience in two stages corresponding to her two books, we see a journey from (relative) privilege as a writer and member of a cultured elite to one of solidarity with the oppressed. In the phase of *The Glass Rings* we see a young woman facing the threat of the coming war with her creative talent. The book's publication was a triumph and brought her immediate notoriety. The second book, *Prison Diaries*, represents a different kind of trial, one that morally, on one level, seems to defeat her spirit, even though her writing about her defeat is a way of redeeming it. The witness she gives in her writing to the suffering of those around her becomes a somber celebration of the community of the oppressed. It opens a gate to a redemption from within, beyond the freedom brought about by the arrival of Allied troops. It reminds us that a journey into "moral and religious memory" to which John Paul II exhorts us cannot be achieved without humility.

Notes

1. Luise Rinser, *Gefaengnistagebuch* (Frankfurt a.M.: Fischer Verlag, 1963), 7.

2. John Paul II, "Accompanying Letter to Cardinal Cassidy" to "We Remember: A Reflection on the 'Shoah' " by the Vatican's Commission for Religious Relations with the Jews, *Origins* 27/40 (March 26, 1998): 671-72.

3. Ibid., 671.

4. "Joint Communique of International Catholic-Jewish Liaison Committee Meeting at Vatican," *Origins* 27/42 (April 9, 1998): 702-4.

5. Catholic-Jewish Liaison Committee, "Care for the Environment: A Religious Act," *Origins* 27/42 (April 9, 1998): 705-6.

6. *Origins*, 27/18 (October 16, 1997): 303.

7. Michael J. Farrell, "Becoming a Saint Trickier Than Going to Heaven," *National Catholic Reporter* (October 23, 1998): 2.

8. See also Michael Phayer and Eva Fleischner, *Cries in the Night: Women Who Challenged the Holocaust* (Kansas City: Sheed and Ward, 1997).

9. Daniel Goldhagen, *Hitler's Willing Executioners: Ordinary Germans and the Holocaust* (New York: Knopf, 1996).

10. Pamela Kirk, "Reflections on Luise Rinser's *Gratwanderung, "Philosophy and Theology* (Spring 1998): 293-300. See also Pamela Schaefer, "Karl Rahner's 22-Year Romance," *National Catholic Reporter* (December 18, 1997): 5-7.

11. Sigrid Weigel, "Luise Rinser," *Kritisches Lexikon zur deutschsprachigen Gegenwartsliteratur*, 7 (Munich: Heinz Ludwig Arnold, 1992): 2 .

12. Elke Frederiksen, "Luise Rinser," *Dictionary of Literary Biography*, 69, Contemporary German Fiction Writers, First Series, ed. Wolfgang Elfe and James Hardin (Detroit: Gale Research Co., 1988), 258.

13. Ibid., 259.

14. Detlev J. K. Peukert, "Working-Class Resistance: Problems and Options," *Contending with Hitler, Varieties of German Resistance in the Third Reich*, ed. David Clay Large (Washington, D.C.; Cambridge: German Historical Institute and Cambridge University Press, 1991).

15. Fritz Stern, "Address," in Large, *Contending*.

16. Martin Broszat, "A Social and Historical Typology of the German Opposition to Hitler," in Large, *Contending*, 25.

17. Luise Rinser, *Den Wolf Umarmen* (Frankfurt a.M.: Fischer Verlag, 1979), 149. (All translations are mine.)

18. Ibid., 74-78.

19. Ibid., 335-37.

20. Ibid., 11.

21. Ibid.

22. Luise Rinser, *Die gläsernen Ringe* (Frankfurt a.M.: Fischer Verlag, 1966), 7.

23. Rinser, *Wolf,* 25-27.

24. Ibid., 364-65.

25. Ibid., 366.

26. Ibid., 367.

27. Ibid., 375-76.

28. For accounts of other women political prisoners see: Gerda Szepansky, *Frauen leisten Widerstand: 1933-1945. Lebensgeschichten Nach Interviews und Dokumenten* (Frankfurt a.M.: Fischer Verlag, 1993).

29. Since April was the month just before the capitulation in which Bonhoeffer and numerous others were executed, Rinser asks herself in amazement: "Who kept the letter from Berlin from arriving in Bavaria until after the war?" *Wolf,* 45.

30. Ibid., 157.

31. Ibid., 146-47.

32. Ibid., 144-46.

33. Ibid., 154.

34. Rinser, *Gefaengnistagebuch,* 7.

35. Rinser, *Wolf,* 381-82.

36. Rinser in *Wolf,* 388, cites *Gefaengnis.*

37. Another area in which the church has grounds for repentance: "When Jehovah's Witnesses were suppressed in Bavaria on April 13 [1933] the church even accepted the assignment given it by the Ministry of Education and Religion of reporting on any member of the sect still practicing the forbidden religion." Guenter Lewy, *The Catholic Church and Nazi Germany* (New York: McGraw Hill, 1964*),* 43.

38. Claudia Koonz, *Mothers in the Fatherland: Women, Family Life, and Nazi Ideology, 1919-1945* (New York: St. Martin's Press, 1987), 331: "The most cohesive group of resisters were sustained by religion. From the first, Jehovah's Witnesses did not cooperate with any facet of the Nazi state. Even after the Gestapo destroyed their national headquarters in 1933 and banned the sect in 1935, they refused to do so much as say '*Heil Hitler.*' About half (mostly men) of all Jehovah's Witnesses were sent to concentration camps, a thousand of them were executed, and another thousand died between 1933 and 1945."

39. Rinser, *Gefaengnis,* 21.

40. Ibid., 22.

41. Ibid., 26.

42. Rinser, *Wolf,* 23. See also Rachel Feldhay Brenner, *Writing as Resistance: Four Women Confronting the Holocaust* (University Park, Penn.: The Pennsylvania State University Press, 1997), 5, about Stein, Franke, Hillesum and Weil: "The four resisted Hitlerian tyranny through the act of writing."

43. Rinser, *Gefaengnis,* 49.

44. Ibid., 119-20.

45. Brenner, in *Writing as Resistance,* 5, also warns that "idolization of testimonies of the women's final moments is symptomatic of the post-Holocaust proclivity to make Holocaust suffering more manageable. Reverence enshrines

these individuals, separating them from masses of other victims. Such attitudes attenuate the victim's experience of pain, suffering, and despair."

    46. Ibid., 6-7.
    47. Ibid., 75.
    48. Ibid., 39-40.
    49. Ibid., 81-84.

Cotton Patch Justice, Cotton Patch Peace: The Sermon on the Mount in the Teachings and Practices of Clarence Jordan

Ann Coble

Introduction

The setting is Louisville, Kentucky, in the late 1930s, and racial tensions are at a peak. A group of angry black men has assembled in a small room to plan a retaliation against an incidence of violence known to have been perpetrated by some white men in the community. The voices grow louder as the men, obviously the recipients of years of injustice, seek retribution, an eye for an eye. One of the men swings a section of iron pipe and declares, "Just like the whites kill a Negro for this, I'm going to kill a white man." As the crowd is at the point of taking up weapons, the only white man at the meeting steps forward and says, "If a white man must die for this. . . let it be me. Do it now." Clarence Jordan's words shock these men, many of them his friends, into silence. The crowd looks at the situation through new eyes, and after some discussion they work for a different response to this injustice.[1]

Who is this man Clarence Jordan? What made him work for racial reconciliation in the South? In the face of repeated incidents of racial violence, what made him choose peaceful means of fighting racial hatred? Clarence Jordan was an ordinary, Southern Baptist good-old-boy who was willing to take a peaceful stand against racial violence from both sides. Why? As I will demonstrate through many examples from Jordan's life, he chose to take a stand against racial injustice and to use nonviolent means because of his commitment to living out his understanding of the Sermon on the Mount.

In order to explain Clarence Jordan's ideas about and practice of the Sermon on the Mount, I first give a brief history of Jordan and the communal group he founded, Koinonia Farm. Jordan made his own paraphrase of the Sermon on the Mount, and I include a section of that so you can get the feel of his approach to this text. I then use illustrations from Jordan's writings and sermons and anecdotes from his life to show that Jordan's ideas of justice and peace were derived from his simple and straightforward interpretation of the Sermon on the Mount. I lastly show how Jordan, a Southern Baptist, came to the attention of Dorothy Day and also the Hutterites, and how Jordan's vision of the Sermon on the Mount became the cornerstone for Habitat for Humanity.

Koinonia Farm

Clarence Jordan was born in 1912 in Talbotton, Georgia, a rural area in south-central Georgia. He was raised in a Southern Baptist family, and he "went forward," that is, experienced a personal conversion, at a revival meeting when he was ten. He studied agriculture at the University of Georgia in Athens and then went on for a Master of Divinity and Doctor of Philosophy in New Testament from Southern Baptist Theological Seminary in Louisville, Kentucky. Through his college and seminary years, Jordan became increasingly interested in bridging the gap between the white and black subcultures. While at Southern Seminary, Jordan taught New Testament at Simmons College, a training school for black preachers, and he also was superintendent of a city mission.[2]

In 1942, Clarence Jordan, with his wife, Florence, and Martin and Mabel England, moved to a small farm in Sumter County, Georgia, and started an agricultural-based religious community. Jordan met Martin England, a Baptist missionary on furlough, because Jordan was intrigued by a letter which England wrote that began, "I have not been able to explain away the Sermon on the Mount or the 13th chapter of First Corinthians, or lots of other passages in the New Testament, about loving your neighbors."[3] Jordan and England shared similar visions of pacifism, working for racial reconciliation, and living communally. Jordan named the community Koinonia Farm; *koinonia* as it is used in the New Testament is a rich word that includes the ideas of fellowship, community, sharing, generosity, and close relationship.[4] The Englands soon left to return to their missionary work in Burma, but within the first ten years a few new individuals and families moved to the community. Although leadership responsibilities were rotated among the adults, Clarence Jordan functioned as the unofficial leader. During this time, Jordan focused on applying new techniques in agriculture and teaching them to the nearby farmers and sharecroppers. Like many similar communities, Koinonia Farm members shared their finances in common. Unlike many similar communities, Koinonia Farm was not intended to be a separatist endeavor; farm members were active in the local community, attended the local churches, and sold their crops at the local grain elevator and at a neighborhood roadside market.

Jordan had seen some of the effects of racism during his early life in rural Georgia, and during his time at Southern Baptist Theological Seminary in Louisville, Kentucky. However, it was at Koinonia Farm that Jordan took a series of small but significant stands against the racist practices around him. In the early years Koinonia Farm hired local people to help with the farming, some white and some black. It was here that Jordan began his controversial practices such as having all the workers, black and white, eat the noon meal together, and paying all the workers the same wages.

In addition, Jordan's pacifism and preaching of non-violence together with the common ownership of property and income led the people of Sumter County to hold Koinonia Farm in suspicion of anti-American and Communist activities. All through the 1950s and early 1960s, Koinonia Farm endured a period of persecution. There were frequent acts of violence by the Ku Klux Klan, resulting in the injury of a few Koinonia members and the repeated bombing of their roadside market. The Sumter County judicial system viewed Koinonia with distrust, fearing the group to be pro-Communist, and Koinonia members themselves were blamed for inciting the violent acts. Meanwhile, local feed stores refused to sell fertilizer or seed to Jordan or other members, and the local grain elevators boycotted Koinonia Farm produce. To offset this, Koinonia Farm members began their mail-order business, which is still their main source of farm income. The local Baptist church excommunicated the Jordans and other members of the Koinonia community on the grounds that they were allowing the races to mix.[5]

From the mid-1950s until 1969, Jordan worked on his Cotton Patch versions of the New Testament. These were loose paraphrases of the books of the New Testament, rewritten so that the setting for the events in Jesus' life was twentieth-century Georgia, and the main tension was between black and white.[6] Jordan traveled throughout the United States, preaching mostly from the New Testament and speaking about ways to take a stand against racism. While remaining numerically small, Koinonia Farm became well known in Baptist circles, among the rising Christian counter-culture, and among a slice of both the liberal and conservative churches that were interested in community life and fighting racism. By the time Jordan died in 1969, he had become a public figure and Koinonia Farm was considered a model community because of the non-violent stand against racial injustice.[7]

Jordan's Cotton Patch versions of the New Testament books, particularly the Gospels, are a fascinating window into rural Southern culture in the late 1950s and early 1960s. Jordan retold the story of the Gospels as though it were set in Georgia in the 1950s. Jesus is born in Gainsville, Georgia, his family flees to Mexico instead of Egypt, and the main city is Atlanta rather than Jerusalem. Here are a couple short sections from the Sermon on the Mount. The beatitudes:

> The spiritually humble are God's people, for they are citizens of his new order. They who are deeply concerned are God's people, for they will see their ideas become reality. They who are gentle are his people, for they will be his partners across the land. They who have an unsatisfied appetite for the right are God's people, for they will be given plenty to chew on. The generous are God's people, for they will be treated generously. Those whose motives are pure are God's people, for they will have spiritual insight. Men of peace and good will are God's people, for they will be known throughout the land as his children.[8]

Listen to Matthew 5:43-44: "Another thing you've always heard is, 'Love your own group and hate the hostile outsider,' but I'm telling you, love the outsiders and pray for those who try to do you in, so that you might be sons of your spiritual Father."[9]

While being socially quite liberal for his time, and therefore often considered to be theologically liberal as well, Jordan actually held to a simple hermeneutic. He read the text as though it were written to him in his situation and then he based his actions on what he had read. He was not concerned with gray areas, subtleties, or nuances.

Justice and Peace

While a child, Jordan learned the familiar children's song "Jesus Loves the Little Children," which said, "Jesus loves the little children, all the children of the world; red and yellow, black and white, they are precious in His sight. Jesus loves the little children of the world." When in graduate school, in his personal journal Jordan reflected on his experience of singing that song as a child:

> The question arose in my mind, "Were the little black children precious in God's sight just like the little white children?" The song said they were. Then why were they always so ragged, so dirty and hungry? Did God have favorite children?
> I could not figure out the answers to these puzzling questions but I knew something was wrong. A little light came on when I began to realize that perhaps it wasn't God's doings, but man's. God didn't turn them away from our churches—we did. God didn't pay them low wages—we did. God didn't make them live in another section of town and in miserable huts—we did. God didn't make ragged, hungry little boys pick rotten oranges and fruit out of the garbage can and eat them—we did. Maybe they were just as precious in God's sight, but were they precious in ours? My environment told me that they were not very precious in anybody's sight.[10]

As Dallas Lee comments, Jordan's memory probably added quite a bit to his childhood thoughts, but it is clear that by the time he wrote this during his seminary years, Jordan was beginning to question the discontinuity between what he saw in church and what he was experiencing in the streets.[11]

During his college years, Jordan was also participating in the Reserved Officers Training Corps. It was in ROTC that Jordan made his first significant break with Southern society. In 1932, a professor recommended him for a special summer course that would lead to a commission as a second lieutenant. He attended the summer boot camp course in 1933, and it was here that he began to question his views on the military. Dallas Lee has pointed out that an officer's position in the U. S. Cavalry was a dream for many Southern gentlemen. "Now

Clarence Jordan mounted on a bold black steed, a pistol in one hand and a saber in the other, was the fulfillment of a mysterious compulsion common to most sons of southern aristocracy."[12] Jordan had returned to Talbotton for vacation, proudly showing his boots and spurs.[13] He was moving toward the life of a successful Southern aristocrat, but he was beginning to question this dream.

Jordan spent his free time at cavalry boot camp absorbing Jesus' words in the Sermon on the Mount. As he considered his training, he came to the decision that the teachings of the Sermon on the Mount were in conflict with his boot camp experience. One day he was memorizing Matthew 5:43, "You have heard it said, 'You shall love your neighbor, but hate your enemy.' But I say to you, Love your enemies . . ."[14] Later that day, Jordan and his cavalry group were engaged in maneuvers in which they charged through a wooded area, shooting or hacking a series of dummies that were set up for the drill. Jordan later recalled,

> Soon I spotted a target. Drawing a bead, I pressed the trigger of my pistol . . . a tiny white spot appeared in the black circle of the dummy's head.
>
> "But I say to you, LOVE YOUR ENEMIES."
>
> But he's not my enemy, he's only a dummy. Besides, I'm just practicing. . . . Well, someday it will be a real man, but after all one must be prepared to defend himself.
>
> "But I say to you, love your ENEMIES."
>
> Another dummy. I was well past it before I saw it, and my hand was trembling. . . . When I arrived on the other side there was only one empty cartridge in my pistol. . . . It was crystal clear that this Jesus was going one way and I another. Yet I called myself his follower.[15]

Moments later, as he came out of the woods, he dismounted, approached his commanding officer, and resigned his commission. During this conversation, the officer suggested that Jordan might become a chaplain. Jordan remembers, "I told him that that would be worse than ever. I could not encourage someone else to do what I myself would not do."[16] Eventually this same officer told him, "Son, I hope someday you make my job impossible."[17] From that day onward Jordan was a confirmed pacifist; he advocated nonviolent solutions to problems and he would not support any preparations for war.

Jordan's non-violent approach was a hot topic in the rural South, especially since he was advocating pacifism during World War II. He had tried to register as a conscientious objector, but the draft board registered him as exempt due to the fact that he was a minister.[18] While a pacifist, he did not consider himself to be passively accepting his circumstances. Jordan explained his non-violent approach to fighting racism in this story from his life:

> An old farmer stated to him with obvious distaste: "I heard you won't fight." Clarence replied: "Who told you that? We sure will fight."
>
> Surprised, the farmer said: "Well, you won't go in the Army, will you?"
>
> Clarence said: "No, we don't fight that way. Let me explain. You see that mule over there? Well, if that mule bit you, you wouldn't bite it back, would you?" "Nope," the farmer allowed, "I'd hit him with a two-by-four."
>
> "Exactly," Clarence replied. "You wouldn't let that mule set the level of your encounter with him. You would get a weapon a mule couldn't use and knock his brains out. That's what Christians are supposed to do—they are supposed to use weapons of love and peace and goodwill, weapons that the enemy can't handle."[19]

Just because he was committed to non-violence does not mean Jordan was never angry. More than once Jordan asked people if they would like him to put his "Christianity on hold for 15 minutes and beat the tar" out of some racist person. Most of the time he did not mean it. He was using this suggestion for shock value. Once, though, he really thought he would do it. All of the children from Koinonia Farm were treated badly at school. School administrators turned a blind eye, and although the children were rarely physically beaten, they had to endure years of emotional trauma. On one such occasion, Jordan's daughter, who was in high school, came to him and said she did not know if she could continue. One of the boys at school frequently embarrassed her by running up to her and shouting horrible names at her. Faced with his daughter's pain, Jordan asked her if he should take matters into his own hands, including the possibility of threatening the boy and his family with physical harm. His daughter did not take him seriously, and she laughed at him and declined his offer. Two weeks later, Jordan asked her how things were with this boy, and she explained that she had solved the problem herself. Whenever, she saw him, she would run up to him grinning and gushing as though she had a crush on him. The boy was now avoiding her at all cost. Jordan remarked that he was both amused and humbled by his daughter's creative solution.[20]

Jordan's commitment to living out the Sermon on the Mount brought him into contact with a variety of individuals and groups with similar convictions. Two of these that are of particular interest are Dorothy Day, co-founder of the Catholic Worker movement, and the Hutterites, an Anabaptist communal group. Dorothy Day visited Koinonia Farm in an effort to learn more about rural communal living. Biographer William Miller mentions that local KKK members shot at Day's car as she arrived at the farm.[21] The Hutterites also expressed an interest in Koinonia Farm. At one point Koinonia Farm members considered becoming a Hutterite community.[22] I suggest that the common thread that drew both Day and the Hutterites to Jordan's farm appears to be the centrality of the Sermon on the Mount. Jordan's passion for the Jesus of the Gospels, his interest in communal living, his pacifism, and mission to the poor inspired both the radical urban Catholic worker and the rural, separatist Hutterites.

Conclusion

Clarence Jordan lived a fascinating life, full of interesting events that provide a window into the racial conflict in the rural South. His focus on the Sermon on the Mount, and in particular the passages about loving the enemy or the outsider, led Jordan to first work toward loving the African-Americans whom he saw were treated as outsiders. Over time, it led him to work toward loving the racist, violent white people who treated him as though he were the enemy.

Jordan was not only a storyteller, he was a visionary. Many of his ideas did not come to fruition, but one well-known organization owes its start to Jordan and his ideas about living out the Sermon on the Mount. A year before Jordan's death in 1969, Millard Fuller, a disillusioned millionaire from Alabama, came to Koinonia Farm for lunch. Lunch turned into weeks, and Fuller eventually helped Jordan write up some new ideas for Koinonia Farm that would help it expand its ministries. This new vision, called Koinonia Partners, fostered a number of new ventures such as a daycare and after-school program for local children and teenagers. Probably the most well-known of the Koinonia Partners ministries was started by Millard Fuller soon after Jordan's death. Fuller was the sort of person who attracted money and thought big, and after seeing how the people at Koinonia Farm helped each other build homes, he began what became Habitat for Humanity.[23]

Before Jordan wrote the Cotton Patch versions of the New Testament books, he had written a book on the Sermon on the Mount. His comments on "loving your enemy" seem to be a fitting end to a paper on justice and peace. He wrote,

> The truth might be that in its initial stages unlimited love is very impractical. Folks who are determined enough to hold on to it usually wind up on a cross, like Jesus. Their goods get plundered and they get slandered. Persecution is their lot. Surely nobody would be inclined to call this practical. Yet in its final stages, unlimited love seems to be the only thing that can possibly make any sense.[24]

Notes

[1] Henlee H. Barnette, *Clarence Jordan: Turning Dreams into Deeds* (Macon, Ga.: Smith & Helwys Publishing, Inc., 1992), 6.

[2] For Jordan's early life, see Tracy Elaine K'Meyer, *Koinonia Farm: Building the Beloved Community in Postwar Georgia* (Ann Arbor, Mich: University of Michigan Press, 1993), 13-40; Dallas Lee, *The Cotton Patch Evidence: The Story of Clarence Jordan and the Koinonia Farm Experiment (1942-1970)* (Americus, Ga.: Koinonia Partners, Inc., 1971), 1-34; P. Joel Snider, *The "Cotton Patch" Gospel: The Proclamation of Clarence Jordan* (Lanham, Md.: University Press of America, Inc., 1985), 7-13; Clarence Jordan, Koinonia Partners tape collection, #CJ56, "Clarence Jordan Tells the Koinonia Story," n.d.

[3] Lee, *The Cotton Patch Evidence*, 27.

[4] Walter Bauer, *A Greek-English Lexicon of the New Testament and Other Early Christian Literature*, second edition, translated and adapted by William F. Arndt and F. Wilbur Gingrich, revised and augmented by F. Wilbur Gingrich and Frederick W. Danker (Chicago: University of Chicago Press, 1979), 438-39.

[5] For the history of Koinonia Farm, see K'Meyer, *Koinonia Farm*, 41-260; Lee, *The Cotton Patch Evidence*, 35-236; Snider, *The "Cotton Patch" Gospel*, 13-25;

Jordan, Koinonia Partners tape collection, #CJ56, "Clarence Jordan Tells the Koinonia Story," n.d.; Barnette, *Clarence Jordan*, 25-59.

[6] See Clarence Jordan, *The Cotton Patch Version of Matthew and John*, (Clinton, N.J.: New Win Publishing, Inc., 1970). Note that Jordan only finished the first eight chapters of John. See *The Cotton Patch Version of Hebrews and the General Epistles*, (Clinton, N.J.: New Win Publishing, Inc., 1970); *The Cotton Patch Version of Luke and Acts: Jesus' Doings and the Happenings*, (Clinton, N.J.: New Win Publishing, Inc., 1969); *The Cotton Patch Version of Paul's Epistles*, (Clinton, N.J.: New Win Publishing, Inc., 1970).

[7] Although it was highly respected across the United States, Koinonia Farm was still being boycotted by businesses in Sumter County. The police would not come to the farm when Jordan died, and neither would an ambulance. Although he was obviously dead, the members of the farm put Clarence in a station wagon and drove him to the hospital so he could be pronounced legally dead. See Lee, *The Cotton Patch Evidence*, 232-33.

[8] Jordan, *The Cotton Patch Version of Matthew and John*, 22.

[9] Jordan, *The Cotton Patch Version of Matthew and John*, 25.

[10] Lee, *The Cotton Patch Evidence*, 7-8.

[11] Lee, *The Cotton Patch Evidence*, 8.

[12] Lee, *The Cotton Patch Evidence*, 12.

[13] James McClendon, *Biography as Theology* (Nashville: Abingdon Press, 1974), 92.

[14] Lee, *The Cotton Patch Evidence*, 13; Snider, *The "Cotton Patch" Gospel*, 10.

[15] Snider, *The "Cotton Patch" Gospel*, 10.

[16] Lee, *The Cotton Patch Evidence*, 14.

[17] McClendon, *Biography as Theology*, 92.

[18] Lee, *The Cotton Patch Evidence*, 54.

[19] Lee, *The Cotton Patch Evidence*, 58; also Barnette, *Clarence Jordan*, 27-28.

[20] Barnette, *Clarence Jordan*, 32-34.

[21] William D. Miller, *A Harsh and Dreadful Love: Dorothy Day and the Catholic Worker Movement* (New York: Liveright, 1973), 441.

[22] For a description of the interaction between Koinonia Farm and various Hutterite locations, see Lee, *The Cotton Patch Evidence*, 164-79.

[23] Barnette, *Clarence Jordan*, 41-59.

[24] Clarence Jordan, *The Sermon on the Mount* (Valley Forge, Penn.: Judson Press, 1952), 67-68.

Part IV

NEW PRAXIS

Liberty in an Age of Coercion and Violence

Franklin H. Littell

I count it a professional and personal privilege to stand at the spot where John Howard Yoder was expected to appear. John Howard and I were friends from the time we were both in service in post-war Europe. We both owed a great deal to one of the spiritual and intellectual giants of the past generation: Harold S. Bender of Goshen College and Seminary. John Howard's *Täufertum und Reformation in der Schweiz* (1962) and *Täufertum und Reformatoren im Gespräch* (1968) are definitive works of scholarship that no serious student of the Radical Reformation and the Free Churches can detour around. The publication of his *The Politics of Jesus* (1972) was a landmark in biblical ethics by which many still chart their way. While these studies were being written he gave dozens of addresses and lectures, both at the level of the congregation member and among professors and graduate students—as recorded in the valuable *Comprehensive Bibliography* compiled by Mark Thiessen Nation and published by the Mennonite Historical Society in 1997. John Howard Yoder was, in sum, a Christian intellectual of the first water and a grade "A+" Christian activist.

The topic to which I invite your attention is one that was close to John Howard's heart: "Liberty in an Age of Coercion and Violence."

The Culture of a Violent Age

Every newspaper, radio, and TV broadcast brings into the public mind pictures and sound bytes of all levels of violence.[1] A recent study reports on school children's use of leisure hours. Generally, the average child leaves elementary school having watched 8,000 murders and more than 100,000 acts of violence on TV. Even the schoolyards have become arenas of mayhem. We are learning what it means when children are constantly exposed to a culture of violence.

The Language of Assault has become systematized and heavily financed, emerging as a shaper of culture rather than a mere pathological motif exhibited only in sporadic outbursts when someone temporarily loses self-control.

Such massive forces as TV, movies, and the Internet—driven by nothing but a trade-off of maximum sensation for maximum profit—drive and form this culture of the general society. They also shape international relations. This was brought home to me some months ago when I was watching CNN in the capital of a distant country in the Commonwealth of Independent States, south of Siberia—a country of which it used to be said that "you can't get there from here." Virtual reality was being created by television's excited pursuit of the latest rumors and backyard gossip about the President of the United States—a pursuit on which the most reactionary and destructive forces in the American republic have thus far spent tens of millions of dollars in a fishing expedition.

I realized that Mrs. Littell was surfing and perhaps glimpsing the same scenes and fantasies—cut loose from primary sources!—at the very same time. It came to me that the face (*prosopon*) of America was being defaced abroad. In the United States, all the polls indicate that the common sense of the American people has rejected—at least at the political level—the pornographic assault on the President. The effort of the reactionaries to get even for the exposure of Nixon's defiance of the Constitution by criminalizing what was at worst uncivil behavior is stalled politically, but our paparazzi still swarm over the sewers of popular prurience.

Abroad, however, the popular effect of this morbidity is a major factor in international affairs. A patriotic American overseas suddenly realizes how "the Great Satan" appears to peoples who have never been taught the scientific, critical, analytical way of verification. Moreover, their intellectual innocence is harnessed to an austere morality and frequently fanatical moralism. Not long ago, realizing how widely Hollywood movies had been spread, we used to wonder about the misunderstanding of America created by feature films of violence and sex. For that matter, we can still wonder what view of America is created by a pornographic film like *Deconstructing Harry*, the latest degenerate offering from a once great talent. With movies, however, we could always hope that there would be a canny awareness that someone had cunningly contrived an exhibition, that it was after all a piece of theatre, not the real thing. Not so with TV: it is not only instantaneous, it creates its own reality. It generates acceptance as it goes, a real acceptance at home by children with guns and abroad an acceptance as a true portrayal of America by peoples not accustomed to a flood of exhibitionist sex and casual violence.

In modernity, the question has become, "When does 'virtual reality' become, as it were, incarnate reality?" No such problem tormented our forefathers, who had both time and distance covering their errors. When Andrew Jackson and Jean Lafitte led the famous (and only) American victory against the British in the War of 1812, the war had been over for six weeks. A peace treaty had been signed at Ghent in Belgium. But in those days news travelled by clipper ship across the Atlantic, then along the Cumberland Trail, and then down the Ohio and Mississippi to the scene of action, New Orleans, the glorious battle that propelled Jackson toward the presidency. Today the news we see is viewed in Hong Kong, Seoul, Ankara and Cape Town, at the same moment. The time lag is no longer there to cushion our mistakes. And the great distances that would have hidden our shame, if Americans had then confused liberty with license, have been eliminated.

Of course the most particular and specific recent decline of American influence in international affairs is due to the fact that—thanks to a bureaucratic bottleneck exploited by Senator Tobacco of North Carolina—we are now the worst deadbeat nation in the United Nations. We may have a budget surplus, but we just won't pay our long overdue dues. We demand the space to flex our muscle, flaunting NATO in the face of the Russians, who are still struggling to crawl their way up out of the ruins of the USSR and need a friendly welcome, not encouragement to their own militarists and macho politicians. We expect our European allies to fall into line behind American policy vis-à-vis Iran and Iraq, Burundi and Rwanda, as well as in the ruins of the former Yugoslavia and, now, India and Pakistan. Yet we allow the senility rule governing chairmanships in the U.S. Senate to create a situation in which we shamelessly, after months of stalling, still fail to pay our fair share of the basic costs of international cooperation. We want to have our way on the cheap, and the bottleneck senator symbolizes our irresponsibility.

In the long haul, however, most damaging to America and its standing in international affairs is the unabashed promotion of a culture of violence on TV. It came blindingly clear to me in the situation I mentioned before, deep in the Caucasus and so far away from home, surrounded by populations dominated by a Muslim fundamentalist morality: "God pity us! If that's what they see hour after hour, we Americans *truly deserve* to be called 'the Great Satan.' "

From "Virtual Reality" to Genocide

On the large map, in the twentieth century violence and coercion have ranged far more widely than liberty. In fact, the century from which we are emerging is known to many scholars as "The Age of Genocide." Genocide, defined in the International Genocide Convention of 1951 as the targetting by a government of specific minorities for extinction, is a most extreme and comprehensive form of violence and constraint.

The doctrine of genocide in international law, like the invented word itself—a welding of *genos* and *cidere*—came out of the Holocaust. The inventor, and the man who more than any other was responsible for establishing the beginnings of law in this sector of the jungle, was a refugee from Hitler's Europe: Rafael Lemkin.

There is a debate as to whether the Holocaust refers to the *circa* six million systematically targeted and murdered in the Nazi genocide of the Jews ("Final Solution to the Jewish Problem," as the program was euphemistically and pretentiously termed) or to the total of *circa* eleven million who perished in the German concentration camps. Elie Wiesel defends the former position; Simon Wiesenthal takes the latter and more inclusive stance.

In either case, there can be no debate as to the nexus between individual responsibility and a culture of ultimate violence. No one has staked out the high ground better than good Pope John XXIII in *Pacem in Terris* (April 10, 1963). "True freedom, freedom worthy of the sons of God, is that freedom which most truly safeguards the dignity of the human person." He proclaimed throughout the message the high religious value of the liberty, dignity, and integrity of the human person. In his affirmation he specifically designated the rights of minorities affirmed in the United Nations Declaration of Human Rights and in the International Genocide Convention.

Once the high ground is abandoned, once the liberty and dignity and integrity of the human person are surrendered, once a culture and politics of coercion and violence is permitted to prevail, a nation enters on the slippery slide that savages personal morality and destroys peoples and nations. The yoking of personal salvation with the destiny of a society can easily be seen in the slide that, unless checked, gathers speed in the destruction of peoples.

The Slide to Genocide

Again: the high ground, aerated by the dialogue of free men and women,[2] is grounded in affirmation of the liberty, dignity, and integrity of the human person.

Reflect with me on the signposts that slip by in increasing tempo as a people, turning away from the Law of God, slides downward and self-destructs. The mode runs from individual flaw to social sin to the hell of Man in revolt against his God and against his own true being.

Tolerance, the first personal step downward[3]: "We'll put up with 'the Other' if we have to."

Contempt, where the stain begins to show through

Bigotry

Prejudice

The Language of Assault, where incipient violence becomes a barely disguised call to action—so different from the Language of Dialogue, the style of civilized men and women on campus and in the public forum. At this point social structures and policy take over from the individual orientation.

Harassment

Discrimination

Repressive Measures, where government decrees enter the picture

Targeting of Potential Victims

Isolation (ghettoization)

Military Alert, with genocide enabled by mobilization of the bureaucratic and technological specialists of modernity, and usually facilitated by a state of war

GENOCIDE. According to the leading specialist, nearly one hundred and fifty-two thousand people were murdered from 1900 to 1987 BY THEIR OWN GOVERNMENTS, which is almost three times as many as have died in international and civil wars during the same period of time.[4]

Who Commits Genocide?

When we think of war, the ultimate expression of coercion, aggression and violence, we are still conditioned to think of world wars and, sometimes, civil wars. But in fact the supreme denial of the liberty and dignity and integrity of the human person in our lifetime has been expressed in the intentional, systematic, technically mounted, bureaucratically administered crime of *genocide*. Genocide is the crime of some regime against internal targeted and powerless victims. It is war against one's own. Since 1951 genocide has been defined as a crime by international law, a crime where no claim of national autonomy in defining and effecting such policy has any standing. Every government has the right, indeed the legal duty, to intervene across borders to stop such crime and to apprehend the criminals.

How does a regime find and train individuals to commit genocide? Hannah Arendt found the essence of the enterprise, staffed for the most part by clerks and desk-top killers, in "the banality of evil." Her concept was challenged by some writers and students of the Holocaust, from Jacob Robinson to Daniel Goldhagen, because it seemed to diminish the evil ambience and the personal responsibility of the perpetrators.

Our task as Christians is to translate the statistics—the six million or the eleven million—into the human measure, the destiny of a human person. This is as true for understanding the perpetrator as it is for empathizing with the victim. One of the shorter writings of the martyr Dietrich Bonhoeffer describes the petty bureaucratic tyrant, who in his small domain of minor authority takes pride in his short moments of domination. This fragment, written in prison before his martyrdom by the gigantic Nazi killing machine, concludes "Many well-meaning people of our class have been accustomed to laugh at these petty criminals . . . This laughter is as foolish and irresponsible as laughter about a tiny measure of bacteria . . ."[5]

A better metaphor than the well-known expression "the desk-top killer" is "the bicycle man." The "bicycle man" bends far over toward those before him and treads down with vigor upon what is below his feet. The "bicycle man" is the ideal instrument of a totalitarian regime, his resentment at life being directed toward those beneath him and his love of death directed toward the assigned victims of genocide.

Significantly, the opposite of the "bicycle man" is the upright man or woman, the person who is not the *subject* of a despotism or dictatorship but a *citizen* in a free society (constitutional monarchy, republic, or simple democracy). Even more significantly, the studies show that the more totalitarian and less democratic a regime, the more genocide and the greater the annual rate of genocide it commits.[6]

Contrary to what many assume, there is *no* correlation between diversification in a nation's culture, including the presence of large minorities, and the propensity to commit genocide. The danger lies *not* in pluralism of race, culture or creed, but in the misuse of power. According to Professor Rummel of the University of Hawaii, "The degree of a regime's power along a democratic to totalitarian scale is a direct underlying cause of domestic democide, including genocide ... At the extremes of power, totalitarian governments have slaughtered their people by the *tens of millions*, while many democracies can barely bring themselves to execute even serial murderers."[7]

Early Warning

The initial political task is to marshal the joint action of free peoples to halt genocide. The second task is to apprehend those who have committed genocide, and to punish them publicly, because justice must be served, and also to inhibit others who may be contemplating a similar crime. Finally, the task is to apply an Early Warning System to identify potentially genocidal movements and stop them from infiltrating and acquiring power.

We write and speak often of the message and lessons of the Holocaust, what the sociologists call—an awful expression—"the model case" of twentieth-century genocide. I prefer the prophet Amos' metaphor of the plumbline which, unique in its characteristics, can be held up against similar tragic events in the experience of other peoples, thereby relating the genocide of the Jews to other genocides.

At Yom Hashoah, now an official calendar day in Israel and America, and more recently in Germany and Austria, we remember in meditation and prayer the violent event and its victims. At other times, especially at the anniversary of *Kristallnacht* (November 9-11), we itemize and teach the lessons. Of the lessons, the first is this: the Nazi genocide of the Jews didn't have to happen. Already in 1923 the National sozialistische Deutsche Arbeiter partei (NSDAP) was an identifiable, potentially genocidal conspiracy.

Ingmar Bergman, the Swedish cinema genius, made a movie some years ago on the rise of the Nazi Party during the Weimar Republic. He called it "The Serpent's Egg," and in another season it certainly would have won Academy awards. He was asked about the name and the metaphor, and he said, "With the serpent's egg, the membrane is so thin you can already see the perfectly formed body of the reptile." By 1923, the NSDAP was a perfectly formed, genocidal reptile. The time to stop the movement in its tracks was 1923. Early 1933, the year of the Enabling Act, was too late. 1938, the year the Nazi Party flaunted its internal violence in the face of other nations, was much too late.

We do not have a scientific solution when someone writes a careful report on an epidemic or plague. We have a science when it is possible for seasoned specialists to gather about a long table and *predict* that, given certain unchecked developments, an epidemic or plague *will* occur.[8]

We now have that capability in respect to genocide, and you and I as citizens in a republic have the responsibility to insist that our government act decisively in respect to the crime where it is found or where it is threatened. We educate and preach, of course, against contempt and bigotry here at home, with an eye to raising up better children and grandchildren than their parents and grandparents. In the meantime, we are concerned for the uses of power. As a people of liberty we expect our government to be concerned for those less privileged than we, in a world where over two-thirds of the peoples live under despotisms or dictatorships, under regimes structured in coercion, infused with violence, and incipiently genocidal.

The Christian Component

What does confrontation with a culture that popularizes violence and a politics where governments too often act aggressively toward other peoples and also their own minorities have to do with Christian witness? A simple summary is to state bluntly that to be a member of the Christian people is to be constrained by a counter-culture. John Howard Yoder came from the Old Mennonites, a people who have shunned violence and political coercion consistently. A movement that began in Zürich in 1524, they did not even vote until two generations ago in America. It was one of Yoder's contributions to relate for his Anabaptist/Mennonite brethren the connections of scriptural faithfulness with political and social concerns of conscience.

Although the Anabaptist/Mennonite communities wintered through the savage persecution of Roman Catholic and Lutheran state churches in the sixteenth century, it was not until the seventeenth century in England that their spiritual descendents were able to bear witness to their convictions about the nature of a political process that God could approve. Their solution was both naive and radical: the method of decision making that Jesus had taught his followers was to be applied to civil life. We are entitled to believe, they said, that Jesus gave his people the pattern of government that was most pleasing to God. [9] The pattern of discussion and prayer, leading to consensus and collective action, was, they thought, appropriate for both church and town.

As a besieged and persecuted minority for generations, they practiced government by consensus in the little house churches. With the end of the Stuart absolute monarchy, when the way was opened in England and New England for the rise of parliamentary government, the teaching was advanced that the town meeting should take its lessons from the congregational meeting. What had been learned?

> in "the small democracy of the Christian congregation . . . the insight into the purposes of life which the common life and discussion of a democratic society can give [guidance] as nothing else can. . . . The root of the matter is that if the discussion is at all successful, we discover something from it which could have been discovered in no other way. [10]

Thus the medieval Christian concept of the *consensus fidelium* became in the radical Reformation and through their Free Church spiritual descendants [11] a principle of governance for the church and a standard by which the quality of civil governments might also be tested. Best known to those outside this tradition have been such concepts as "centering down," "the sense of the meeting," "soul liberty," and so forth, by which Quakers and Baptists and some others have found their way in *both* churchly *and* public affairs.

Especially, even when there is no explicit discipline of biblical non-resistance or modern pacifism, the Free Churches that hewed to the line of the radical Reformation have commonly identified Satan as the initiator of violence in the civil society and the sponsor of coercion in the churches. As they have assimilated to the general society in America, a tendency exponentially augmented by the mass media since World War II, the onetime neuralgic reaction of the Free Churches to coercion and violence has flagged and sometimes failed altogether.

Let me give some quick examples of the power of the American society that, unlike European "Christendom," not only does not persecute the Free Churches but actually seduces them to affirm its values and style of life. First, take the Mennonites. Going into World War II, more than half of the Old Mennonite farmers offered to mortgage their farms, if necessary, to support the pacifist Alternative Service of their conscientious objectors. Both men and women were then wearing the plain clothes, as were the students on campuses like Goshen (Indiana) and Eastern Mennonite (Harrisonburg, Virginia). To find the plain clothes now, one must travel far into rural enclaves. A recent study shows less than 17 percent of the Mennonites still living and working on the farm.

Second, take the Baptists. The largest Protestant denomination in America has within the decade been subject to a series of takeovers of boards and agencies and seminaries by *putschistes*, operating in the ruthless style of corporate takeovers and in defiance of the most elementary Baptist principles of decision making. As the forefathers would say, the winners in these material aggressions "have gone over to the world."

The experience of considerable numbers of Southern Baptists, who were quietly doing the Lord's work and not paying attention until very late to the intrigue that preceded open coercion and violence in the churches, has brought greater pain than that recorded recently in most of the denominations. But many of them, including my own (United Methodist), are at one broken barricade or another learning the spiritual cost of accommodation to the spirit of the times.

The *Zeitgeist* is the false god of populist politics, both in the church and in the civil society, and it opens the door to coercion and violence *within* the churches. Let me speak of the Methodists. In 1963 I wrote on the Methodists[12] for *The Christian Century* series on "What's Ahead for the Churches?" I diagnosed the malaise of assimilation and prescribed a recovery of Wesleyan standards, including training for membership. The minister of one of our largest congregations wrote me a letter of protest, advocating inclusiveness. He said they think their task is to "get them in and then Christianize them." He need not have worried: the denomination has been so well adjusted to the general society that it has lost nearly 35 percent of its membership in a decade. The open door to the world allows passage in either direction.

The final argument in our day and age, in politics as in the churches, is always the appeal to the unfettered "will of the people," a *volonté générale* expressed in license rather than liberty. Of all the crimes of modernity, genocide has been one of the most popular, and it is the one that most clearly demonstrates the wickedness of which the "Common Man," if unchecked by law and unformed by the Gospel, is enthusiastically capable. Every murderous despot or dictator in the twentieth century has claimed to speak for "the will of the people." Justified in practice by constant and demonstrative misuse of plebiscites, genocide has been justified in theory by the blasphemous declaration, *Vox populi, vox dei.* Who can stand against a populist system of violence, terror or coercion, especially if it claims to be blessed by the gods?!

In the churches, treason toward the Spirit of Truth (John 16:13) is popularly demonstrated by abandonment of the liberty that we have in Christ Jesus for a spurious freedom, for the licentious life-style of a world that is every day more evidently coming apart at the seams. The ever more reckless affirmation of terror, coercion, and violence by most regimes on the globe—and even on occasion by legitimate governments (as, for instance, by our own government in respect to the murders of American citizens in the Waco and Ruby Ridge outrages)—is nothing less than rebellion against God and God's purposes for humankind.

Against movements driven by killing ideologies and against government misuse of authority through terror and violence, as democratic citizens we are committed to the rule of law—in the defense of human rights and the elimination of the crime of genocide—at the end of the slippery steps that lead downward into the pit. This is our democratic task, anchored in a sound understanding of the liberty, dignity, and integrity of the human person.

Against the culture of coercion and violence, as men and women of faith we confess a Christian community woven together by dialogue and prayer and, being healed of sinful aggression, reaching out to the Other in brotherhood love (*agape*). This is our Christian witness, a counter-culture until in the fullness of time all things are restored to the perfection God still purposes for his creation.

Notes

[1] For an excellent survey, see Sissela Bok's *Mayhem: Violence as Public Entertainment* (Reading, Mass.: Addison-Wesley, 1998).

[2] The now classic "Dialogue Decalogue" was authored by Leonard Swidler, editor of *Journal of Ecumenical Studies*, and published in the journal in the first issue of 1983; see also his *After the Absolute: The Dialogical Future of Religious Reflection* (Philadelphia: Fortress Press, 1990), 42-44.

[3] *Tolerance* as a personal attitude, lower in value than empathy, is of course different from *toleration* as a governmental policy.

[4] Prof. R. J. Rummel of the University of Hawaii, author of *Democide: Nazi Genocide and Mass Murder* (New Brunswick, N.J.: Transaction Publishers, 1992), *Death by Government* (New Brunswick, N.J.: Transaction Publishers, 1994), and *Statistics of Democide: Genocide and Mass Murder since 1900* (Charlottesville, Va.: Center for National Security Law, School of Law, University of Virginia, 1997), in a paper entitled "Explaining Twentieth Century Genocide and the Role of Demonization" for the Vidal Sassoon Center for the Study of Antisemitism, MSS page 9.

[5] Published in *Unterwegs* 4 (1954): 196-205, and found in translation as Appendix No. 1 in my *Wild Tongues: A Handbook of Social Pathology* (New York: Macmillan Co., 1969).

[6] Rummel, 17f.

[7] Ibid., 25.

[8] On the Early Warning System see my article in III *Holocaust & Genocide Studies* 4 (1988): 483-90.

[9] "He must needs be presumed to have made choice of that Government as should least Expose his People to Hazard, either from the Fraud, or Arbitrary measures of particular men." John Wise, *A Vindication of the Government of the New-England Churches . . . 1717*, re-issued with an Introduction by Perry Miller (Gainesville, Flor.: Scholars' Facsimiles & Reprints, 1958), 62.

[10] A. D. Lindsay, *The Essentials of Democracy* (Philadelphia: University of Pennsylvania Press, 1929), 19, 37.

[11] A classical presentation of this spiritual descent, with its relevance for democratic societies and its inherent repudiation of totalitarianism, was written by a scholar of the Church of the Brethren, Donald F. Durnbaugh, *The Believers' Church* (New York: Macmillan Co., 1968).

[12] LXXX *The Christian Century* (1963) 26: 826-28.

Celibacy and Sexual Malpractice: Dimensions of Power and Powerlessness in Patriarchal Society

Brian F. Linnane

In recent years, ethicists like Karen Lebacqz and Marie Fortune have helped to focus the attention of Christian communities on the problem of clerical sexual malpractice, that is, the sexual manipulation or abuse of adult parishioners. Sexual relations between pastor and parishioner, even if apparently consensual, have the strong potential, it is argued, to be abusive of the parishioner due to the greater social and religious power that adheres to the role of the clergy member. The parishioner is said to be the victim of sexual abuse because the power inequity involved undermines the capacity for authentic consent and due to the suffering that can result from the betrayal of trust in a professional and pastoral relationship. Because reports of such malpractice are often anecdotal, the extent of this problem is difficult to determine. The statistics available suggest that the problem is a serious one for the churches.[1]

In the Roman Catholic community, concerns about clerical sexual malpractice often focus on the culpability of the individual priest. This paper suggests that this phenomenon may also reflect the way that power relations are structured in the Catholic church rather than simply the immoral and unprofessional behavior of individuals. Particular attention will be paid to the discipline of celibacy, as it is presently experienced by a significant number of priests, and clerical sexual malpractice. My purpose is not to suggest a rejection of hierarchical authority in Roman Catholicism or of clerical celibacy, but rather to ask questions about how these institutions are currently structured—do they serve to promote the counter-cultural dimensions of the Christian message or are they serving the interests of a prevailing power structure in a way that might be contrary to the gospel? Before turning to this question, it will be helpful to consider briefly the ways in which the new histories of sexuality have served to alert Christian ethicists to the dynamics of power in gender relationships and to the potential for abuse and manipulation in sexual relationships between adults.

The New Histories of Sexuality: Attending to the Cultural Dynamics of Power in Sexual Relations

Many scholars point to the publication of Michel Foucault's *La Volonté de savoir*[2] in 1976 as a turning point for contemporary histories of sexuality and gender relations.[3] His work served to undermine essentialist notions of human sexuality; that is, that human sexuality is only a biological given and so a constant in human history. Sexuality, Foucault suggests, is intimately related to the subtle dynamics of the interplay between power and knowledge in particular societies. Far from being hidden and repressed, concern for human sexuality in the modern West has generated multiple authoritative (scientific) "discourses" that serve to catalogue and characterize human sexual response. While such discourse is construed as objective, Foucault and his interpreters see that it actually reflects the interests of the powerful. So, then, for a sexual practice/pleasure to be characterized as perverse indicates, at least in part, that it does not serve the interests of prevailing power structures in a given society. While Foucault does not claim that there is a unified intention or beneficiary behind these power relationships, he does suggest that traditional and economic values are reinforced.[4] In this regard he writes,

> For was this transformation of sex into discourse not governed by the endeavor to expel from reality the forms of sexuality that were not amenable to the strict economy of reproduction: to say no to unproductive activities, to banish casual pleasures, to reduce or exclude practices whose object was not procreation? . . . All this garrulous attention which has us in a stew over sexuality, is it not motivated by one basic concern: to ensure population, to reproduce labor capacity, to perpetuate the form of social relations: in short, to constitute a sexuality that is economically useful and politically conservative?[5]

The idea that what has been held to be normative in human sexuality and gender relations is not so much a reflection of what is natural as it is a reflection of power relationships within a particular culture has had an enormous impact on Christian sexual ethics.

Influenced by Foucault and his followers, many Christian ethicists have moved away from an understanding of sexual morality as a matter of private, personal ethics solely concerned with issues of love, fidelity, procreation, and the like to a view of sexual ethics as a sociocultural concern focusing on justice and social transformation.[6] Feminist thinkers, for example, have argued that social arrangements are constructed so as to denigrate the sexual experience of women and so to limit their sexual (and thus personal) autonomy. Their work has shown the central role of domination and the potential for violence even in socially approved gender relations while exposing the limits of consent in a patriarchal culture.[7] Thus there has been an increased awareness of power inequities within gender relations and a concern to develop means to protect and promote authentic consent in such relations. In addition, feminist Christian ethicists and others have highlighted the potential for abuse of adults within professional relationships, including the minister-parishioner relationship. This phenomenon is often treated as a problem of professional ethics; however, it is the purpose of this paper to look at this issue in light of the ways in which power is structured in the contemporary church.

Sexual malpractice is a distinct form of sexual abuse in that it involves sexualizing a professional relationship in which the client's consent is presumed due to his or her age and general competence. In another context, I have addressed the issue of clerical sexual malpractice in the Roman Catholic tradition not as a problem of the discipline of celibacy (as is often suggested) but as a power violation, pointing to the power inequity between the priest as pastoral counselor and the parishioner/counselee in crisis.[8] In this paper, I intend to push that assertion by examining how celibacy functions in a power structure that can be perceived as authoritarian. Power accrues to the priest due to his status in the church and society. In the pastoral counseling relationship the priest is more powerful than his client due to his role as healer. Higher levels of education and personal charisma often serve to enhance a priest's power. Finally, in a patriarchal society men are more powerful than women.[9] The inappropriate or manipulative use of the priest's or counselor's power to sexualize a pastoral relationship always, I argued, undermines the potential for free consent on the part of the client and has enormous potential to inflict greater harm on that already vulnerable person.

What I want to address in this essay is the situation of the priest-abuser. Are there any clues in the situation of Catholic priests or other clerics that would shed some light on this alarming phenomenon? It does not seem, at least on first glance, to be an issue of imposed clerical celibacy—the experience of many adult women and men who have been sexually manipulated and abused by noncelibate, married clerics supports this perception. Nor is this essentially an issue of psychopathology or paraphilia, for I am not addressing the problem of clerical pedophiles or ephebophiles, that is those members of the clergy who gratify their sexual urges with (and so abuse) children or adolescents. Nonetheless, there does seem reason to suspect that at least part of the answer might be found in the "stress factors" that affect members of the ordained clergy at the present time. These factors are said to generate poor morale among members of the clergy, whose situation is often characterized by a sense of isolation, irrelevance, and powerlessness.[10] While these stress factors may go some way in explaining the phenomenon of sexual malpractice, it may be the case that these factors are symptoms of a larger, systemic issue characteristic of the structure of power relations in church communities organized around patriarchal principles. The next section of this paper will address these "symptoms" before turning to a discussion of what some have perceived as a systemic problem.

Power Experienced as Powerlessness

In the post-war period, there have been many cultural, social, and religious shifts—if not revolutions—that have affected the Roman Catholic priesthood. The huge increase in vocations following World War II dropped off markedly in the mid-1960s, a period that also saw the beginning of an unprecedented departure rate from the priesthood and religious life. This has resulted in a crisis of meaning for those priests who remain *and* has meant an increased—and often solitary—workload. In addition, the secularization of Western society has meant that the church, and so the priest, has been "de-centered." To large segments of the population the church is simply irrelevant; in other segments the priest and church teaching are no longer the only or principal sources of moral and religious guidance. Nowhere is this more clear than in the realm of sexual morality. Virtually every dimension of traditional Christian sexual ethics has been called into question. The value of sexual self-denial, which had pride of place in a religiously sanctioned ethic of duty, obedience to authority, and self-sacrifice have given way to contemporary society's ethic of self-fulfillment,[11] of which sexual self-fulfillment is at the heart.

Given these changes, particularly changes in understandings of human sexuality and intimacy, it is not surprising that the discipline of celibacy is a significant cause of low priestly morale.[12] The culture itself denigrates celibacy and sexual abstinence; far from an heroic stance, the media bombards the celibate with the message that there is something profoundly askew in his lifestyle, that he is an oddity. The priest then is not likely to perceive himself as particularly powerful. Rather, he can feel a victim, caught between the demands of an unbending hierarchy and the enticements of a permissive culture. Thus, it is not difficult to see that "acting out" sexually may be one way of dealing with the frustrations inherent to the contemporary experience of ordained ministry.[13] Psychologist William Perri confirms this when he writes, "unconscious feelings of victimization and sexual inadequacy, both of which can be associated with enforced celibacy, may lead to a search for power and abusive control in relationships."[14] Celibacy, then, insofar as it is experienced as "forced" rather than freely embraced, can be symptomatic of a malaise that serves as a breeding ground for abusive relationships.[15]

While sexual renunciation itself does not explain clerical sexual malpractice, the experience of being a victim of sexually confining and controlling power might. Commenting on the traditional Christian tendency to view sex and sexuality in a negative way, Marvin Ellison writes,

> One consequence of this control system is that prevailing sexual moral discourse, in both its conservative and liberal guises, remains overwhelmingly judgmental, fear-ridden, and punitive. Another consequence is that people become both self-hating and pleasure deprived. When deprived of pleasure, and especially pleasurable touch, people are not only more prone to violence, but also more compliant with external authorities.[16]

To see the priest-abuser as victim (which in no way absolves him of responsibility for sexual malpractice) can help us to expose the patriarchal power dynamic in which all women are dominated by men and all are dominated by a few men.[17] This will also help us to see the difficulties before us in preventing sexual malpractice.

At the most basic level, the understanding of priest-abusers as victims themselves demonstrates the difficulties church authorities and mental health professionals face in educating members of the clergy about abuses of power and boundary violations. If these persons do not perceive themselves as powerful, it may be difficult—if not impossible—for them to identify their own manipulative actions as power abuse.[18] Consider the case studies J. A. Loftus cites. The stories of "The Loneliness of Father-Uncle," "The Repentant Pedophile," and "The Wealthy Prostitute,"[19] all point to sad, lonely, and vulnerable men. None of these men experiences himself as powerful. There is the additional problem of self-deception among clerical abusers. Neil and Thea Ormerod report that the cleric "often does not see that he has done anything wrong, and can even rationalize his actions as somehow beneficial to his victims."[20] These examples demonstrate the ineffectiveness of the language of power in helping the priest-abuser understand his offense as well as in educating other priests about the problem of sexual malpractice as an abuse of power.

Ultimately such discussions are not effective because of appeals to power imbalance or of harm to pastoral clients, but because of consequences, that is, of legal and ecclesial punishment. Fear of negative consequences does not provide a strong moral evaluation of the damage such behavior causes. Nonetheless, the most effective message seems to be "the times have changed; if you engage in certain types of activity you are going to get into trouble." John Allan Loftus's book, *Understanding Sexual Misconduct by Clergy*,[21] an introductory handbook for pastoral ministers, reflects this message. While Loftus is no stranger to the complexity of the issue of sexual malpractice and abuse and he clearly states that the message of the churches must be more than simply "c-y-a,"[22] his book does take on a pragmatic tone that seeks to assist members of the clergy in establishing boundaries.[23] Further, Loftus worries about the credibility of the church and its ministries if we do not face the problem of sexual malpractice among the clergy.[24] Little attention is paid to the reality of the victim of power abuse and the destructive potential of such activities.

To view *clerical* sexual malpractice solely, or even primarily, as a matter of professional ethics—as many writers do[25]—may also represent a mistaken strategy. Such a strategy tends to isolate the priest-abuser from the systemic context of patriarchal and hierarchical control. It allows church authorities and others to claim that the problem of clerical sexual malpractice has to do with weak or deviant individuals and not with the discipline of celibacy as it is presently structured or the organizational character of the church.

Another approach to the problem of sexual malpractice by Roman Catholic priests is that of a psychological/spiritual approach, which seeks to help the priest embrace celibacy as a healthy, apostolically effective life-style. In other words, it seeks to help the priest overcome the effects of poor morale. The subtitle of a work I have already referred to, William Perri's book, *A Radical Challenge for Priesthood Today: From Trial to Transformation*, indicates that it falls in this category.[26] This approach, heavily influenced by psychotherapy, helps the priest deal with his reality in a constructive way. It encourages him to recognize his own need for human intimacy and to seek appropriate ways to fulfill that need.

Celibacy, Power, and Sexual Control

The danger with this approach and others like it is that it may not offer the critical leverage necessary to attend to the destructive tendencies inherent in the priest's "reality." These approaches tend to address the symptoms of a problem that is much deeper. We come again to the problematic nature of patriarchy. For it seems that sexual malpractice by members of the clergy—which is, of course, nothing new—ultimately serves to expose the pattern of power relation between women and men as well as between those few men in the higher reaches of the hierarchical power structure and those men lower down. Feminist writers show us that this pattern of power relationship is one of dominance and submission. If we are to rid our culture of the abuse of clerical sexual malpractice we must honestly assess the power dynamics of patriarchal society, the church's role in maintaining that structure, and the resources of Christianity for generating an equitable and just pattern of relationship between women and men and so throughout society.

The insights culled from the feminist analysis of patriarchy are widely known.[27] In most societies, men are, on the whole, more powerful than women and so society is organized to maintain this power inequity and the benefits for the more powerful that accrue from it. This power, feminists argue, "takes the form of male domination of women in all areas of life; sexual domination is so universal, so ubiquitous and so complete that it appears 'natural' and hence becomes invisible."[28] What sexual malpractice by members of the clergy does, then, is expose the pattern of dominance and submission that characterizes the sexual relations of men and women generally and that is otherwise invisible due to its "natural" character.

While there is a radical feminist critique of patriarchy that argues that all sexual relations between men and women are expressions of violence or rape and advocates a rejection of heterosexuality, mainstream Christian feminists have argued that an adequate sexual ethic must account for the differences in power between women and men in patriarchal society.[29] Karen Lebacqz's 1990 Presidential Address to the Society of Christian Ethics, "Love Your Enemy: Sex, Power, and Christian Ethics,"[30] is illuminating in the regard. Lebacqz suggests that for a woman to fall in love with a man—given the circumstances of patriarchy—is to fall in love with the enemy; using "the term 'enemy' to indicate the man's role as representative of those who have power in this culture."[31] It is obvious that not every man seeks to harm or dominate the woman he is romantically attracted to, but Lebacqz argues persuasively that a realistic ethic of heterosexual relations must "take seriously the power that attaches to a man in this culture simply because he is a man (no matter how powerless he may feel), the power that he has as representative of other men, and the power that he has for women as representative of the politics of dominance and submission and as representative of the threat of violence in women's lives."[32]

All persons in contemporary American society—women and men—are socialized to view sexual relations as a matter of dominance and to equate the erotic with the violent. Thus Shulamith Firestone claims that "[l]ove, perhaps even more than child-bearing, is the pivot of women's oppression today."[33] It is argued that love between a man and woman is essentially oppressive in our culture because it cannot be based upon equality; rather it reflects, as Valerie Bryson suggests, "women's economic and social dependency and ensures that they will not challenge their subordinate position."[34] I hope that my point is clear: sexual abuse of adult women by members of the clergy is simply a blatant example of the destructive logic of patriarchy.[35] It is of course dangerous not merely to its victims but also to those who benefit from patriarchal arrangements. Such arrangements are exposed not as natural but as violent and dehumanizing—for both women and men. Yet the deep-seated fear of loss of power explains the patterns of avoidance: ignoring the problem of clerical malpractice, blaming the victim, at best dealing with the effects and external manifestations.

If we reconsider Kate Millet's concise statement of the principles of patriarchy: "male shall dominate female, elder male shall dominate young,"[36] and recall what I have already said about the moral problems of the Roman Catholic clergy as victims of an unbending power structure, we can see something of the church's complicity in the pattern of domination and submission.

The literature on the patriarchal nature of Christianity generally and Roman Catholicism in particular is, of course, vast. I do not intend to rehearse the arguments of that literature but rather to reflect on celibacy as a religious means of controlling sexuality and its implications for women. For as Richard Sipe has put it, "Celibacy is . . . a factor in the power system of the church and is intimately connected with its abuses."[37] Nor can I sketch a historical development of the Roman tradition of celibacy.[38] What can be said, however, is that whatever spiritual or theological justifications one can muster for a celibate clergy, two "worldly factors" cannot be denied. First, the controlled sexuality of priests conforms with the power interests of the church hierarchy. And, secondly, sex and thus women are perceived as dangerous to this power structure. With regard to the first point, David Rice writes, "Compulsory celibacy is, or was, incredibly efficient—the ultimate management technique, giving total control and total mobility of personnel, and rendering priests independent of this-worldly interests and free of lay control."[39] Or from the psychological point of view, Sipe cites the truism, "Control a person's sexuality and you control the person."[40] Here we do well to recall the link between the experience of being controlled engendered by mandatory celibacy and the search for power and abusive control in one's relationships cited by William Perri and others.[41]

With regard to the celibate power structure and the perception of women as dangerous, it is clear that this power structure is threatened by sex and by those identified with sex—that is the submissive, the passive, in other words, women. Sipe cites ample evidence to support his claim that "the male celibate/sexual system functions with a deep ambivalence—even fear and hostility—toward them."[42] Traditionally, priests have been taught that women and relationships with women were a source of danger, that these relationships themselves threaten the vocation of the priest. Sipe then points to a pattern of idealization and denigration in which women are perceived in accord with the archetypes of "the virgin/mother" and "the seducer/whore."[43] This pattern allows for the control of celibate men by fear and the oppression/objectification of women. As such, it is a pattern capable of destructive and dehumanizing manifestations.

If we can claim, then, that the sexual abuse of women by clergy is simply a particularly blatant and distasteful manifestation of the patriarchal power that is fostered by, and sustaining of, the Christian church, what—if any—are the prospects for repentance and renewal? For we must face the question, is the essence of Christianity so tied up with the destructive dimensions of patriarchy that it must be abandoned, at least by self-respecting women? My own conclusion is that such a drastic response is neither necessary nor particularly helpful. As the feminist theologian, Mary Ann Hinsdale, has argued, "Separatism simply reinforces power relationships; it does not change the order nor recognize seriously enough that allowing separate spaces can be a subtle way of maintaining dominance . . . separatism functions to serve the needs of the order."[44] With this in mind, the final part of this article will point to a few resources available to the Christian community for re-imagining itself as a force to dismantle patriarchy and to construct a culture of equality and justice.

Responsibility and Renewal

Using the Roman Catholic church as a test case, I have argued that clerical sexual malpractice is not entirely a problem of professional ethics that can be solved by better screening of candidates for orders or careful seminary training on respecting boundaries. The roots of this serious problem are to be found, I have suggested, in the power structure of this church, which is patriarchal and hierarchical. In this final section of the paper, I want to suggest two sources for conversion and renewal for Catholic Christianity with regard to this systemic issue: New Testament sexual ethics, particularly as developed by Lisa Sowle Cahill, and feminist ecclesiologies.

It is possible, in discussions such as this, to seem to impute culpability or blameworthiness to the Christian church for the evils of patriarchy; to claim that the logic of Christian doctrine is necessarily patriarchal or that church authorities plan to harm women and less powerful men. This is not my intention. I view patriarchy and the abuses it generates as a manifestation of social sin or "the sin of the world." This enables us to examine the church's responsibility to rectify this sin without blaming the church as the source of this abuse. Social sin is not traceable to the action of one individual or group. It is a structure of human existence that affects human actions negatively; like original sin, it is prior to individual choice. According to Judith Merkle, some of the manifestations of social sin include: "blindness toward human actions as to their real import; a system of personal or communal desires that is satisfied with less-than-human conditions in the world; and, a satisfaction with the lack of change in the human spirit."[45] The first characteristic of social sin, "blindness to the real import of actions" readily applies to the Christian church and its inability to see how its actions, disciplines, and ethics endorse a set of practices that are destructive of human well-being and flourishing.

There is a tendency, when confronted with the realities of social sin, to think that because no one person or group is directly to blame for it, no one is responsible for this evil. Such a view is inaccurate. Individuals and groups are responsible to be aware of "the signs of the times" and to be open to conversion away from "false consciousness." The cries of persons who have been sexually used by a priest, who are themselves caught up in a patriarchal power structure, call out in judgment and in hope to that organization which promises more abundant life to all persons. This community and its leaders must address the problem of patriarchal abuse, and its complicity in it, if it is to be true to the message it is missioned to proclaim.[46]

It is ironic to note that the example for the church's conversion may be found in the witness of its scriptures and early faith communities. Lisa Sowle Cahill's work in the biblical roots of Christian sexual ethics is particularly helpful here.[47] Cahill's thesis is that "Jesus' preaching of the reign or kingdom of God represents a new experience of the divine presence in history, an experience which transforms human relationships by reordering relations of dominance and violence toward greater compassion, mercy, and peace, expressed in active solidarity with 'the poor.' "[48] New Testament sexual teaching served as a radical challenge to the oppressive and violent dimensions of socially approved gender roles and familial relations in the ancient world. Further, Cahill argues that the sexual conduct that New Testament writers sought to proscribe were "status-making, boundary-erecting, other-dominating, and self-promoting actions and practices."[49] It is not, Cahill argues, the concrete sexual norms generated by the New Testament that should draw our attention—our cultures and worldviews are too distinct; rather it is the radical social challenge of early Christianity that seeks to dismantle all social structures that dehumanize and marginalize persons. She writes,

> The continuing norm of New Testament ethics is compassion and solidarity which brings into community those who have not been looked upon or treated as fellow human beings with interests, needs, and potentials for development and contribution which are as important as those of the "ruling class." Both the success of early Christian morality in its own setting and its authority for our own must be evaluated by this core moral component of our faith. Although this core is not unique to Christianity, Christian faith, centered on Jesus as the inauguration of God's reign, throws it into relief and gives it ultimate moral importance.[50]

Cahill's careful reading of the New Testament sources offers support for those who look to the church to respect and promote the full moral agency of all persons.

If we are able to find a compelling connection between clerical sexual malpractice and the patriarchal/hierarchical dimensions of the church, the problem that we face is ultimately an ecclesiological one. While there have been a number of proposals for a more inclusive, participatory model of church,[51] I will point briefly to some Catholic feminist proposals. For among all of the current theologies of liberation, the greatest concern for interecclesial justice is found in feminist theologies.

Heightened feminist consciousness in the last thirty years has resulted in a conflict for many Catholic women with the structure of their church. Their exclusion from ordained ministry and the decision-making processes of the church has caused some women of faith to move away from the institutional church, while others have worked vigorously to bring about change. While much of this work has focused on opening ordination to women, many Catholic feminists now see the need for what Mary Hines refers to as "[a] massive transformation of the church's structures [to] free them from the patriarchal, hierarchical, and clerical assumptions that prevent the church from becoming a prophetic community of equal disciples committed to the task of liberation for all people."[52]

Roman Catholic feminist ecclesiologies[53] are generally characterized by two common elements: a commitment to the post-Vatican II shift away from understanding the church as a "perfect society," to the understanding of the church as the pilgrim people of God—a community marked by both grace and sin; and a commitment to grassroots change, which flows from the experience of women and other marginalized persons. To take the first point seriously requires that Christians honestly evaluate those dimensions of their ecclesial existence that foster and perpetuate the social sin of patriarchy. It entails a commitment not to continue business as usual but rather to listen and learn from those persons who are abused, victimized and exploited by the current power arrangements in the church. The second element points to new ecclesial movements *within* the church such as Women-Church. Such a community emphasizes the equality of all disciples, highlighting the common baptismal responsibility for the evangelizing and liberating mission of the church. In this regard, Hines writes,

> Imagining the church as a discipleship of equals undermines the pervasive influence of patriarchy epitomized in the hierarchical structures of the church. Since all are followers of Jesus and sharers in his liberating ministry, there is no room for an absolute centralizing power and authority in the hands of the dominant few males. Structures that legitimate relationships of dominance and subordination have no place in a community of equal disciples.[54]

If such an experience of church and ministry is to emerge, feminists argue, it is most likely to have its genesis in small grassroots communities of faith. For our purposes, it is important to note that such an ecclesial vision can offer some hope for a remedy to the pattern of dominance and submission that we discerned in the ongoing problem of clerical sexual malpractice.

It is similarly important to acknowledge that possessing the resources for revisioning ecclesial life is no guarantee that such resources will be utilized. Indeed, there is strong resistance within church authority structures to those ecclesiologies perceived to be overly inclusive and democratic. While, in themselves, such theological developments will not produce dramatic change within church communities, they can be understood to reflect and support incremental change in the way that power relations are structured in church and society. They do so by exposing unjust and de-humanizing dynamics within the churches and by offering an alternative view of relationality and community for those who are striving to be faithful to the Christian gospel.

Conclusion

This paper began by reflecting on the importance of postmodern histories of sexuality for understanding the potentially abusive dynamics of power that adhere to contemporary constructions of human sexuality and gender relations, abusive dynamics not unknown in the Christian churches. These histories, then, make an important contribution to uncovering what is de-humanizing and abusive while fueling a drive for liberation from that which undermines the human spirit. Yet there is need for caution. As Lisa Sowle Cahill has pointed out, postmodern histories and theories are often better at unmasking oppression than they are at articulating an account of authentic liberation.[55] So, then, while postmodern histories can help Catholic Christians to grasp the challenges that face this religious communion, there is no need to abandon or despair of this tradition. The Roman Catholic tradition has the resources to address the debilitating aspects of hierarchy and so become a more inclusive community and an effective sign for the liberation of all persons.[56]

Notes

[1] While I have not encountered statistics on the scope of this problem specifically within the Catholic church, statistics available from other denominations are illuminating. The General Assembly of the Presbyterian Church (USA) reports that "statistical evidence suggests that between ten and twenty-three percent of clergy nationwide have engaged in sexualized behavior or sexual contact with parishioners, clients, employees, etc., within a professional relationship," ("Policies and Procedures on Sexual Misconduct," 1991). Neil and Thea Ormerod point to a 1990 United Methodist survey of sixteen hundred laypersons,

which showed that "twenty-three percent of laywomen said they had been sexually harassed, seventeen percent by their own pastor and nine percent by another minister," (Ormerod, Neil and Thea, *When Ministers Sin: Sexual Abuse in the Churches* [Alexandria, Australia: Millennium Books, 1995], 7).

[2] Published in English as Volume 1 of *The History of Sexuality* (New York: Random House, 1978).

[3] Martha Vicinus, in a review essay focusing on seven histories of sexuality written shortly after the publication of the English edition of Foucault's history, cites the already pervasive influence of his work, "Sexuality and Power: A Review of Current Work in the History of Sexuality," *Feminist Studies* 8 (1982): 138.

[4] Foucault, *The History of Sexuality*, 106-7.

[5] Ibid., 36-37.

[6] In this regard, see Marvin M. Ellison, *Sexual Justice: A Liberating Ethic of Sexuality*, (Louisville, Kentucky: John Knox Westminster Press, 1996). He writes, "By and large, even liberal Christians either regard patriarchal control as socially necessary or dismiss sexuality as rather indifferent matter that bears little consequence compared to 'larger,' more 'legitimate' social issues. For many people the link between sexuality and justice is muddled at best. By not paying attention to sexual oppression, people fail to grasp how a multiplicity of interconnected social oppressions operate in the small and large places of their lives, in and on their bodies and the body politic. . . . *They fail to see that sexual oppression is intimately bound up with race, gender, and class oppression*" (90, emphasis added).

[7] Karen Lebacqz, for example, writes in her Presidential Address to the Society of Christian Ethics, "I argue that an adequate Christian sexual ethic must attend to the realities of the links between violence and sexuality in the experiences of women. It must attend to male power and to the eroticizing of domination in this culture. Because domination is eroticized, and because violence and sexuality are linked in the experiences of women, the search for loving heterosexual intimacy is for many women an exercise in irony: women must seek intimacy precisely in an arena that is culturally and experientially unsafe, fraught with sexual violence and power struggles," ("Love Your Enemies: Sex, Power, and Christian Ethics," *The Annual of the Society of Christian Ethics* [1990]: 3-4).

[8] "Playing with Sore Hearts," *The Tablet* (12 October 1996): 1321-22.

[9] While it is the case that some individual women are more powerful than some individual men (a dynamic that can be exacerbated by the politics of race and class), the point here is that individual men do represent the patriarchal power arrangements in contemporary society. See my discussion of Karen Lebacqz on this point (p. 234 above).

[10] See National Conference of Catholic Bishops, *Reflections on the Morale of Priests* (Washington, D.C.: United States Catholic Conference, 1988). John Allan Loftus, S.J., also finds evidence of "a keen sense of isolation and loneliness" in priests who "act out" in a sexually inappropriate way, *Understanding Sexual Misconduct by Clergy*, (Washington, D.C.: The Pastoral Press, 1994), 39.

[11] For a brief discussion of the ethics of authenticity or self-fulfillment, see

William Schweiker, *Responsibility and Christian Ethics* (Cambridge: Cambridge University Press, 1995), 27-28.

[12] This is acknowledged by the Roman Catholic bishops of the United States in their document, *Reflections on the Morale of Priests*. Also see William D. Perri's discussion, *A Radical Challenge for Priesthood Today* (Mystic, Conn.: Twenty-Third Publications, 1996), 58-60. Perri quotes Daniel Nelson's analysis of the bishops' study on morale, "This document identifies the lack of openness by church administration to discuss optional celibacy in the context of changing understandings of sexuality and sexual orientation as a major factor to the current low morale among Catholic clergy. It identified this rigidity towards mandatory celibacy as a major reason a) for leaving the priesthood, b) for the shortage of vocations, and c) for loneliness and personal unhappiness of those who stay . . ." (59). David Rice's *Shattered Vows* (London: Michael Joseph, 1990), a journalistic approach to the issue of priestly celibacy, also asserts a link between "forced" celibacy and low priestly morale (222-26).

[13] Karen Lebacqz and Ronald G. Barton also point to the stresses of contemporary ordained ministry as reason for "sexual acting-out on the part of pastors (*Sex in the Parish* [Louisville, Ky.: John Knox/Westminster, 1991], 18).

[14] Perri, *A Radical Challenge*, 66.

[15] It is, of course, somewhat problematic to refer to the Roman Catholic priest's pledge of celibacy as "forced." No one is forced to be a priest. Nonetheless, rather than experiencing a call to a celibate life, some priests may view it simply as a (more or less coercive) requirement to ordained ministry.

[16] Ellison, *Sexual Justice*, 22.

[17] Kate Millet, *Sexual Politics* (London: Virago, 1985), 25.

[18] Loftus makes this point in his book, *Understanding Sexual Misconduct*, 16.

[19] Ibid., 27-28, 31-32, 22-23, respectively.

[20] Ormerod, Neil and Thea, *When Ministers Sin*, 75.

[21] Loftus, *Understanding Sexual Misconduct*.

[22] "cover-your-ass"; ibid., 58.

[23] Ibid., 43-53. The cases cited in Chapter Three also seem to make this point (19-35).

[24] Ibid., 56.

[25] Neil and Thea Ormerod (*When Ministers Sin*) write that sexual contact between a minister and parishioner or client is " 'unprofessional' in much the same way that such behavior would be unprofessional in a doctor, counselor or teacher" (72). Karen Lebacqz and Marie Fortune, although sensitive to questions of patriarchy and abuse in the churches, also tend to frame the problem of clerical sexual malpractice in terms of professional ethics. See Fortune's "Is Nothing Sacred? The Betrayal of the Ministerial or Teaching Relationship," *Violence against Women and Children*, ed. Carol Adams and Marie Fortune (New York: Continuum, 1995), 351-60, esp. 353-56; or her "Clergy Misconduct: Sexual Abuse in the Ministerial Relationship," *Concilium: Violence against Women*, 1994/1, ed. M. S. Copeland and E. Schüssler Fiorenza; and Lebacqz and Barton, *Sex in the Parish*.

[26] Perri, *A Radical Challenge*. The fifth chapter of this book, "From Abusive Power to Intimacy," deals with the issues of power and abuse.

[27] For a very helpful overview, see Valerie Bryson, *Feminist Political Theory* (London: Macmillan, 1992), esp. 181-232.

[28] Ibid., 185. The natural and invisible character of the "constructed" pattern of dominance and submission is important to my argument. I do not want to suggest that the response (or lack of response) of religious hierarchies to such arrangements represents "bad faith."

[29] See, for example, Lisa Sowle Cahill, *Sex, Gender, and Christian Ethics* (Cambridge: Cambridge University Press, 1996) or Marie M. Fortune, *Love Does No Harm: Sexual Ethics for the Rest of Us* (New York: Continuum, 1995).

[30] *The Annual of the Society of Christian Ethics* (1990): 3-23.

[31] Ibid., 12.

[32] Ibid., 11.

[33] Shulamith Firestone, *The Dialectic of Sex* (London: Women's Press, 1979), 121.

[34] Bryson, *Feminist Political Theory*, 201.

[35] This same logic explains the homosexual abuse of men by members of the clergy. Feminist and gay critics have persuasively linked the subordination of women with the abuse of homosexuals. See Rosemary Radford Ruether, "Homophobia, Heterosexism, and Pastoral Practice," *Homosexuality in Priest-hood and Religious Life*, ed. Jeannine Gramick (New York: Crossroad, 1989) and Beverly Wildung Harrison, "Misogyny and Homophobia: The Unexplored Connections," *Making the Connections: Essays in Feminist Social Ethics*, ed. Carol S. Robb (Boston: Beacon Press, 1985).

[36] Millet, *Sexual Politics*, 25.

[37] A. W. Richard Sipe, *Sex, Priests, and Power: Anatomy of a Crisis* (London: Cassell; New York: Brunner-Mazel, 1995), 46.

[38] Sipe offers a balanced and concise account of this development, ibid., 96-111.

[39] Rice, *Shattered Vows*, 229.

[40] Sipe, *Sex, Priests, and Power*, 99.

[41] Perri, *A Radical Challenge*, 66.

[42] Sipe, *Sex, Priests, and Power*, 101.

[43] Ibid., 100-8. Also see Susan A. Ross's discussion of women's bodies as symbols of the sexual and the corruptible in the Christian tradition, " 'Then Honor God in Your Body' (1 Cor. 6:20): Feminist and Sacramental Theology on the Body," *Horizons* 16/1 (Spring, 1989): 7-27, esp 15-23. Ross writes, "The denigration of the female body has been evident in ritual proscriptions against female contact with the holy, in the classification of women as ontologically different from (and consequently, inferior to) men, and in a negatively obsessive concern with sexual matters in a tradition where women symbolize the sexual to celibate men" (18).

[44] Hinsdale, Mary Ann, "Power and Participation in the Church: Voices from the Margins," *Warren Lecture Series in Catholic Studies* 13, The University of Tulsa, October 28, 1990, 9.

[45] Merkle, Judith A., "Sin," *The New Dictionary of Catholic Social Thought*, ed. J. Dwyer (Collegeville, Minn.: The Liturgical Press, 1994), 883-88.

[46] William Schweiker writes, "In so far as an institution represents its identity through interpretive practices (reports to shareholders, accounting practices, political traditions, social histories, communal memories) and thus constitutes itself through time, then it is rightly held responsible for respecting and enhancing the integrity of life" (*Responsibility and Christian Ethics*, 184).

[47] Cahill, *Sex, Gender, and Christian Ethics*, esp 121-216. Also see Sally B. Purvis, *The Power of the Cross: Foundations for a Christian Feminist Ethic of Community* (Nashville, Tenn.: Abingdon Press, 1993).

[48] Ibid., 121.

[49] Ibid., 157.

[50] Ibid., 163.

[51] In this regard, see Terrence L. Nichol's recent book, *That All May Be One: Hierarchy and Participation in the Church* (Collegeville, Minn.: The Liturgical Press, 1997). Nichols argues for a participatory hierarchy and holarchy, a concept that allows for unique traditions and practices in local churches while maintaining a principle of unity.

[52] Hines, Mary E., "Community for Liberation," *Freeing Theology*, ed. C. M. LaCugna (New York: Harper Collins, 1993), 163-64.

[53] Here I include the work of Rosemary Radford Ruether, Elisabeth Schüssler Fiorenza, Mary Hines, and Mary Ann Hinsdale.

[54] Hines, "Community for Liberation," 175.

[55] Cahill, *Sex, Gender, and Christian Ethics*, 28.

[56] I am grateful to an anonymous reader of this article and to my colleague, Mary E. Hobgood, for their comments and suggestions on earlier drafts of this paper. I am also grateful to the Christian Survivors of Sexual Abuse (UK) for first inviting me to reflect systematically on the problem of clerical sexual malpractice.

Experiential Learning in Service of a Living Tradition

Margaret R. Pfeil

Perhaps there is no better way to appreciate the value of experiential learning in theological education than to be a graduate student instructor, a position which is itself predicated on the assumption that acquiring experience as a teacher is a constitutive step in the process of becoming a professor of theology. Under such auspices, I had the opportunity to construct and teach a second-level theology class at the University of Notre Dame entitled, "Catholic Social Teaching: A Living Tradition."

Based on insights gleaned from this experience, I would like to address the way in which the use of experiential learning in the theological curriculum may serve to elucidate a religious tradition unfolding in "lived" time. As a prelude to subsequent methodological considerations, I will begin with a description of the structure of the class and then devote attention to the manner in which this course shed light on Catholic social teaching as a living tradition via the two objectives of skillful textual interpretation and testing the applications of knowledge gained. Finally, I will address the significance of the community-based learning method in advancing the theological project of the class.

The Structure of the Class

It may be helpful to begin by noting a few particulars of the theology curriculum at Notre Dame. All undergraduates are required to take at least two theology classes. The first course functions as a prerequisite and consists of a treatment of scripture and the early church. In structuring my second-level class, I was able to presume this foundational knowledge, but I was also aware of the fact that the vast majority of my students were not theology majors. In fact, for many of them, this class would be their last encounter with formal theological education as undergraduates.

Within this context, I developed the course in consultation with the staffs of Notre Dame's Center for Social Concerns and the Kaneb Center for Teaching and Learning.[1] The structure reflected two main objectives. First, it was designed to help students develop skills for textual interpretation. Thus, they were asked to write two short analytical papers, which entailed choosing a particular text, locating it in its historical context, identifying a principal theme or operative principle, and reflecting on the significance of the document for the ecclesial community of the time.[2]

Second, the course asked students to examine the applications and implications of their growing knowledge of Catholic social teaching via one of two means. First, students could choose among three possible community-based learning sites where they were to work for fifteen hours over the course of the semester. This option culminated in a final paper in which they were asked to integrate their experience with the course material. The alternative, a research paper, was chosen by six out of the seventy students enrolled in this class over two semesters.

The three service-learning sites available were the South Bend Center for the Homeless, La Casa de Amistad (a Latino community center), and Earthworks (a faith-based organic farming project). At each site, a staff member worked with me to coordinate the placement of students. In offering the experiential learning option, the site coordinators and I presupposed the definition of community-based learning developed by Dr. Kathleen Maas Weigert of Notre Dame's Center for Social Concerns. It involves six dimensions, which together are intended to distinguish community-based learning from community service and other forms of experiential education:

> Three of the elements focus more on the community side of the equation; the other three focus more on the campus side. On the community side: the student provides some meaningful service (work) that meets a need or goal that is defined by a community (or some of its members). On the campus side: the service

provided by the student flows from and into course objectives, is integrated into the course by means of assignments that require some form of reflection on the service in light of course objectives, and the assignment is assessed and evaluated accordingly.[3]

Ongoing written assignments were designed to facilitate such appropriation of the material in accord with both course objectives. First, all of the students were asked to make weekly one-page entries in an integration notebook. Those who chose the community-based learning option used this forum to correlate their experience with particular aspects of the texts and class discussions. Those who opted for the research paper were asked to choose an article from a scholarly or popular journal or newspaper and to relate this to the course material.

Second, students met in small discussion groups of five to eight people for the first twenty minutes of each class. Group members took turns in facilitating the discussion by posing two or three critical questions drawn from the assigned readings. These questions were collected and evaluated as part of the students' class participation. After concluding the discussion, each facilitator offered a brief summary of the group's conversation to the rest of the class. I then attempted to incorporate these insights into a forty-minute lecture.

Hermeneutics: Elucidating a Religious Tradition Unfolding in "Lived" Time

The course title described Catholic social teaching as a living tradition, but in what sense is it to be considered "living"? In taking up this question, we might turn to John Paul II for some guidance. Among the objectives of his 1987 encyclical, *Sollicitudo Rei Socialis*, he cited the reaffirmation of the continuity as well as the "constant renewal" of Catholic social doctrine:

> This twofold dimension is typical of . . . [the Church's] teaching in the social sphere. On the one hand it is constant, for it remains identical in its fundamental inspiration, in its "principles of reflection," in its "criteria of judgment," in its basic "directives for action," and above all in its vital link with the Gospel of the Lord. On the other hand, it is ever new, because it is subject to the

necessary and opportune adaptations suggested by the changes
in historical conditions and by the unceasing flow of the events
which are the setting of the life of the people and society.[4]

For the purposes of our class, appreciation of Catholic social teaching
as a tradition at once constant and ever new involved the development
of a hermeneutic: Even as we were participants in history's unfolding,
we were also attempting to assess its significance. How were we to
situate a particular text historically? And, in turn, from what standpoint were we to interpret that text? In engaging this twofold hermeneutical task, we were on our way to meeting the first course objective.

   This endeavor also provided students with the conceptual categories necessary to correlate their community-based learning experiences
with the course material. While the experiential-learning method was
most operative in the students' movement toward the second course
objective (testing the applications and implications of their knowledge of Catholic social teaching), this goal presupposed substantial
progress toward the first objective of skillful textual interpretation. I
would also venture to say that active engagement of the implications
of Catholic social teaching in the lived experiences of community-
based learning spurred many of my students to fresh critical insight as
textual interpreters. So, a brief examination of the hermeneutical issues involved in the interpretive dimension of the course may prove
helpful in assessing the role of the experiential-learning method in
shaping the students' understanding of Catholic social teaching as a
living tradition.

   Taking up the first part of the hermeneutic, our initial challenge
was to test a presupposition held by many of the students that the
church's teaching has generally remained constant over time. This
dimension of our studies led to some cognitive dissonance. For example, our reading revealed that Leo XIII's treatment of private property in *Rerum Novarum* was not precisely consonant with the Thomistic
tradition that he purported to retrieve. In addition, we learned that
subsequent papal teaching would correct the Leonine interpretation of
Aquinas on this point. Pondering the implications of this particular
thread of the tradition, one student asked, "But does that mean that
Leo was *wrong* about private property in *Rerum Novarum*?" Suddenly,
the magisterial phrase often invoked to bridge the vicissitudes of his-

tory, "As the church has always taught . . .," was called into question.

Apart from the issue of private property, we encountered numerous other shifts in doctrine regarding particular social issues, including religious liberty, conscientious objection, and capital punishment. At every turn, it became increasingly clear that responsible interpretation required that the content of a particular text be situated against its historical horizon. This task involved cultivating an appreciation of the author's intentions, the ecclesial issues at stake, and the church's understanding of its relationship to state and society at a given historical juncture.

We discovered that not only particular aspects of doctrine but also the methods used in Catholic social teaching texts were historically conditioned. For example, Nell-Breuning's account of drafting *Quadragesimo Anno* in isolated secrecy[5] stood in sharp contrast to the elaborate consultative processes used by the U.S. bishops in crafting their peace and economic pastoral letters. At Nell-Breuning's invitation, students soon began to ask normative questions about the methods employed in the composition of ecclesial texts.

Often, students registered surprise not so much at the fact that a particular textual point or method may have been inadequate for the task at hand, but rather at how very *human* was the process by which Catholic social teaching unfolded. Resonating with John Paul II's assessment in *Sollicitudo Rei Socialis*, it was not difficult for us to think of the Catholic social teaching tradition, in terms of both particular points of doctrine and textual mechanics, as *living*. As this description implies, the tradition embodies a dynamic interrelationship of change and continuity over time.[6]

Addressing the first hermeneutical issue of the historical location of the documents necessarily entailed consideration of the second hermeneutical aspect, the standpoint of the interpreter. By raising questions of content and method, students were taking up their own interpretive stances, even as they were beginning to wonder exactly where their feet were planted conceptually.

By way of illustration, it may be useful to consider their general interpretive approach to one central historical marker in the course, the Second Vatican Council. The majority were not familiar with Vatican II, but as the semester unfolded, they began to appreciate the fact that the ecclesial events of 1962 through 1965 fundamentally shaped their understanding of Catholicism. Reading Rahner's interpretation of the Council as the point at which the church became a world church,[7] they began to analyze *Gaudium et Spes* and *Dignitatis Humanae* against the horizon of the church's global social mission. In turn, as I will describe in greater detail below, they came to some insights regarding their own roles in this ecclesial mission as they attempted to draw connections between their community-based learning experiences and the magisterial texts. In a real sense, the tradition of Catholic social teaching was rendered living by their careful analysis and attempted application of it.

The Community-based Learning Method in Service of Theological Content

In the third part of this paper, I will consider the ways in which the experiential learning method facilitated the elucidation of Catholic social teaching as a tradition unfolding in "lived" time. Within the academic discipline of theology, the curricular subfield of ethics, and particularly the ethical niche occupied by Catholic social thought, aptly lends itself to the pedagogical use of experiential learning. In this course, for example, the experiential learning component afforded many students a very effective means by which to build on their progress toward the first course objective, textual interpretation, while advancing toward the second objective of testing the applications and implications of their knowledge of Catholic social teaching. Over time, a mutual correlation between the experiential learning method and the theological content conveyed in the classroom became evident in many students' written work.

For the purpose of learning the skill of disciplined textual analysis, I encouraged them to read the documents of Catholic social teaching with an eye toward identifying seven fundamental principles often used to anchor textual argumentation in this genre.[8] For the great majority of the students, these principles and, in turn, the thrust of the documents in which they appeared, only took root intellectually when they were enfleshed experientially. As one student reflected,

> The community-based learning option . . . was an integral part of my introduction to the principles of Catholic social teaching. Though I learned a great deal through reading the various encyclicals and pastoral letters, my volunteer project at the South

Bend Center for the Homeless made me truly realize how applicable the content of the texts was to my individual lifestyle. ... [I]n *living* these teachings, we can better see how Catholic principles should affect everything we do on a day-to-day level.

The first principle, that humans are endowed with dignity by virtue of their creation *imago Dei*, was not difficult for students to identify as the departure point of virtually every social teaching text from *Rerum Novarum* forward. But, what did it really mean theologically and ethically? Of the thirty-five students who worked at the Center for the Homeless during the spring semester, about thirty made some reference in their notebooks and/or final papers to the way in which their community-based learning project had led them to a deeper understanding of the meaning of human dignity. Imagine what our society would be like, they urged, if each of us really treated one another with full awareness of the significance of our creation in God's image. Encountering people who were stripped of even the most basic material possessions and often of their dignity as well, these students were challenged to consider the intrinsic worth of every human life and the corresponding obligations incumbent upon society to protect and nurture the human dignity of each and of all.

Closely related to this first principle are the second, third, and fourth: Each human being is the subject of rights and duties, and all of society is responsible for safeguarding the common good, while the state alone is charged with securing public order. As a society, we cannot speak of achieving the common good if not all members can partake in shaping it. Such participation is predicated upon fundamental respect for human rights and duties.[9] As we examined documents such as *Pacem in Terris* and *Economic Justice for All*, class discussions of human rights and duties in relation to the common good invariably came around to the question of practical application. These documents establish very high ideals, but how "realistic" is it to expect society to fulfill them? At this point, someone would usually refer back to his or her community-based learning experience. Those who tutored children at the homeless center or at La Casa de Amistad often wondered aloud whether these children would ever be able to fully participate in shaping the common good. And, as the semester unfolded, many also drew the conclusion that the voicelessness of these children was everyone's loss: The systematic exclusion of citizens from integral participation in society ultimately represented a severe impediment to achievement of the common good in its fullness.

At this conceptual juncture, some were also able to draw a connection to the fifth principle, the option for the poor. The economic pastoral urged Americans to adopt the perspective of society's most vulnerable in making socioeconomic decisions.[10] Comprehending this teaching, much less attempting to live in accordance with it, was a nearly impossible task for these students, who had come from middle- to upper-income homes to the insular environs of Notre Dame and were now seated in one of the nation's most technologically advanced classroom buildings. If our educational journey had been confined strictly to classroom learning, I am certain that the bishops' call for economic justice would have been summarily dismissed as an unattainable utopian ideal.

But, through the experiential learning component, students almost inevitably found themselves grappling with the implications of the bishops' call to embrace the option for the poor. Through playing cards every Friday night with Robert, an underemployed man struggling to find affordable housing, one student began to write about the real structural injustices manifested in our society's socioeconomic priorities as well as the immeasurable value of accompaniment, walking with the poor. As he recounted in his notebook entry after one particular night at the homeless center, he realized that he was not in a position to effect any transformative changes in housing policy at the moment, but he also understood that the significance of his community-based learning extended far beyond the game of hearts that he had lost that night. He acknowledged Robert as a teacher who was revealing to him a new and frightening perspective on the society to which they both belonged. It was the view from society's periphery, seen by those who had been forced to the margins of societal participation and reduced to the bare minimum of human fulfillment.[11]

I will round off the correlation of the social teaching principles with the experiential method by turning to the sixth principle, subsidiarity, and the seventh principle regarding the constitutive place of voluntary associations in the fabric of societal interrelationship. These two principles often served as methodological tools in the hands of those students engaged in community-based learning. Grassroots involvement in voluntary associations like the Center for the Homeless, La Casa de Amistad, and Earthworks turned the sometimes opaque notion of subsidiarity into an intelligible means of assessing the proper level of social organization at which to engage a particular social problem.

From this brief look at how the experiential method served to enhance the students' understanding of these principles of Catholic social teaching, I would like to draw a more synthetic insight. I suggest that the use of community-based learning in the context of this Catholic social teaching course served to ground the theological content of the course as well as pedagogical claims about the experiential learning method itself. Turning to the first aspect of this argument, as I mentioned earlier, one of the main themes of the course was the centrality of Vatican II to the church's understanding of its social mission and of those called to incarnate this mission through social ministry.[12] As Bishop Malone has suggested, in the wake of the council all members of the ecclesial community could be perceived as both teachers and learners at some level.[13] Both teaching and learning are integral aspects of Christian discipleship for a church that describes itself as the people of God.

This point is closely connected to the notion of a religious tradition unfolding in "lived" time. As Lucien Richard has described, the conciliar understanding of the *sensus fidelium* viewed against the background of the Holy Spirit's action among the people of God "implies that not only the magisterium but the whole ecclesial body is an organ of tradition."[14] It is one thing to emphasize the theological point that tradition is rendered living only in its *active* reception and transmission;[15] it is quite another for undergraduate students of theology to move from an academic understanding of this Vatican II ecclesiology to responsible appropriation of its meaning and implications in their own lives of Christian discipleship. To begin to see oneself as an active participant, an integral part of the people of God, is to begin to take up the gift and task of shaping the church's tradition in "lived" time.

The method of experiential learning conveyed this aspect of the course content very well, and in the process, it bore out claims made in contemporary scholarship about the experiential learning method itself. In the case of the student's encounter with Robert, the community-based learning component reinforced the post-Vatican II articulation of the significance of membership in the ecclesial community by demonstrating what Barbara Jacoby has taken to be one of the hall-

marks of experiential learning: reciprocity. Just as Christian discipleship entails walking with others, and especially with the poor, community-based learning involves acting "*with* others rather than *for*
them," which presupposes a relationship of mutual respect in which
the participants learn from one another.[16]

Such convergence of theological content and experiential method
also occurred in relation to the virtues of charity and justice. Turning
to the issue of method, we might note with Jacoby that the notion of
reciprocity "implies a concerted effort to move from charity to justice,
from service to the elimination of need."[17] While one semester of accompanying the men at the homeless center on Friday nights afforded
the above-mentioned student little opportunity for effecting structural
change, it did inspire a shift in his own assessment of what he was
doing. His notebook entries evidenced a movement from concern that
he was not "giving enough" to these men toward a budding realization
that what was really needed here was not one-sided charity, in the
sense of almsgiving, but rather justice, and specifically social justice.

Once again, this particular emphasis of community-based learning
served the course content well. In virtually every Catholic social teaching document since *Rerum Novarum*, there is some operative understanding, whether expressed or implied, about the relationship of charity
to justice. The U.S. bishops and John Paul II, for example, have been
particularly insistent that charity in the form of almsgiving is simply
not sufficient to fulfill the obligations of justice, while charity understood as love of God and neighbor is the *sine qua non* of acting justly.[18]

This grounding of the essential link between charity and justice
facilitated the students' understanding of the strong emphasis in Catholic social teaching on the integral relationship between personal conversion and action.[19] In cultivating an awareness of the significance of
this theme, community-based learning was at least beneficial if not
essential. While I did not conduct any formal empirical studies to prove
this connection, I would affirm Judith Boss's conclusion drawn from
a controlled experiment involving her ethics class: "Engaging in community service work helps students to define themselves as effective
moral agents."[20]

In the context of a course on Catholic social teaching, such realized
moral agency was understood as one component of the process of
formation of conscience and responsible discernment. It was treated
as one part of the larger task of articulating and living Christian iden-

tity in the contexts of both church and society. As the U.S. bishops wrote in *Economic Justice for All*, "[C]onversion is a lifelong process. And, it is not undertaken alone. It occurs with the support of the whole believing community, through baptism, common prayer, and our daily efforts, large and small, on behalf of justice."[21]

The 1971 Synod of Bishops emphasized that such action on behalf of justice is a constitutive dimension of preaching the gospel,[22] and this point was driven home by Paul VI in *Evangelii Nuntiandi*: The witness of an authentically Christian life is the first means of evangelization. In some fashion, all Christians are called to such witness by acting on behalf of justice.[23] For many of my students, coming to understand themselves as evangelizers was the beginning of insight. Gradually, some of them began to approach the community-based learning experience as an opportunity to witness to what they were learning academically and professing ecclesially. Reflecting on his experience at the homeless center, one student concluded in his final integration paper,

> It is only through continuous teaching and learning that we can fully integrate Catholic social teaching into our lives, so that when we are called to act in a morally responsible way, we will be ready. . . . As the U.S. Catholic bishops state in *Economic Justice for All*, "Our faith is not just a weekend obligation, a mystery to be celebrated around the altar on Sunday. We cannot separate what we believe from how we act in the community" (para 25).

Conclusion

Based on my limited experience in teaching this theology class to seventy students over two semesters, I can affirm that the tradition of Catholic social teaching is vibrantly alive, both in its historical continuity and in its "constant renewal" via, in part, careful study and application of it by contemporary students of theology. The experiential learning method employed in this class served to render the tradition intelligible and meaningful, thereby facilitating the students' appropriation of it. The correlation of theological content with the experiential method also underscored some pedagogical claims about experiential models of education, particularly the centrality of reciprocity and the relationship of charity and justice. While I trust that there are many viable models for structuring a theology class on the Catholic social teaching tradition, I would say that this particular method served my students extremely well in their efforts to grasp the thrust of the subject matter. Beyond that, I am quite certain that the experiential learning component was instrumental to our collective rendering of Catholic social teaching as a living tradition, at once ever constant and ever new.

Notes

[1] I would like to thank Fr. Don McNeill, C.S.C., Dr. Kathleen Maas Weigert, and Dr. Barbara Walvoord for their patient, insightful guidance and experiential wisdom.

[2] For a list of the primary and secondary readings used in this course, please see the Appendix.

[3] Kathleen Maas Weigert, "Academic Service Learning: Its Meaning and Relevance," *New Directions for Teaching and Learning, No.73, Academic Service Learning: A Pedagogy of Action and Reflection,* ed. Robert Rhoads and Jeffrey P. F. Howard (San Francisco: Jossey-Bass Publishers, 1998), 5.

[4] John Paul II, *Sollicitudo Rei Socialis* in *Catholic Social Thought,* ed. David O'Brien and Thomas Shannon (Maryknoll: Orbis Books, 1992), n. 3. For the quoted phrases in this passage, John Paul II cites *Octogesima Adveniens,* n. 4, and the Congregation for the Doctrine of the Faith, *Libertatis Conscientia* (Instruction on Christian Freedom and Liberation) (22 March 1986), n. 72.

[5] Oswald von Nell-Breuning, "The Drafting of *Quadragesimo Anno,*" in *Readings in Moral Theology No. 5: Official Catholic Social Teaching,* ed. Richard McCormick, S.J., and Charles Curran (Mahwah: Paulist Press, 1986), 60-68.

[6] For a treatment of change and continuity in relation to tradition, see John O'Malley, S.J., *Tradition and Transition: Historical Perspectives on Vatican II* (Wilmington: Michael Glazier, 1989), 19-81.

[7] See Karl Rahner, "Towards a Fundamental Theological Interpretation of Vatican II," *Theological Studies* 40 (1979): 716-27.

[8] For a similar list of Catholic social teaching principles, see *Economic Justice for All* in *Catholic Social Thought,* nn. 13-18.

[9] See *Pacem in Terris,* nn. 8-38, in ibid., and *Economic Justice for All,* nn. 14-15, 17-18.

[10] See *Economic Justice for All,* nn. 16, 87.

[11] For a treatment of the expanded notion of the role of "teacher" that is involved in experiential learning, see Weigert, "Academic Service Learning," 6, and idem, "Experiential Learning: Contributions to the Development of Values," in *Value Development in the University Classroom,* ed. Daniel G. Ross, S.J. (Taiwan: Fu Jen University, 1993), 382-412.

[12] See J. Bryan Hehir, "The Social Role of the Church: Leo XIII, Vatican II, and John Paul II," in *Catholic Social Thought and the New World Order,* ed. Oliver F. Williams, C.S.C., and John W. Houck (Notre Dame: University of Notre Dame Press, 1993), 29-50, and idem, "Church-State and Church-World," *Proceedings of the Catholic Theological Society of America* 41 (1986): 54-74.

[13] Bishop James W. Malone, "The Role of the Bishop as Teacher and Listener," in *Shepherds Speak: American Bishops Confront the Social and Moral Issues That Challenge Christians Today,* ed. Dennis M. Corrado and James F. Hinchey (New York: Crossroad, 1986), 11-19.

[14] Lucien Richard, O.M.I., "Reflections on Dissent and Reception," in *The Church in the Nineties: Its Legacy, Its Future,* ed. Pierre M. Hegy (Collegeville, Minn.: The Liturgical Press, 1993), 10.

[15] Ibid., 9-10. Regarding this point, Richard is relying on Yves Congar, O.P., *Tradition and Traditions,* trans. M. Naseby and T. Rainborough (London: Burns & Oates, Ltd, 1966), 253.

[16] "Service-Learning in Today's Higher Education," in *Service Learning in Higher Education,* ed. Barbara Jacoby et al. (San Francisco: Jossey-Bass Publishers, 1996), 8. See also J.C. Kendall, "Combining Service and Learning: An Introduction," in *Combining Service and Learning: A Resource Book for Community and Public Service,* vol.1, ed. J.C. Kendall (Raleigh, N.C.: National Society for Experiential Education, 1990), 22.

[17] Ibid., 9.

[18] Note the centrality of the dual love command in *Economic Justice for All,* n.43, 356-57, 365. See also John Paul II, *Centesimus Annus,* nn. 57-58, in *Catholic Social Thought,*

[19] E.g., *Economic Justice for All,* nn. 23-29.

[20] Judith A. Boss, "The Effect of Community Service Work on the Moral Development of College Ethics Students," *Journal of Moral Education,* 23:2 (1994): 192.

[21] *Economic Justice for All,* n. 24.

[22] *Justice in the World,* in *Catholic Social Thought,* 289.

[23] Cf. *Evangelii Nuntiandi,* n. 41, in ibid.

Appendix:
A List of Course Readings

Primary

Consejo Episcopal Latinoamericano (CELAM). "Evangelization in Latin America's Present and Future" (Puebla Final Document), in *Puebla and Beyond: Documentation and Commentary,* ed. John Eagleson and Philip Scharper. Maryknoll, N.Y.: Orbis Books, 1979, 123-39, 263-72, 369-70.

———. "Medellín Documents," in *The Gospel of Peace and Justice,* ed. Joseph Gremillion. Maryknoll, N.Y.: Orbis Books, 1976, 445-76.

Ellsberg, Robert, ed. *By Little and By Little: The Selected Writings of Dorothy Day.* Maryknoll, N.Y.: Orbis Books, 1992.

John Paul II. *Evangelium Vitae.* Washington, D.C.: U.S. Catholic Conference, 1995, para. 52-56.

———. "A Letter to Women," *The Tablet* (15 July 1995), 917-19.

Maurin, Peter. *The Green Revolution* (rev. 1961). Fresno, Calif.: Academy Guild Press, 1949.

O'Brien, David, and Thomas Shannon, eds. *Catholic Social Thought.* Maryknoll: Orbis Books, 1992.

Pius XII. "The Anniversary of *Rerum Novarum*" (Pentecost, 1941), *The Major Addresses of Pope Pius XII,* Vol. I, ed. Vincent Yzermans. St. Paul: The North Central Publishing Co., 1961, 26-36.

———. "Communism and Democracy" (1956), in *The Major Addresses of Pope Pius XII,* Vol. II: *Christmas Messages,* ed. Vincent A. Yzermans. St. Paul: The North Central Publishing Co., 1961, 213-28.

———. "Religious Freedom" and "Declaration on Religious Freedom," in *The Documents of Vatican II,* ed. Walter M. Abbott. New York: Corpus Books, 1966, 672-96.

U.S. Bishops. "Communities of Salt and Light: Reflections on Parish Social Mission," *Origins* 23:25 (2 December 1993), 443-48.

———. "The Economy Pastoral Ten Years Later," *Origins* 25 (1995), 389-93.

———. "Statement on Capital Punishment," *Origins* 10:24 (27 November 1980), 373-77.

Secondary

Baum, Gregory. "John Paul II's Encyclical on Labor," *The Ecumenist* (1981), 1-4.

Bernardin, Joseph Cardinal. "The Post-Cold War Agenda for Peace," *Origins* 23:1 (20 May 1993), 1, 3-7.

Bohlen, Celestine. "Pope Says 'Unjust' Teachings by Christians Helped Fuel Persecution of Jews," *The New York Times* (1 November 1997), A6.

Bokenkotter, Thomas. *A Concise History of the Catholic Church* (rev. ed.). New York: Image Books, 1990.

Carlen, Claudia. "Introductory Note," *Papal Pronouncements,* Vol. 1. Ann Arbor: The Pierian Press, 1990.

Claver, Bishop Francisco. "The Church and Revolution: The Philippine Solution," *America* (3 May 1986), 356-59.

———. "The Church and Revolution: The Philippine Solution (Part II)," *America* (10 May 1986), 376-78.

Coleman, John. "Development of Church Social Teaching," *Origins* 11 (4 June 1981), 33, 35-41.

Curran, Charles. "American Catholic Social Ethics, 1880-1965," in *Directions in Catholic Social Ethics.* Notre Dame: University of Notre Dame Press, 1985, 71-104.

———. "The Changing Anthropological Bases of Catholic Social Ethics," *The Thomist* 45:2 (1981), 284-318.

Dorr, Donal. *Option for the Poor: A Hundred Years of Catholic Social Teaching* (rev. ed.). Maryknoll, N.Y.: Orbis Books, 1992.

Gracida, Bishop Rene H. "Capital Punishment and the Sacredness of Life," in *Shepherds Speak: American Bishops Confront the Social and Moral Issues That Challenge Christians Today*, ed. Dennis M. Corrado and James F. Hinchey. New York: Crossroad, 1986, 108-25.

Hehir, J. Bryan. "Church and State: Basic Concepts for an Analysis," *Origins* 8 (November 1978), 377-81.

———. "Church-State and Church-World," *Proceedings of the Catholic Theological Society of America* 41 (1986), 54-74.

———. "John Paul II: Continuity and Change in the Social Teaching of the Church," in *Co-Creation and Capitalism: John Paul II's Laborem Exercens*, ed. John W. Houck and Oliver F. Williams. Washington, D.C.: University Press of America, 1983, 124-40.

Hollenbach, David. "Human Rights Chart," in *Claims in Conflict: Retrieving and Renewing the Catholic Human Rights Tradition*. New York: Paulist Press, 1979, 98.

Land, Philip. *Catholic Social Teaching as I Have Lived, Loved, and Loathed It*. Chicago: Loyola University Press, 1994, 18-35.

Mahoney, John. "Nature and Supernature," in *The Making of Moral Theology. A Study of the Roman Catholic Tradition*. Oxford: Clarendon Press, 1987, 72-115.

Malone, Bishop James W. "The Role of the Bishop as Teacher and Listener," in *Shepherds Speak: American Bishops Confront the Social and Moral Issues That Challenge Christians Today*, ed. Dennis M. Corrado and James F. Hinchey. New York: Crossroad, 1986, 11-19.

Miller, Amata, I.H.M. "Catholic Social Teaching: What Might Have Been if Women Were Not Invisible in a Patriarchal Church," in *Rerum Novarum: A Symposium Celebrating 100 Years of Catholic Social Thought*, ed. Ronald F. Duska. Lewiston: The Edwin Mellen Press, 1992, 21-47.

Mueller, Franz. "The Church and the Social Question," in *The Challenge of Mater et Magistra*, ed. Joseph N. Moody and Justus George Lawler. New York: Herder and Herder, 1963, 13-154.

Rahner, Karl. "Towards a Fundamental Theological Interpretation of Vatican II," *Theological Studies* 40 (1979), 716-27.

Rhodes, Anthony. "The New Pope, Pius XII, and the Outbreak of War, 1939," in *The Vatican in the Age of the Dictators (1922-1945)*. New York: Holt, Rinehart, and Winston, 1974, 219-33.

Romero, Archbishop Oscar. "The Political Dimension of the Faith from the Perspective of the Option for the Poor," in *Voice of the Voiceless*, trans. Michael J. Walsh. Maryknoll, N.Y.: Orbis Books, 1985, 177-87.

Von Nell-Breuning, Oswald. "The Drafting of *Quadragesimo Anno*," in *Readings in Moral Theology No. 5: Official Catholic Social Teaching*, ed. R.

McCormick and C. Curran. Mahwah, N.J.: Paulist Press, 1986, 60-68.

Weakland, Archbishop Rembert. "A Gospel Life-style in a Consumer Society," in *Shepherds Speak: American Bishops Confront the Social and Moral Issues That Challenge Christians Today,* ed. Dennis M. Corrado and James F. Hinchey. New York: Crossroad, 1986, 171-79.

———. "The Urban Poor and the Churches," *Origins* 26 (November 1996), 360-64.

Contributors

Michael Horace Barnes is professor of religious studies at the University of Dayton, and the author of *In the Presence of Mystery* (Twenty-Third Publications, 1990) and the forthcoming *Stages of Thought: The Co-Evolution of Religious Thought and Science* (Oxford University Press).

Elizabeth A. Clark is John Carlisle Kilgo Professor of Religion at Duke University. She is the author or editor of ten books on early Christianity; her *Reading Renunciation: Asceticism and Scripture in Early Christianity* will appear in 1999. She is the past president of the American Academy of Religion, the American Society of Church History, and the North American Patristics Society, and is the co-editor of the *Journal of Early Christian Studies* and an editor of *Church History*.

Ann Coble is a doctoral student in Historical Theology at Saint Louis University. Her area of specialization is American Christianity.

James T. Fisher holds the Danforth II Chair in Humanities at Saint Louis University. He is the author of *The Catholic Counterculture in America, 1933-1962* and *Dr. America: The Lives of Thomas A. Dooley, 1927-1961*.

Barbara Green, O.P., is professor of biblical studies at the Dominican School of Philosophy and Theology at the Graduate Theological Union in Berkeley. She has written two books and several articles and is currently working on the usefulness of the thought of philosopher and literary critic Mikhail Bakhtin for biblical interpretation, specifically the text of 1 Samuel.

Justo L. González is executive director of the Hispanic Theological Initiative and director of the Hispanic Summer Program in Theological Education. He is the author of numerous books, including the three-volume *A History of Christian Thought,* as well as a number of books on biblical hermeneutics and Hispanic theology.

Pamela Kirk is associate professor in the Department of Theology and Religious Studies at St. John's University, New York. She has recently published a book on the Mexican poet, dramatist and religious writer, *Sor Juana Ines de la Cruz: Religion, Art and Feminism.* She has written numerous articles and reviews on women's role in the church, past and present.

Brian F. Linnane is assistant professor of religious studies at the College of the Holy Cross, Worcester, Massachusetts. In addition to writing on issues of sexuality and gender relations, he has published articles on fundamental moral theology and medical ethics.

Franklin H. Littell is Professor Emeritus at Temple University. In 1996-97, he held the Ida King Distinguished Visiting Professor in Holocaust Studies at the Richmond Stockton College of New Jersey. He is a foremost authority both in Holocaust studies and in the Anabaptist tradition.

Vincent J. Miller is assistant professor of theology at Georgetown University, Washington, D.C. His contribution to this volume is part of a larger project articulating a contemporary theology of tradition. Other interests include the function of doctrine in consumer culture and the relationship between eschatology and political theology.

Margaret R. Pfeil is a doctoral candidate in moral theology/Christian ethics at the University of Notre Dame.

Ann R. Riggs recently finished her Ph.D. in systematic theology at Marquette University in Milwaukee. Her article is based on her dissertation, "Rahner, Self, and God: The Question of the Cartesian Ego in the Theology of Karl Rahner."

Donna Teevan is assistant professor of theology at Seattle University. She received her Ph.D. from the University of St. Michael's College (Toronto School of Theology) in 1994 with a dissertation on the relationship between Lonergan's theological method and hermeneutics. Her current research interests also include liberation theologies, especially feminist theology.

Terrence W. Tilley is immediate past president of the College Theology Society. He has taught at Georgetown University, St. Michael's College (Vermont), Florida State University, and currently chairs the Religious Studies Department at the University of Dayton. He is author of five books in philosophy of religion, methodology, and narrative theology, co-editor of two books, and has written scores of reviews, essays and articles for learned journals.